Active Server Pages 3.0

Your visual blueprint for developing interactive Web sites

Visual

From
maranGraphics™

&

IDG Books Worldwide, Inc.
An International Data Group Company
Foster City, CA • Indianapolis • Chicago • New York

Active Server Pages 3.0

Published by
IDG Books Worldwide, Inc.
An International Data Group Company
919 E. Hillsdale Blvd., Suite 400
Foster City, CA 94404

Copyright© 2000 by maranGraphics Inc.
5755 Coopers Avenue
Mississauga, Ontario, Canada
L4Z 1R9

Library of Congress Catalog Card No.: 00-103976

ISBN: 0-7645-3472-6

Printed in the United States of America
10 9 8 7 6 5

1V/QR/QX/QQ/MG

Distributed in the United States by IDG Books Worldwide, Inc.

Distributed by CDG Books Canada Inc. for Canada; by Transworld Publishers Limited in the United Kingdom; by IDG Norge Books for Norway; by IDG Sweden Books for Sweden; by IDG Books Australia Publishing Corporation Pty. Ltd. for Australia and New Zealand; by TransQuest Publishers Pte Ltd. for Singapore, Malaysia, Thailand, Indonesia, and Hong Kong; by Gotop Information Inc. for Taiwan; by ICG Muse, Inc. for Japan; by Intersoft for South Africa; by Eyrolles for France; by International Thomson Publishing for Germany, Austria and Switzerland; by Distribuidora Cuspide for Argentina; by LR International for Brazil; by Galileo Libros for Chile; by Ediciones ZETA S.C.R. Ltda. for Peru; by WS Computer Publishing Corporation, Inc. for the Philippines; by Contemporanea de Ediciones for Venezuela; by Express Computer Distributors for the Caribbean and West Indies; by Micronesia Media Distributor, Inc. for Micronesia; by Chips Computadoras S.A. de C.V. for Mexico; by Editorial Norma de Panama S.A. for Panama; by American Bookshops for Finland.

For corporate orders, please call maranGraphics at 800-469-6616.
For general information on IDG Books Worldwide's books in the U.S., please call our Consumer Customer Service department at 800-762-2974.
For reseller information, including discounts and premium sales, please call our Reseller Customer Service department at 800-434-3422.
For information on where to purchase IDG Books Worldwide's books outside the U.S., please contact our International Sales department at 317-572-3993 or fax 317-572-4002.
For consumer information on foreign language translations, please contact our Customer Service department at 800-434-3422, fax 800-550-2747, or e-mail rights@idgbooks.com.
For information on licensing foreign or domestic rights, please phone 650-653-7000 of fax 650-653-7500.
For sales inquiries and special prices for bulk quantities, please contact our Sales department at 650-655-3200.
For information on using IDG Books Worldwide's books in the classroom or for ordering examination copies, please contact our Educational Sales department at 800-434-2086 or fax 317-572-4005.
For press review copies, author interviews, or other publicity information, please contact our Public Relations department at 650-653-7000 or fax 650-653-7500.
For authorization to photocopy items for corporate, personal, or educational use, please contact maranGraphics at 800-469-6616.

Trademark Acknowledgments

Permissions

ABOUT IDG BOOKS WORLDWIDE

Welcome to the world of IDG Books Worldwide.

IDG Books Worldwide, Inc., is a subsidiary of International Data Group, the world's largest publisher of computer-related information and the leading global provider of information services on information technology. IDG was founded more than 30 years ago by Patrick J. McGovern and now employs more than 9,000 people worldwide. IDG publishes more than 290 computer publications in over 75 countries. More than 90 million people read one or more IDG publications each month.

Launched in 1990, IDG Books Worldwide is today the #1 publisher of best-selling computer books in the United States. We are proud to have received eight awards from the Computer Press Association in recognition of editorial excellence and three from Computer Currents' First Annual Readers' Choice Awards. Our best-selling ...For Dummies® series has more than 50 million copies in print with translations in 31 languages. IDG Books Worldwide, through a joint venture with IDG's Hi-Tech Beijing, became the first U.S. publisher to publish a computer book in the People's Republic of China. In record time, IDG Books Worldwide has become the first choice for millions of readers around the world who want to learn how to better manage their businesses.

Our mission is simple: Every one of our books is designed to bring extra value and skill-building instructions to the reader. Our books are written by experts who understand and care about our readers. The knowledge base of our editorial staff comes from years of experience in publishing, education, and journalism — experience we use to produce books to carry us into the new millennium. In short, we care about books, so we attract the best people. We devote special attention to details such as audience, interior design, use of icons, and illustrations. And because we use an efficient process of authoring, editing, and desktop publishing our books electronically, we can spend more time ensuring superior content and less time on the technicalities of making books.

You can count on our commitment to deliver high-quality books at competitive prices on topics you want to read about. At IDG Books Worldwide, we continue in the IDG tradition of delivering quality for more than 30 years. You'll find no better book on a subject than one from IDG Books Worldwide.

John Kilcullen
Chairman and CEO
IDG Books Worldwide, Inc.

Eighth Annual Computer Press Awards ≥1992

Ninth Annual Computer Press Awards ≥1993

Tenth Annual Computer Press Awards ≥1994

Eleventh Annual Computer Press Awards ≥1995

IDG is the world's leading IT media, research and exposition company. Founded in 1964, IDG had 1997 revenues of $2.05 billion and has more than 9,000 employees worldwide. IDG offers the widest range of media options that reach IT buyers in 75 countries representing 95% of worldwide IT spending. IDG's diverse product and services portfolio spans six key areas including print publishing, online publishing, expositions and conferences, market research, education and training, and global marketing services. More than 90 million people read one or more of IDG's 290 magazines and newspapers, including IDG's leading global brands — Computerworld, PC World, Network World, Macworld and the Channel World family of publications. IDG Books Worldwide is one of the fastest-growing computer book publishers in the world, with more than 700 titles in 36 languages. The "...For Dummies®" series alone has more than 50 million copies in print. IDG offers online users the largest network of technology-specific Web sites around the world through IDG.net (http://www.idg.net), which comprises more than 225 targeted Web sites in 55 countries worldwide. International Data Corporation (IDC) is the world's largest provider of information technology data, analysis and consulting, with research centers in over 41 countries and more than 400 research analysts worldwide. IDG World Expo is a leading producer of more than 168 globally branded conferences and expositions in 35 countries including E3 (Electronic Entertainment Expo), Macworld Expo, ComNet, Windows World Expo, ICE (Internet Commerce Expo), Agenda, DEMO, and Spotlight. IDG's training subsidiary, ExecuTrain, is the world's largest computer training company, with more than 230 locations worldwide and 785 training courses. IDG Marketing Services helps industry-leading IT companies build international brand recognition by developing global integrated marketing programs via IDG's print, online and exposition products worldwide. Further information about the company can be found at www.idg.com.

1/26/00

maranGraphics is a family-run business
located near Toronto, Canada.

At *maranGraphics*, we believe in producing great computer books–one book at a time.

Each maranGraphics book uses the award-winning communication process that we have been developing over the last 25 years. Using this process, we organize screen shots and text in a way that makes it easy for you to learn new concepts and tasks.

We spend hours deciding the best way to perform each task, so you don't have to!

Our clear, easy-to-follow screen shots and instructions walk you through each task from beginning to end.

We want to thank you for purchasing what we feel are the best computer books money can buy. We hope you enjoy using this book as much as we enjoyed creating it!

Sincerely,

The Maran Family

Please visit us on the Web at:

www.maran.com

CREDITS

Author:
Paul Whitehead

Copy Editors:
Kelleigh Johnson
Wanda Lawrie

Project Manager:
Judy Maran

Editors:
Raquel Scott
Janice Boyer
Stacey Morrison
Teri Lynn Pinsent
Andrea Carere
Luis Lee

Screen Captures & Editing:
James Menzies

Layout Design:
Treena Lees
Ted Sheppard
Sean Johannesen

Cover Illustration:
Russ Marini

Screen Artist:
Jimmy Tam

Indexer:
Kelleigh Johnson

Post Production:
Robert Maran

**Senior Vice President,
Technology Publishing
IDG Books Worldwide:**
Richard Swadley

**Editorial Support
IDG Books Worldwide:**
Barry Pruett
Martine Edwards

ACKNOWLEDGMENTS

Thanks to the dedicated staff of maranGraphics, including
Jennifer Amaral, Cathy Benn, Janice Boyer, Andrea Carere,
Sean Johannesen, Eric Kramer, Wanda Lawrie, Luis Lee,
Treena Lees, Jill Maran, Judy Maran, Robert Maran, Ruth Maran,
Russ Marini, James Menzies, Suzana Miokovic, Stacey Morrison,
Teri Lynn Pinsent, Steven Schaerer, Raquel Scott, Ted Sheppard,
Jimmy Tam, Roxanne Van Damme, and Kelleigh Johnson.

Finally, to Richard Maran who originated the easy-to-use
graphic format of this guide. Thank you for your
inspiration and guidance.

TABLE OF CONTENTS

ACTIVE SERVER PAGES 3.0:
Your visual blueprint for
developing interactive Web sites

3) USING VBSCRIPT

TABLE OF CONTENTS

4) USING ACTIVE SERVER PAGES WITH HTML

5) SEND INFORMATION TO A CLIENT

6) RETRIEVE INFORMATION FROM A CLIENT

ACTIVE SERVER PAGES 3.0:
Your visual blueprint for
developing interactive Web sites

7) WORK WITH THE WEB SERVER

8) WORK WITH USER INFORMATION

9) CREATE A WEB APPLICATION

TABLE OF CONTENTS

ACTIVE SERVER PAGES 3.0:
Your visual blueprint for
developing interactive Web sites

14) USING PREPROCESSING DIRECTIVES

15) HANDLING ERRORS

16) REFERENCE

APPENDIX

HOW TO USE THIS BOOK

Active Server Pages 3.0: Your visual blueprint for developing interactive Web sites uses simple, straightforward examples to teach you how to create powerful, dynamic Web pages and sophisticated Web applications.

To get the most out of this book, you should read each chapter in order, from beginning to end. Each chapter introduces new ideas and builds on the knowledge learned in previous chapters. Once you become familiar with Active Server Pages (ASP), this book can be used as an informative desktop reference.

Who This Book Is For

Because you are interested in authoring dynamic Web pages, we assume you have experience using HyperText Markup Language (HTML) to create Web pages. However, if you are not familiar with HTML, you can find the basics you need to get started in this book.

No prior experience with Web server software is required, but familiarity with the Microsoft Windows operating system installed on your computer is an asset.

Experience with VBScript programming is also an asset, but even if you have no programming experience, you can use this book to learn the VBScript essentials you need to work with ASP.

What You Need To Use This Book

To perform the tasks in this book, a computer with Microsoft Windows 2000 installed that is running Internet Information Server (IIS) 5.0 is required. A computer with Microsoft Windows 95 or 98 installed that is running Personal Web Server 4.0 can also be used to perform most of the tasks in this book. Both server software programs include a version of Active Server Pages and are ideal for learning about Web servers and ASP.

You do not require any special development tools to use ASP. All you need is a text editor—we use Notepad in the examples throughout this book—and a Web browser, such as Microsoft Internet Explorer.

The Conventions In This Book

A number of typographic and layout styles have been used throughout *Active Server Pages 3.0: Your visual blueprint for developing interactive Web sites* to distinguish different types of information.

Courier Font

Indicates the use of HTML code such as tags or attributes, scripting language code such as statements, operators or functions and ASP code such as objects, methods or properties.

Bold

Indicates information that must be typed by you.

Italics

Indicates a new term being introduced.

Apply It

An Apply It section usually contains a segment of code that takes the lesson you just learned one step further. Apply It sections offer inside information and pointers that can be used to enhance the functionality of your code.

Extra

An Extra section provides additional information about the task you just accomplished. Extra sections often contain interesting tips and useful tricks to make working with ASP easier and more efficient.

ACTIVE SERVER PAGES 3.0:
Your visual blueprint for
developing interactive Web sites

The Organization Of This Book

Active Server Pages 3.0: Your visual blueprint for developing interactive Web sites contains 16 chapters and an appendix.

The first chapter, Getting Started, shows you how to install and configure Web server software. Once you have installed the Web server software of your choice, you can immediately begin creating Active Server Pages code.

Chapter 2, entitled Work with Web Pages, reviews the basics of HTML. If you are already familiar with HTML, feel free to skim over the contents of this chapter and then proceed to the remainder of the book.

Chapter 3, Using VBScript, introduces you to the essentials of VBScript, the default scripting language used by ASP. This chapter also covers the fundamentals of programming, which enables you to use the material in the following chapters to create your own ASP pages. If you are already familiar with VBScript or another scripting or programming language, you may want to read over this chapter quickly before continuing through the book.

The fourth chapter, Using Active Server Pages with HTML, gets you started using ASP and shows you how to employ ASP to make your HTML forms more powerful.

Chapters 5 through 9 provide an in-depth examination of the five most important ASP objects—Response, Request, Server, Session and Application. You are shown in detail how to access and utilize each of these fundamental elements of ASP.

Chapter 10, Using the Global.asa File, and Chapter 11, Using External Code, demonstrate how you can create and use one section of code in several of your Web pages. This can help you create Web pages much more efficiently.

Chapters 12 through 14 describe some of the most popular technologies used with Active Server Pages, including databases, components and preprocessing directives. This book teaches you the basic principles of implementing and working with these advanced technologies.

Chapter 15, Handling Errors, illustrates how you can create custom error messages for your Web applications.

The final chapter contains a reference section. Once you are familiar with the contents of this book, you can use the VBScript and ASP references to obtain at-a-glance information for some of the most commonly used VBScript and ASP statements.

What Is On The CD-ROM Disc

The CD-ROM disc included in this book contains the sample code from each of the two-page lessons. This saves you from having to type the code and helps you quickly get started creating ASP code. The CD-ROM disc also contains several shareware and evaluation versions of programs that can be used to work with Active Server Pages. An e-version of the book and all the URLs mentioned in the book are also available on the disc.

INTRODUCTION TO ACTIVE SERVER PAGES

A ctive Server Pages (ASP) is technology developed by Microsoft that is used to create powerful and dynamic Web pages and sophisticated Web applications.

Web Servers

You do not require a dedicated Web server to publish the ASP pages you create. You can simply install Web server software on your own computer. Personal Web Server software and Internet Information Server (IIS) software both include support for Active Server Pages. Personal Web Server allows you to develop a Web site before transferring the site to a Web presence provider. IIS offers many advanced features that allow you to effectively host and manage even the busiest Web sites.

You do not require any special development tools to create and view ASP pages. All you need is a text editor and a Web browser.

Versions

Active Server Pages 3.0 is the latest version of ASP and is available with Internet Information Server (IIS) 5.0. Active Server Pages 2.0 is available with Personal Web Server 4.0. Active Server Pages 3.0 offers more features than previous versions of the technology. The Web server you are running will determine the version of ASP you are using and the tasks you can perform.

Scripting Languages

Scripting languages form the basis of Active Server Pages technology. There are many scripting languages that can be used to write ASP code. ASP supports VBScript and JScript, which is Microsoft's version of JavaScript, by default. If you want to use a different scripting language, such as REXX, PerlScript or Python, you must install the scripting language on the Web server.

Server-side Processing

Active Server Pages uses a DLL component installed on the Web server, so the processing of ASP code takes place on the server. When a user requests a Web page, the server checks to see if the requested file has the .asp file extension. If the file has the .asp extension, the ASP DLL component processes the file and then sends the result as HTML code to the user's Web browser. This allows ASP pages to be viewed by every Web browser.

ASP Objects

There are five main objects in ASP. The Response object sends and controls information from the Web server to a user. The Request object retrieves and controls information sent from a user to the Web server. The Server object creates objects and supplies access to methods and properties on the Web server. The Session object stores session information for individual users as they navigate a Web site. The Application object stores and shares information for use during an active application.

Each ASP object has properties and methods that instruct the object to perform a specific task.

FEATURES OF ACTIVE SERVER PAGES

Create Dynamic Web Sites

Dynamic Web sites contain Web pages that display constantly changing content. Using Active Server Pages, you can determine the content a Web page displays, depending on many different factors. For example, you can have a page automatically present different content to users depending on the current date or the user's location. Dynamic Web pages are more useful to each individual user than static Web pages.

Use Built-in Components

Active Server Pages includes easy-to-use components that can be used to accomplish tasks such as rotating advertisements, tracking user statistics or checking the capabilities of a user's Web browser so a page can be tailored to the browser. For even more flexibility, Active Server Pages allows Web site administrators to create and use their own custom components in the ASP pages they create.

Create Interactive Web Sites

Interactive Web sites contain Web pages that exchange information between the Web site and the user. Active Server Pages allows Web administrators to easily create Web pages that process information from a user and then generate content depending on the information submitted by the user. Interactive Web sites allow Web administrators to tailor the content of Web pages to better appeal to the user.

Work With Databases

An important feature of Active Server Pages is the ability to connect to a database. ASP pages can be used to make information stored in a database available to the users who visit your Web site. Using databases to store information and ASP pages to access the information is an efficient method of displaying up-to-date information in a Web site.

Active Server Pages can also allow users to manipulate the data in a database. For example, you can use an ASP page to add, delete or edit records in a database.

Create Applications

Many people are used to working with applications, such as word processors, appointment schedulers and e-mail readers, on their computers. With Active Server Pages technology, it is possible to create applications that are hosted on a Web site and are accessed by a Web browser. This allows users to run programs written in languages that are not supported by their Web browser and enables users to access a wider range of programs.

Increased Security

Because Active Server Pages code is processed on the Web server, the user cannot access the code used to create an ASP page. This makes it safer to work with sensitive data, such as login names and passwords. If a user views the source code of an ASP page within a Web browser, all the user will see is the HTML code that was generated by the Web server to create the page, not the Active Server Pages code itself.

INSTALL PERSONAL WEB SERVER

Microsoft Personal Web Server is Web server software that allows you to host a single Web site on your own computer to make Web and ASP pages available for viewing.

Personal Web Server was designed for use on small networks, such as a corporate intranet, and is often used by businesses to facilitate the sharing of documents.

Personal Web Server is also often used to develop a Web site before transferring the site to a Web presence provider. This allows

you to test and troubleshoot any problems before making the Web site available on the Internet. Personal Web Server is not suitable for making information available directly to users on the Internet.

Personal Web Server 4.0 is available on the Windows 98 CD-ROM installation disc and includes Active Server Pages 2.0. Personal Web Server 4.0 can be used to perform most of the examples in this book and is ideal for learning about Web servers and Active Server Pages. Once Personal Web Server is installed, you can immediately begin creating ASP pages.

INSTALL PERSONAL WEB SERVER

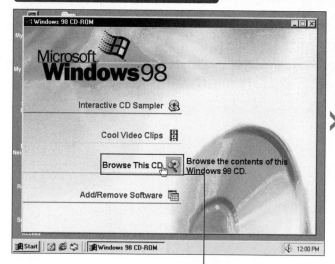

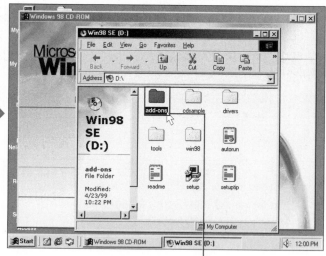

1 Insert the Windows 98 CD-ROM disc into a drive.

■ The Windows 98 CD-ROM window appears.

2 Double-click Browse This CD.

■ The drive window appears.

3 Double-click add-ons.

Extra

In addition to Windows 98, Personal Web Server can be used on a computer running the Windows 95 or Windows NT Workstation operating system. If you do not have your Windows 98 CD-ROM installation disc or you are using Windows 95 or Windows NT Workstation, you can obtain Personal Web Server 4.0 free of charge at the www.microsoft.com/windows/ie/pws Web site. Personal Web Server is part of the Windows NT 4.0 Option Pack.

You do not have to start Personal Web Server manually each time you want to use the software. Once you have installed the Web server software, Personal Web Server will start automatically each time you start your computer.

The Windows 2000 operating system includes its own Web server software called Internet Information Server (IIS) 5.0. IIS is suitable for hosting multiple Web sites and can be used to make Web and ASP pages available on a corporate intranet or on the Internet. IIS 5.0 includes Active Server Pages 3.0, which offers more features than Active Server Pages 2.0. For more information about IIS, see page 14.

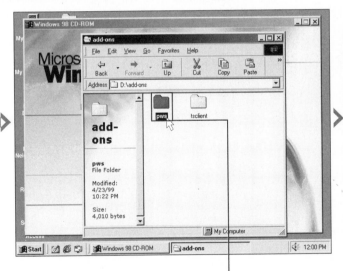

■ The add-ons window appears.

4 Double-click pws.

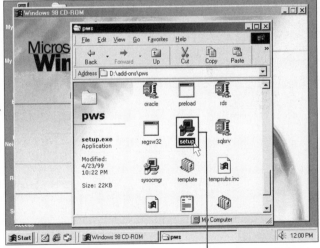

■ The pws window appears.

5 Double-click setup.

CONTINUED

INSTALL PERSONAL WEB SERVER
(CONTINUED)

When installing Personal Web Server, you can choose the installation option that best suits your needs. The Minimum option installs only the files required to run Personal Web Server. This option is useful when installing Personal Web Server on a computer with limited hard drive space available. The Typical option installs the most commonly used Personal Web Server files and is the recommended option. The Custom option allows advanced Web site developers to choose the Personal Web Server files they want to install.

The C:\Inetpub\wwwroot directory is automatically set as the home directory for Personal Web Server.

The home directory is where you will store all the Web and ASP pages you want users to be able to display.

To complete the installation of Personal Web Server, you must restart your computer.

After Personal Web Server is installed, you can use a Web browser to access Web and ASP pages stored in the Personal Web Server home directory. You can access pages using a Web browser installed on the same computer that is running Personal Web Server or a Web browser installed on another computer on the network.

INSTALL PERSONAL WEB SERVER (CONTINUED)

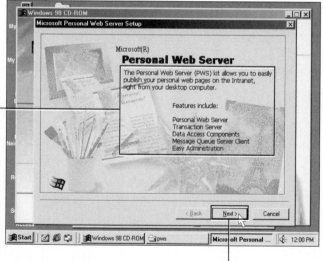

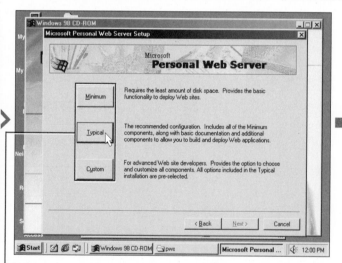

■ The Microsoft Personal Web Server Setup dialog box appears.

■ This area displays information about Personal Web Server.

 Click Next to continue.

7 Click the type of installation you want to perform.

Note: If you choose Custom, the following steps will be different for your installation.

Extra

If you do not want to use the C:\Inetpub\wwwroot directory as the home directory, you can set another directory as the home directory during the installation. This is useful if you already have a directory that stores the pages you want users to be able to display and you do not want to copy the pages to the default home directory. You can also change the home directory for Personal Web Server after the installation is complete. See page 8 for more information.

You can double-click the Personal Web Server icon on the taskbar (🐾) to display the Personal Web Manager window. The Personal Web Manager window allows you to administer your Web site. For example, to stop Personal Web Server and make your Web site unavailable to users, click the Stop button. To restart Personal Web Server, click the Start button.

In addition to wwwroot, several other directories are created when Personal Web Server is installed. In the Personal Web Manager window, you can click C:\Inetpub\wwwroot to display these directories. For example, the iissamples directory contains samples of ASP pages and the scripts directory provides a convenient place to store ASP scripts you create.

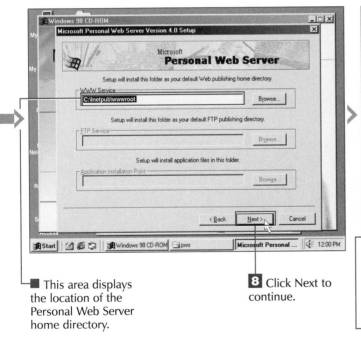

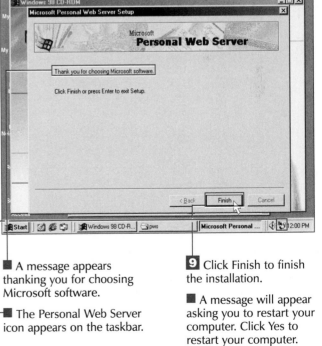

■ This area displays the location of the Personal Web Server home directory.

8 Click Next to continue.

■ A message appears thanking you for choosing Microsoft software.

■ The Personal Web Server icon appears on the taskbar.

9 Click Finish to finish the installation.

■ A message will appear asking you to restart your computer. Click Yes to restart your computer.

CHANGE THE HOME DIRECTORY FOR PERSONAL WEB SERVER

The home directory is the main or root directory of a Web site and is where most users begin navigating a site. All of the Web and ASP pages you want users to be able to access must be stored in the home directory or its subdirectories. Each Web site must have a home directory.

By default, the C:\Inetpub\wwwroot directory is set as the home directory when Personal Web Server is installed, but you can set another directory as the home directory. This is useful

if you already have a directory that stores the pages you want users to be able to display and you do not want to copy the pages to the default home directory.

The home directory is mapped to the name of the Web site. For example, the home directory of C:\files may be mapped to the abccorp.com Web site. If the C:\files directory contains a Web page called info.html, the page can be accessed using the address www.abccorp.com/info.html.

CHANGE THE HOME DIRECTORY FOR PERSONAL WEB SERVER

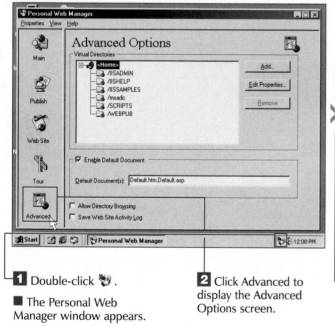

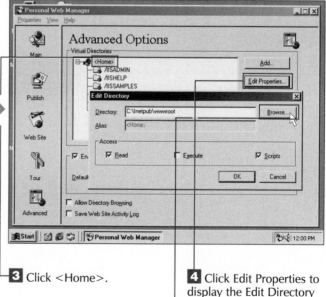

1 Double-click 🌏 .

■ The Personal Web Manager window appears.

2 Click Advanced to display the Advanced Options screen.

3 Click <Home>.

4 Click Edit Properties to display the Edit Directory dialog box.

5 Click Browse to display the Browse for Folder dialog box.

Extra

You can specify how you want a directory, including the home directory, to be accessed. You must specify the access permissions for each directory and subdirectory individually. In the Advanced Options screen, double-click the directory you want to specify access permissions for and then select the appropriate permissions in the Edit Directory dialog box.

Read

This option allows users to access Web pages and must be turned on for a directory containing content you want to be displayed. If this option is turned off, Personal Web Server will generate an error when a user requests a page. This option should be turned off for directories containing programs executed only by Personal Web Server.

Execute

This option allows users to run applications in a directory. For security reasons, this option should be turned off for a directory containing only displayable content.

Scripts

This option allows users to run scripts in a directory and must be turned on for a directory containing ASP pages. If this option is turned off, Personal Web Server will generate an error when a user requests an ASP page.

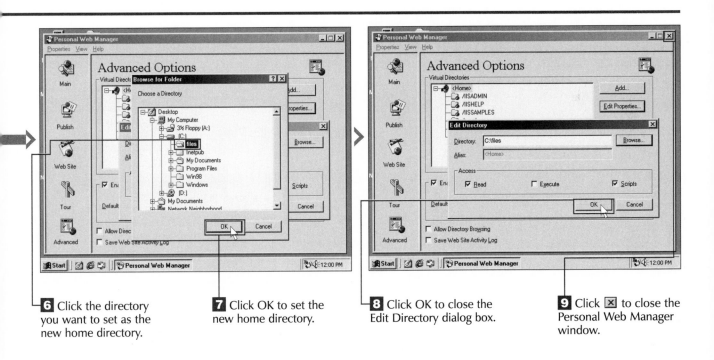

■6 Click the directory you want to set as the new home directory.

■7 Click OK to set the new home directory.

■8 Click OK to close the Edit Directory dialog box.

■9 Click ☒ to close the Personal Web Manager window.

ADD A VIRTUAL DIRECTORY TO PERSONAL WEB SERVER

O nly Web pages stored in the home directory of Personal Web Server or its subdirectories can be displayed by users. By default, the home directory and its subdirectories are found in C:\Inetpub\wwwroot. You can create a virtual directory to make Web pages that are not stored in the home directory or its subdirectories available for viewing. Users displaying pages in a virtual directory will not be able to determine the actual location of the directory on the computer.

You must specify the location of the directory you want to make a virtual directory. You must also give the directory an alias, which is a name that users will use to access pages in the directory. An alias

is often used to shorten a long directory name. For example, a directory named '1999_sales_information' could be assigned the alias 'sales'.

You can specify how you want the virtual directory to be accessed. The Read option allows users to access Web pages and must be turned on for a virtual directory containing content you want to be displayed. The Execute option allows applications to run in the directory and should be turned off for virtual directories containing only displayable content. The Scripts option allows scripts to run in the directory and must be turned on for virtual directories that contain ASP pages.

ADD A VIRTUAL DIRECTORY TO PERSONAL WEB SERVER

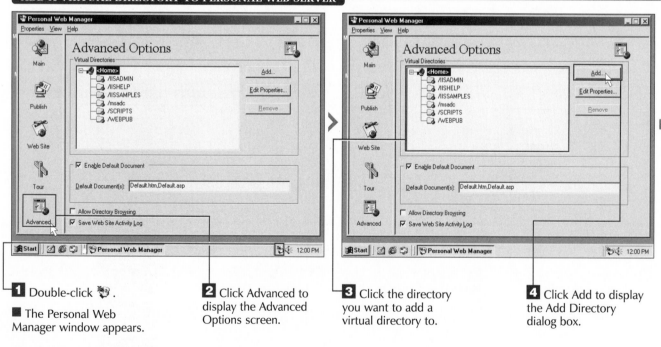

■1 Double-click 🐾.

■ The Personal Web Manager window appears.

■2 Click Advanced to display the Advanced Options screen.

■3 Click the directory you want to add a virtual directory to.

■4 Click Add to display the Add Directory dialog box.

Extra

You can also use Windows Explorer to add a virtual directory to Personal Web Server. Display the Exploring window and select the directory you want to add as a virtual directory. Click the File menu and then choose Properties. In the Properties dialog box, click the Web Sharing tab and then select the Share this folder option. In the Edit Alias dialog box, type an alias for the virtual directory and select the access options you want to use for the directory. Then click OK. Click OK in the Properties dialog box to add the virtual directory to Personal Web Server.

You can easily remove a virtual directory you no longer need from Personal Web Server. Display the Advanced Options screen in the Personal Web Manager window and select the virtual directory you want to remove. Click the Remove button and then click Yes in the warning dialog box that appears. Removing a virtual directory prevents users from accessing pages stored in the directory but does not remove the directory and its contents from the computer.

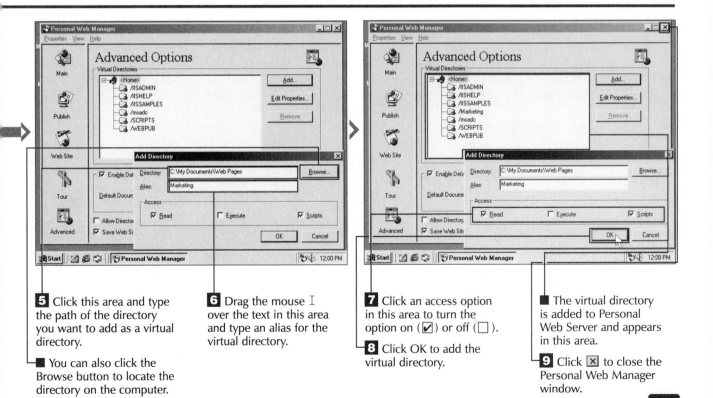

5 Click this area and type the path of the directory you want to add as a virtual directory.

■ You can also click the Browse button to locate the directory on the computer.

6 Drag the mouse I over the text in this area and type an alias for the virtual directory.

7 Click an access option in this area to turn the option on (☑) or off (☐).

8 Click OK to add the virtual directory.

■ The virtual directory is added to Personal Web Server and appears in this area.

9 Click ☒ to close the Personal Web Manager window.

SET PERSONAL WEB SERVER ADVANCED OPTIONS

Personal Web Server offers several advanced options you can set to customize your Web site.

The Enable Default Document option allows you to set a Web page to automatically appear in a user's Web browser when the user specifies a directory, but does not specify the name of the page they want to view. The Web page you want to automatically appear for a directory must be stored in the directory on the server. If a default document is not set, an error message will appear when a user does not specify the name of a page.

If you do not want to use a default document, you can use the Allow Directory Browsing option to allow users to view a list of all the subdirectories and pages a directory contains. When a user does not specify the name of the page they want to display, the user can select a page from the list.

You can use the Save Web Site Activity Log option to keep track of the Web and ASP pages that users access. Logging Web site activity is useful if you need to troubleshoot your pages. Activity logs can get quite large, so you may not want to use this option if storage space on your computer is a concern.

SET PERSONAL WEB SERVER ADVANCED OPTIONS

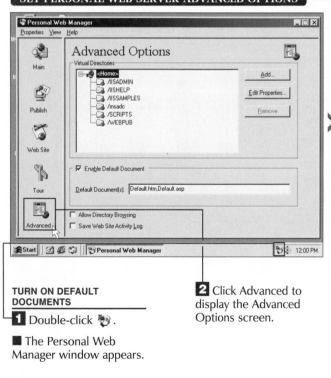

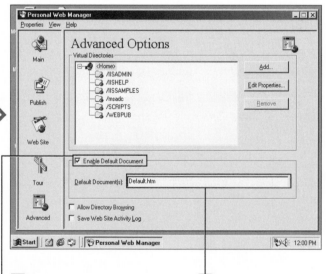

TURN ON DEFAULT DOCUMENTS

1 Double-click 🦋 .

■ The Personal Web Manager window appears.

2 Click Advanced to display the Advanced Options screen.

3 Click Enable Default Document to enable Personal Web Server to display a default document in a user's Web browser (☐ changes to ☑).

Note: This option may be turned on by default.

4 Drag the mouse I over the text in this area and type the name of the default document.

Extra

You can set a different default document for each subdirectory and *virtual* directory of Personal Web Server. Simply save each default document in the appropriate directory. Then enter the name of each default document, separated by a comma, in the Advanced Options screen in the Personal Web Manager window.

Log files are saved as text files and are usually found in the System\LogFiles\W3svc1 folder in the Windows operating system folder. A log file can be viewed using a text editor, such as Notepad.

A log file stores information about Web site activity, including the IP number of the computer that accessed a page, the date and time a page was accessed, the page title and any error numbers that were generated by Personal Web Server while a page was being accessed. Viewing this information can help you pinpoint problems you are experiencing with your pages.

Examples of log file entries:

172.17.224.176 - - [20/Oct/1999:13:05:24 -0800] "GET /index.htm HTTP/1.1" 200 238
172.30.114.201 - - [20/Oct/1999:13:05:26 -0800] "GET /index.htm HTTP/1.1" 200 238
192.168.24.233 - - [20/Oct/1999:13:05:49 -0800] "GET /index.htm HTTP/1.1" 200 284
192.168.74.225 - - [21/Oct/1999:08:57:08 -0800] "GET /index.htm HTTP/1.1" 200 287
172.31.187.193 - - [21/Oct/1999:09:00:36 -0800] "GET /index.htm HTTP/1.1" 200 290

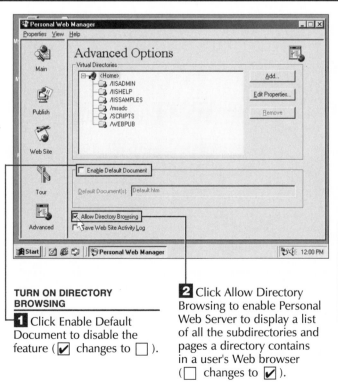

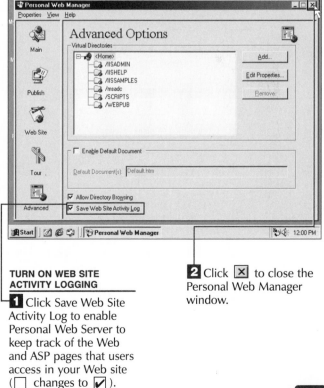

TURN ON DIRECTORY BROWSING

1 Click Enable Default Document to disable the feature (✔ changes to ☐).

2 Click Allow Directory Browsing to enable Personal Web Server to display a list of all the subdirectories and pages a directory contains in a user's Web browser (☐ changes to ✔).

TURN ON WEB SITE ACTIVITY LOGGING

1 Click Save Web Site Activity Log to enable Personal Web Server to keep track of the Web and ASP pages that users access in your Web site (☐ changes to ✔).

2 Click ☒ to close the Personal Web Manager window.

INSTALL INTERNET INFORMATION SERVER

Microsoft Internet Information Server (IIS) 5.0 is Web server software that allows you to host multiple Web sites on the Internet or on a network, such as a corporate intranet.

IIS 5.0 is available on the Windows 2000 Professional CD-ROM disc and includes Active Server Pages 3.0. IIS 5.0 offers many advanced features that allow you to effectively host and manage even the busiest Web sites. Although IIS 5.0 is powerful server software, it can still be used to learn about Web servers and Active Server Pages. IIS 5.0 can be used to perform all of the examples in this book.

To install IIS on a computer, you must add parts of the Internet Information Services component to the computer. The parts of the component that must be added are Common Files, which are the files required to run IIS; Internet Information Services Snap-In, which provides an interface you can use to administer your Web sites; and World Wide Web Server, which allows users to access your Web sites.

After IIS has been installed, you should restart the computer. IIS starts automatically each time the computer is started.

INSTALL INTERNET INFORMATION SERVER

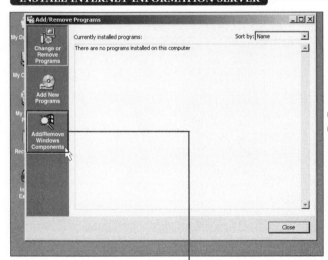

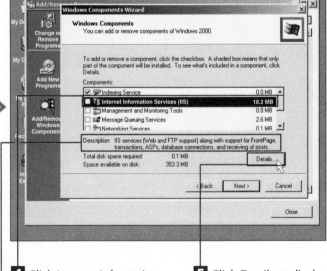

1 Insert the Windows 2000 Professional CD-ROM disc into a drive.

Note: If the Microsoft Windows 2000 CD dialog box appears, click ☒ *to close the dialog box.*

2 In the Control Panel, double-click Add/Remove Programs to display the Add/Remove Programs window.

3 Click Add/Remove Windows Components to display the Windows Components Wizard.

4 Click Internet Information Services (IIS).

■ This area displays a description of the Internet Information Services component.

5 Click Details to display the Internet Information Services (IIS) dialog box.

Extra

The Internet Information Services component includes several optional parts you can install. Documentation provides help files regarding the use of IIS and should be installed. File Transfer Protocol (FTP) Server allows IIS to host FTP sites. FrontPage 2000 Server Extensions allows IIS to use advanced FrontPage features. Personal Web Manager provides a graphical interface you can use to administer your Web sites. SMTP Service allows IIS to send e-mail messages. Visual InterDev RAD Remote Deployment Support allows Visual InterDev to work with IIS.

After IIS is installed, the Internet Information Services window allows you to administer your Web sites. Display the Control Panel and double-click Administrative Tools. In the Administrative Tools window, double-click Internet Services Manager to display the Internet Information Services window.

You can remove IIS from a computer. Perform steps 2 to 9 below, except select each part of the Internet Information Services component you want to remove in step 6 (☑ changes to ☐). Removing IIS from a computer does not remove the Inetpub\wwwroot directory and the files it stores from the computer.

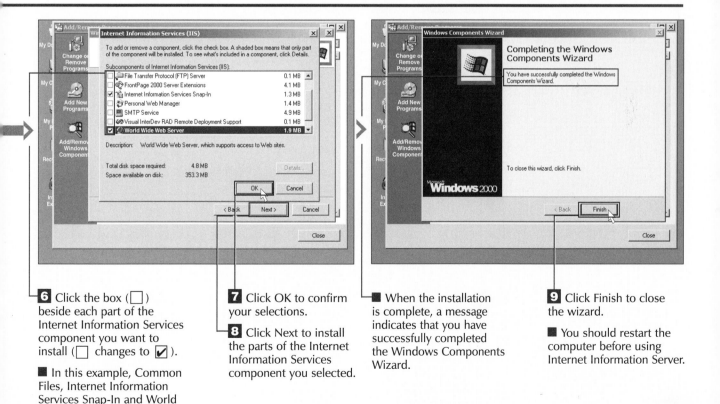

6 Click the box (☐) beside each part of the Internet Information Services component you want to install (☐ changes to ☑).

■ In this example, Common Files, Internet Information Services Snap-In and World Wide Web Server are selected.

7 Click OK to confirm your selections.

8 Click Next to install the parts of the Internet Information Services component you selected.

■ When the installation is complete, a message indicates that you have successfully completed the Windows Components Wizard.

9 Click Finish to close the wizard.

■ You should restart the computer before using Internet Information Server.

CHANGE THE HOME DIRECTORY FOR INTERNET INFORMATION SERVER

The home directory is the main or root directory of a Web site. All of the Web and ASP pages you want users to be able to access must be stored in the home directory or its subdirectories. Each Web site on Internet Information Server (IIS) must have a home directory.

The C:\Inetpub\wwwroot directory is automatically set as the home directory when IIS is installed, but you can set another directory as the home directory. This is useful if you already have a directory that

stores the pages you want users to be able to display and you do not want to copy the pages to the default home directory.

The home directory is where most users begin navigating a Web site and usually contains a default document. When a user specifies the name of a Web site but does not specify the page they want to view, the default document is displayed. For more information about default documents, see page 22.

CHANGE THE HOME DIRECTORY FOR INTERNET INFORMATION SERVER

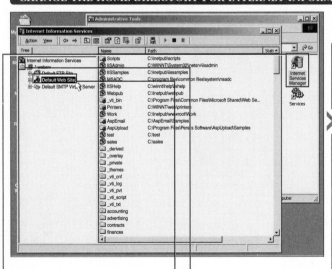

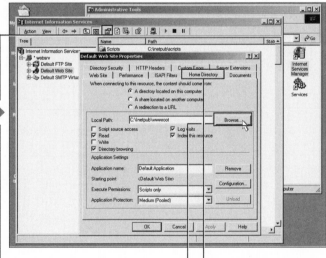

■1 In the Control Panel, double-click Administrative Tools to display the Administrative Tools window.

■2 Double-click Internet Services Manager to display the Internet Information Services window.

■3 Click ⊞ to display a list of Web sites on the Web server (⊞ changes to ⊟).

■4 Click the Web site you want to change the home directory for.

■5 Click 🖼 to display the Properties dialog box.

■6 Click the Home Directory tab.

■7 Click Browse to display the Browse for Folder dialog box.

Extra You can specify the type of home directory you want to set. Perform steps 1 to 5 below to display the Home Directory tab of the Properties dialog box and then select the option you want to use.

OPTION	DESCRIPTION
A directory located on this computer	Allows you to set any directory located on the Web server as the home directory. This includes a directory located on a removable storage device such as a hard drive, DVD-ROM disc or CD-ROM disc.
A share located on another computer	Allows you to set a shared directory stored on another computer on the network as the home directory. Click the Connect As button to specify a user name and password for the shared directory, if necessary.
A redirection to a URL	Allows you to specify a URL as the home directory. Users who access the Web site will be redirected to the Web page specified in the URL. This is useful if your Web site is still being developed.

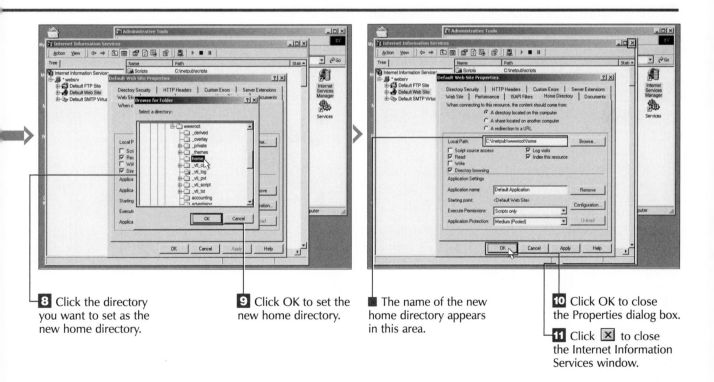

8 Click the directory you want to set as the new home directory.

9 Click OK to set the new home directory.

■ The name of the new home directory appears in this area.

10 Click OK to close the Properties dialog box.

11 Click ✕ to close the Internet Information Services window.

ADD A VIRTUAL DIRECTORY TO INTERNET INFORMATION SERVER

When Internet Information Server (IIS) is installed, a number of directories are created that can be used to store Web pages. By default, these directories are stored in the home directory C:\Inetpub\wwwroot. Only Web pages stored in the home directory or its subdirectories can be displayed by users. You can create a virtual directory to make Web pages that are not stored in the home directory or its subdirectories available for viewing.

You must give the virtual directory an alias, which is a name users will use to access pages in the directory. An alias is often used to shorten a long directory name. For example, a directory named '2000_marketing_information' could be assigned the alias 'marketing'. Short directory names can help make a Web site easier for users to navigate.

Virtual directories allow IIS to make a directory accessible to users of a Web site regardless of the location of the directory. For example, the directory C:\datapages can be added to the abccorp.com Web site as a virtual directory with the alias 'data'. Users can then use the address www.abccorp.com/data/ to access pages in the virtual directory.

ADD A VIRTUAL DIRECTORY TO INTERNET INFORMATION SERVER

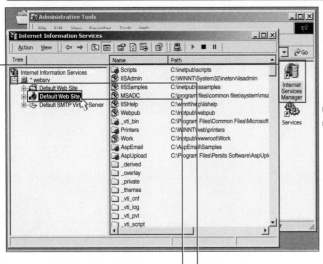

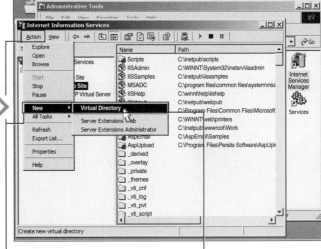

1 In the Control Panel, double-click Administrative Tools to display the Administrative Tools window.

2 Double-click Internet Services Manager to display the Internet Information Services window.

3 Click ⊞ to display a list of Web sites on the Web server (⊞ changes to ⊟).

4 Click the Web site you want to add a virtual directory to.

5 Click Action.

6 Click New.

7 Click Virtual Directory.

Extra

You can also use Windows Explorer to add a virtual directory to IIS. Display the Exploring window and select the directory you want to add as a virtual directory. Click the File menu and then choose Properties. In the Properties dialog box, click the Web Sharing tab and then select the Share this folder option. In the Edit Alias dialog box, type an alias for the virtual directory and select the access and application permissions you want to use for the directory. Then click OK. Click OK in the Properties dialog box to add the virtual directory to IIS.

You can easily remove a virtual directory you no longer need from IIS. Perform steps 1 and 2 below to display the Internet Information Services window and then select the virtual directory you want to remove. Click the Delete button (☒) and then click Yes in the dialog box that appears. Removing a virtual directory prevents users from accessing pages stored in the directory but does not remove the directory and its contents from the computer.

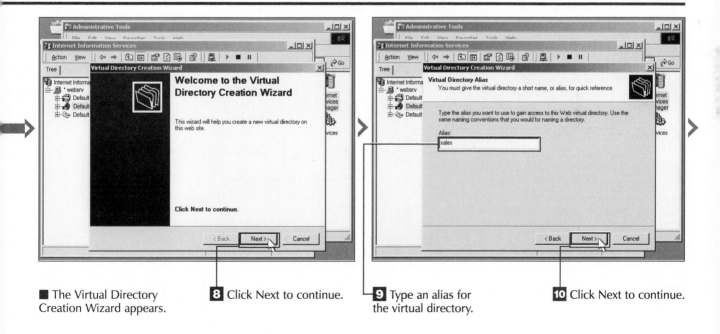

■ The Virtual Directory Creation Wizard appears.

8 Click Next to continue.

9 Type an alias for the virtual directory.

10 Click Next to continue.

CONTINUED ▶

ADD A VIRTUAL DIRECTORY TO INTERNET INFORMATION SERVER

You must specify the location of the directory you want to add as a virtual directory to IIS. You must also specify the access permissions for the directory. Access permissions determine how the Web pages and other files in the directory can be utilized.

The Read permission allows users to access Web pages and must be turned on for a virtual directory containing content you want to be displayed. The Read permission is turned on by default.

The Run scripts permission allows scripts to run in the directory and must be turned on for virtual directories that contain ASP pages. The Run scripts permission is turned on by default.

The Execute permission allows applications to run in the virtual directory. For security reasons, the Execute permission is rarely enabled.

The Write permission allows files to be created in the directory and must be turned on for virtual directories containing ASP pages that create files.

The Browse permission allows users to view a list of all the subdirectories and pages the virtual directory contains. When a user specifies a directory but does not specify the name of the page they want to display, the user can select a page from the list.

ADD A VIRTUAL DIRECTORY TO INTERNET INFORMATION SERVER (CONTINUED)

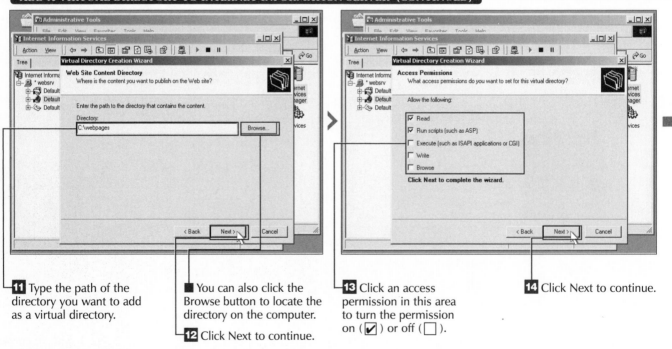

■11 Type the path of the directory you want to add as a virtual directory.

■ You can also click the Browse button to locate the directory on the computer.

■12 Click Next to continue.

■13 Click an access permission in this area to turn the permission on (✔) or off (☐).

■14 Click Next to continue.

Extra

You can later change the properties of a virtual directory you have added to IIS. Display the Internet Information Services window and select the virtual directory whose properties you want to change. Click the Properties button (🖼️) to display the Properties dialog box. You can then change the properties of the virtual directory.

A virtual directory you add to IIS may be affected by folder permissions set by the Windows operating system. Folder permissions restrict who can access the folder and how the files in the folder can be used. For more information about folder permissions, see page 28.

Users accessing a virtual directory you have added to IIS will not be able to determine the actual location of the directory on the computer.

After a virtual directory is created, all the Web pages and files in the directory will be available to users accessing the Web site. You should be careful to store only files and Web pages you want users to be able to view in the virtual directory.

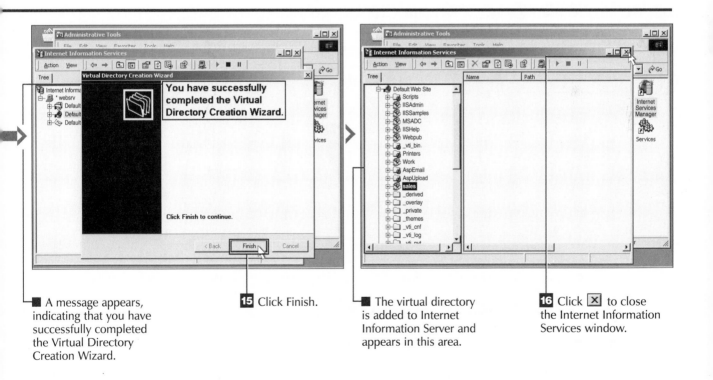

■ A message appears, indicating that you have successfully completed the Virtual Directory Creation Wizard.

15 Click Finish.

■ The virtual directory is added to Internet Information Server and appears in this area.

16 Click ☒ to close the Internet Information Services window.

SET A DEFAULT DOCUMENT FOR INTERNET INFORMATION SERVER

Internet Information Server (IIS) allows you to set a default document for a Web site. A default document is a Web page that automatically appears in a user's Web browser when the user specifies a directory but does not specify the name of the page they want to view. If a default document is not set and a user specifies only the name of a directory, an error message or a list of the subdirectories and pages the directory contains will appear in the user's browser.

A different default document can be used for each directory in a Web site. You must store the default document you want to automatically appear for a directory in the directory on the server. You must also add the name of the default document to the list of default documents in IIS.

When a user enters a directory name but does not specify a page name, IIS compares the name of the first default document in the list to the files stored in the directory. If IIS does not find a match, it searches the directory for the second default document in the list. IIS checks the name of each default document in the list until a match is found in the directory or the list is exhausted. If a match is found, the document is displayed.

SET A DEFAULT DOCUMENT FOR INTERNET INFORMATION SERVER

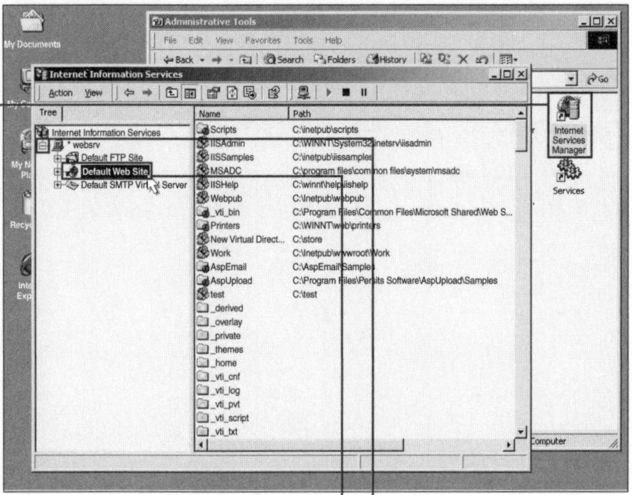

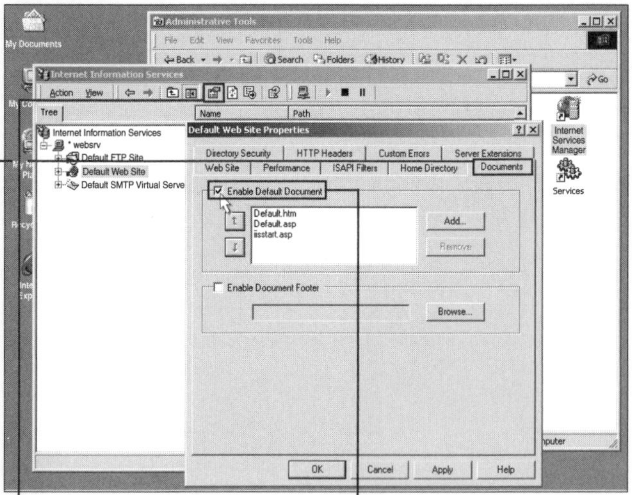

1 In the Control Panel, double-click Administrative Tools to display the Administrative Tools window.

2 Double-click Internet Services Manager to display the Internet Information Services window.

3 Click [+] to display a list of Web sites on the Web server ([+] changes to [−]).

4 Click the Web site you want to set a default document for.

5 Click [Properties] to display the Properties dialog box.

6 Click the Documents tab.

7 To enable IIS to display a default document in a user's Web browser, click Enable Default Document (☐ changes to ☑).

Note: This option may be enabled by default.

Extra

You can use the Enable Document Footer property to easily display the same footer information at the bottom of each Web page in a Web site. Footers are often used to display copyright information, contact information or a company logo.

To add a footer to each page, you must first create the HTML file that stores the footer information you want to display. The code in the footer file should contain only the information and the HTML tags needed to format the information. The code should not contain HTML tags such as <TITLE> or <BODY>.

Perform steps 1 to 6 below to display the Documents tab of the Properties dialog box and click Enable Document Footer (☐ changes to ✔). Then click the Browse button to locate the footer file you created on the computer.

Example of HTML footer file code:

```
<SMALL>Copyright: 2000 James Smith</SMALL>
```

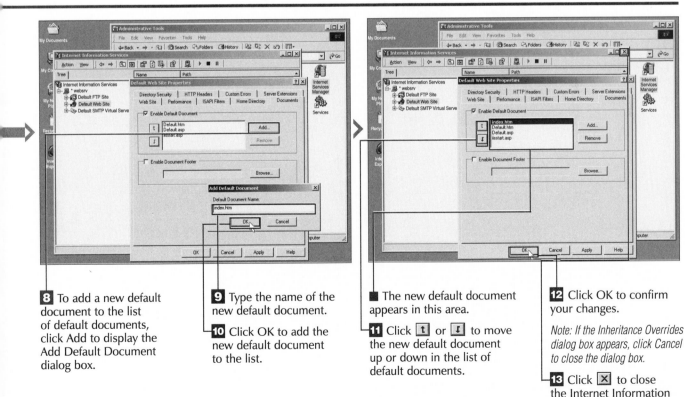

8 To add a new default document to the list of default documents, click Add to display the Add Default Document dialog box.

9 Type the name of the new default document.

10 Click OK to add the new default document to the list.

■ The new default document appears in this area.

11 Click ↑ or ↓ to move the new default document up or down in the list of default documents.

12 Click OK to confirm your changes.

Note: If the Inheritance Overrides dialog box appears, click Cancel to close the dialog box.

13 Click ✕ to close the Internet Information Services window.

CHANGE LOG FILE PROPERTIES OF INTERNET INFORMATION SERVER

An Internet Information Server (IIS) log file keeps track of the requests received by a Web site and can contain information such as the names of the Web pages that were accessed and the IP numbers of clients that accessed the site.

After logging is enabled for a Web site, you can choose to organize the information in the log file using the NCSA Common Log File Format, W3C Extended Log File Format or Microsoft IIS Log File Format. The format you choose depends on the amount of information the log file needs to store and the way the information must be organized. The Microsoft format is suitable for most cases,

unless you intend to use a third-party utility to analyze the log files.

You can specify when you want to create a new log file for a Web site. A busy Web site may need to use an option that creates log files frequently, such as Hourly. A less frequently used Web site may be better suited to an option such as Unlimited file size, which always places logged data in the same file.

You can specify the location of the log file on the Web server. By default, the log file is saved in the System32\LogFiles directory in the Windows operating system directory.

CHANGE LOG FILE PROPERTIES OF INTERNET INFORMATION SERVER

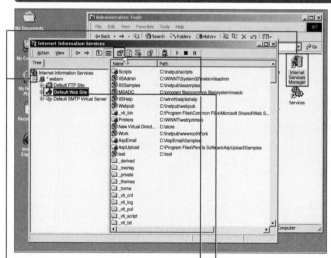

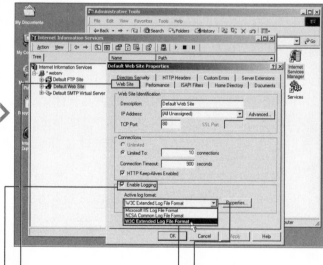

1 In the Control Panel, double-click Administrative Tools to display the Administrative Tools window.

2 Double-click Internet Services Manager to display the Internet Information Services window.

3 Click ⊞ to display a list of Web sites on the Web server (⊞ changes to ⊟).

4 Click the Web site you want to change the log file properties for.

5 Click 🖼 to display the Properties dialog box.

6 Click the Web Site tab.

7 Click Enable Logging to enable the Web site to log information (☐ changes to ✔).

Note: This option may be enabled by default.

8 Click this area to display a list of the available log file formats.

9 Click the log file format you want to use.

Extra

If you chose the W3C log file format, you can specify the information you want to include in the log file. Perform steps 1 to 12 below to set the properties for the log file. Click the Extended Properties tab and then click each extended logging option to enable (✔) or disable (☐) the option. For example, you may want to enable the User Agent option to log information about the type of Web browser people use to access your Web site.

You can disable logging for a specific directory on a Web site. Perform steps 1 to 4 below and then click the directory you no longer want to log. Click 🖻 to display the Properties dialog box and click the Log visits option (✔ changes to ☐).

The name of the log file is displayed at the bottom of the General Properties tab in the Extended Logging Properties dialog box. The first two characters of the log file name indicate the format of the log file. Log files using the W3C format start with 'ex'. Log files using the Microsoft format start with 'in' and log files using the NCSA format start with 'nc'. The rest of the file name indicates the time period selected to create new log files. For example, if you chose the Daily option, the log file name will be in the yymmdd format, such as ex000520.log.

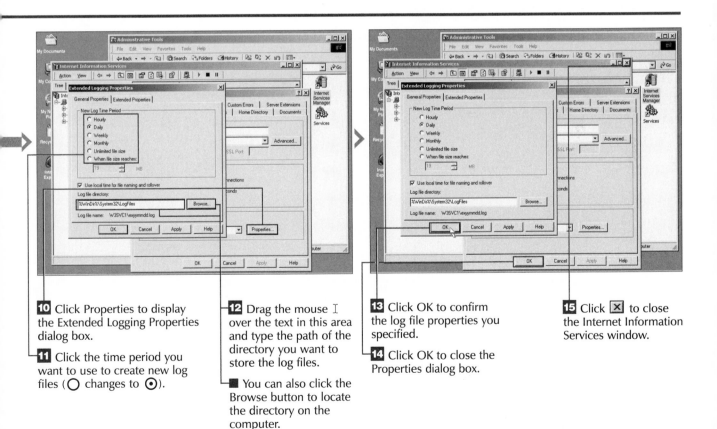

10 Click Properties to display the Extended Logging Properties dialog box.

11 Click the time period you want to use to create new log files (○ changes to ⊙).

12 Drag the mouse I over the text in this area and type the path of the directory you want to store the log files.

■ You can also click the Browse button to locate the directory on the computer.

13 Click OK to confirm the log file properties you specified.

14 Click OK to close the Properties dialog box.

15 Click ⊠ to close the Internet Information Services window.

STOP, START OR PAUSE A WEB SITE

There are times when a Web site needs to be stopped, such as when you need to perform file maintenance, backups or virus checks on the site. Stopping a Web site from running will cause an immediate interruption of service for all users accessing the site. Any activity being performed by the Web site, such as processing an ASP page or creating a file, is stopped immediately.

Some Web site configuration tasks can be performed while the site is running but do not take effect until the site is restarted. You can stop and then start the

site to apply the changes. Starting a Web site you previously stopped also allows users to once again access information on the site.

Web sites can also be paused. Pausing a Web site does not stop the site from completing any activities that are in progress, but it does prevent any new activity on the Web site. For busy Web sites, it is common to first pause the Web site and then wait until all activity has ceased before stopping the Web site.

STOP, START OR PAUSE THE WEB SITE

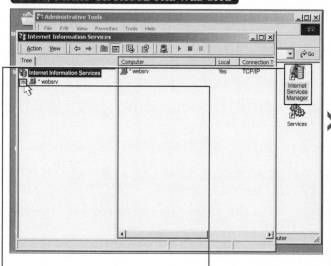

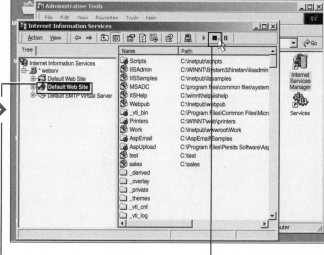

1 In the Control Panel, double-click Administrative Tools to display the Administrative Tools window.

2 Double-click Internet Services Manager to display the Internet Information Services window.

3 Click ⊞ to display a list of Web sites on the Web server (⊞ changes to ⊟).

STOP A WEB SITE

4 Click the Web site you want to stop.

5 Click ■ to stop the Web site.

Extra

You can stop and start a Web server using the `iisreset` command. Using this command to stop or start a Web server will stop or start all the Web sites on the server. At the Command Prompt on the Web server, type **iisreset /** followed by the action you want to perform.

COMMAND	DESCRIPTION
`iisreset /restart`	Stop and then restart the Web server.
`iisreset /start`	Start the Web server.
`iisreset /stop`	Stop the Web server.
`iisreset /reboot`	Restart the computer.
`iisreset /rebootonerror`	Restart the computer if an error occurs while stopping, starting or pausing the Web server.
`iisreset /status`	Display the current status of the Web server.
`iisreset /?`	Display information about the `iisreset` command.

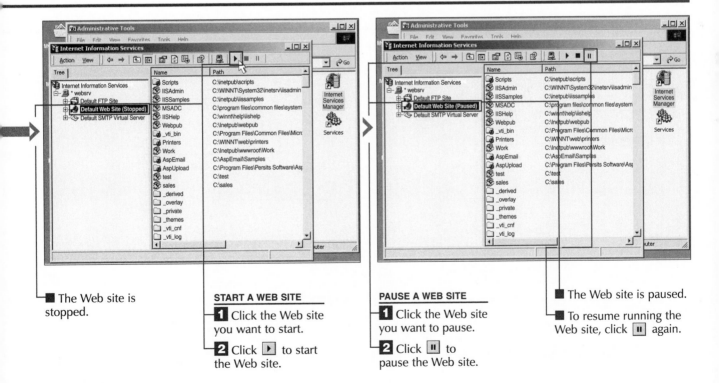

■ The Web site is stopped.

START A WEB SITE

1 Click the Web site you want to start.

2 Click ▶ to start the Web site.

PAUSE A WEB SITE

1 Click the Web site you want to pause.

2 Click ▮▮ to pause the Web site.

■ The Web site is paused.

■ To resume running the Web site, click ▮▮ again.

SET WINDOWS FILE AND FOLDER PERMISSIONS

You can change permissions to grant users and groups of users different types of access to a file or folder on Internet Information Server (IIS).

The type of permissions that can be set for a file or folder depend on the operating system and file system installed on the Web server. The steps below are for use on a server running the Windows 2000 operating system with the NTFS file system.

When IIS is installed, a user account is created called IUSR_ followed by the name of the computer, such as IUSR_WEBSRV. This user account is part of the Everyone group. If you deny the Everyone

group access to a file or folder, you can use the IUSR account to allow users to access information in the file or folder.

You can allow or deny permissions for a user or group to specify how a file or folder can be accessed. Full Control allows users to modify, add, move and delete files, as well as change permissions. Modify allows users to modify, add, move and delete files. Read and Execute allows users to run applications, such as scripts. List Folder Contents allows users to display a list of files and folders stored in a folder. Read allows users to display files. Write allows users to change files.

SET WINDOWS FILE AND FOLDER PERMISSIONS

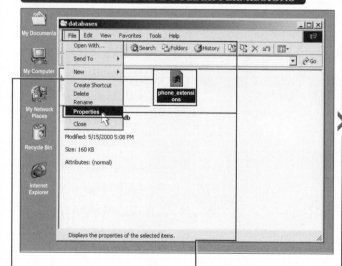

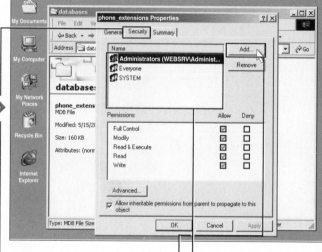

1 Click the file or folder you want to change the permissions for.

2 Click File.

3 Click Properties to display the Properties dialog box.

4 Click the Security tab.

■ This area lists the users and groups that can access the file or folder.

5 Click Add to display the Select Users, Computers, or Groups dialog box.

Extra

Great care must be taken when setting file and folder permissions on a Web server. To gain a full understanding of file and folder permissions and the consequences of changing these permissions, you should consult the operating system and Web server documentation. Incorrectly setting file and folder permissions on a Web server can leave the server vulnerable to a range of problems, from accidental data deletion to serious security breaches. Incorrect file and folder permissions can also prevent all users from accessing the Web server.

Windows file and folder permissions work with the access permissions set in IIS. Access permissions set for a folder in IIS apply to all users who access the folder. Windows folder permissions apply only to the users and groups you specify. When Windows file and folder permissions and IIS access permissions are set differently, the Web server uses the most restrictive permissions. For more information about IIS access permissions, see page 20.

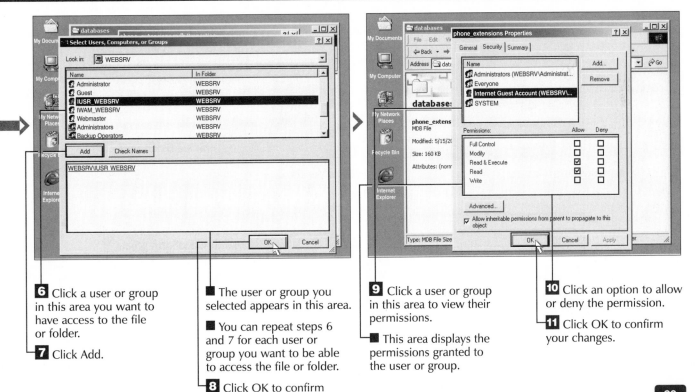

6 Click a user or group in this area you want to have access to the file or folder.

7 Click Add.

■ The user or group you selected appears in this area.

■ You can repeat steps 6 and 7 for each user or group you want to be able to access the file or folder.

8 Click OK to confirm your selection.

9 Click a user or group in this area to view their permissions.

■ This area displays the permissions granted to the user or group.

10 Click an option to allow or deny the permission.

11 Click OK to confirm your changes.

INTRODUCTION TO HTML

HyperText Markup Language (HTML) is a computer language used to create Web pages. Web pages are HTML documents, which consist of text and tags. HTML documents can be created with a simple text editor. A Web browser interprets the tags in an HTML document and displays the document as a Web page.

The major benefit of using Web pages to display information is that Web pages can be displayed on any computer that has a Web browser installed, including computers running a Unix, Windows or Macintosh operating system. Web pages can also be displayed on devices such as handheld computers and some mobile telephones.

Since HTML documents contain only text, they are ideal for transferring information over slow networks, such as the Internet.

HTML ESSENTIALS

Web Browsers

Microsoft Internet Explorer and Netscape Navigator are currently the most popular Web browsers. Microsoft Internet Explorer is included with Windows 98 and Windows 2000. You can also download the browser from the www.microsoft.com/ie Web site. Netscape Navigator is available at the www.netscape.com Web site.

Tags

Tags tell a Web browser about the structure of a Web page. Each tag gives a specific instruction and is surrounded by angle brackets < >. Most tags have an opening tag and a closing tag that affect the text between the tags. Some tags have attributes that offer options for the tag. For example, the <FONT> tag has a COLOR attribute that lets you change the color of text.

Web Browser Support

A Web page may not look the same when displayed in different Web browsers. Not all Web browsers support all the features of HTML and each Web browser may interpret HTML tags differently. Some companies that make Web browsers have also developed their own tags that Web browsers made by other companies may not be able to understand. If a Web browser does not understand a tag, the tag is usually ignored.

HTML Versions

There are several versions of HTML. HTML specifications are constantly evolving and a new version of HTML is released about every two years. Each version offers new features to give users more control when creating Web pages. HTML version 4.01 is the latest version of HTML, although most Web pages conform to HTML 3.2. The World Wide Web Consortium (W3C) regulates the versions of HTML. You can view information about HTML and its versions at the www.w3c.org Web site.

PROGRAMS FOR CREATING WEB PAGES

A text editor is a simple program that allows you to create, modify and save files that contain text, such as HTML documents. Most text editors do not include advanced editing and formatting features. To create a Web page using a text editor, you must add HTML tags to your text to specify how you want the text to appear on the page.

You can also use a word processor, such as Microsoft Word or Corel WordPerfect, to create HTML documents. Word processors provide advanced editing and formatting features to help you create documents, but you must use HTML

tags to format the text on a Web page. Any formatting you apply to text using a word processor's formatting features will not appear when you view the page on the Web.

There are also specialized software tools and programs, such as visual editors and HTML editors, that are specifically designed to help you develop Web pages. Visual editors and some HTML editors allow you to see how your Web page will appear while you are creating the page. Many professional Web masters, however, still use simple text editors to create their Web pages.

PROGRAMS FOR CREATING WEB PAGES

Notepad	Visual InterDev
Microsoft Notepad is a simple text editor included with Microsoft Windows operating systems. Most operating systems contain a text editor similar to Notepad.	Microsoft Visual InterDev is an ideal tool for people who have experience using Microsoft programming products. Visual InterDev is often used to maintain large, highly complicated Web sites. You can find information about Visual InterDev at www.microsoft.com/vinterdev.
UltraEdit	**HomeSite**
UltraEdit is a text-editing program that contains features such as syntax highlighting, which color-codes HTML tags to make the document easier to read, and the ability to save Web pages directly to a Web server. UltraEdit is a shareware program available at www.ultraedit.com.	Allaire's HomeSite is a comprehensive HTML editor designed for creating Web pages. HomeSite is suitable for beginners creating a small number of Web pages and for experienced Web masters producing complicated Web pages and Web sites. HomeSite is available at www.allaire.com.

CREATE A WEB PAGE

You can use a text editor to create a Web page. You should add the <HTML>, <HEAD> and <BODY> tags to every Web page you create.

Each tag gives a specific instruction. Most tags have an opening tag and a closing tag that affect the text between the tags. The closing tag has a forward slash (/). Most people type tags in uppercase letters to make the tags stand out from the text in the Web page.

The <HTML> tag identifies a document as a Web page.

The <HEAD> tag indicates the head of the Web page and can contain information such as the title of the page, the author of the page and keywords to be used by search tools to catalog the page. Information you enter between the <HEAD> and </HEAD> tags will not appear on the Web page.

You must enter the text you want to display on a Web page between the <BODY> and </BODY> tags. You can use alphanumeric characters and symbols to display information on your Web page.

CREATE A WEB PAGE

Untitled - Notepad
File   Edit   Search   Help

```
<HTML>
<HEAD>
<TITLE>Fruit and Flowers</TITLE>
</HEAD>

</HTML>
```

Untitled - Notepad
File   Edit   Search   Help

```
<HTML>
<HEAD>
<TITLE>Fruit and Flowers</TITLE>
</HEAD>
<BODY>
Fruit and Flowers, Inc.
No garden? No problem!
Our special, patented fertilizer lets you grow lush flowers and healthy fruit
INDOORS!
Grow beautiful, exotic flowers and impress your friends!
Grow your own fruit and save on your grocery bills!
Our fruit selection includes:
Popular berries such as strawberries, raspberries and blueberries.
Exotic fruit such as mangos, papayas and kiwis.
Our flower selection includes:
Seasonal plants such as poinsettias, holly and mistletoe.
Tropical flowers such as orchids, birds of paradise and yellow jasmine.

</BODY>
</HTML>
```

1 Start the text editor you will use to create a Web page.

2 Type **<HTML>** at the top of the page. Then press Enter twice and type **</HTML>**.

3 Type **<HEAD>** directly below the <HTML> tag. Then press Enter.

4 Type the information you want the head to contain. Then press Enter.

5 Type **</HEAD>**. Then press Enter twice.

6 Type **<BODY>** directly below the </HEAD> tag. Then press Enter twice.

7 Type **</BODY>** directly above the </HTML> tag.

8 Click directly below the <BODY> tag and type the text you want to display on the Web page.

■ You can now add the HTML tags that will structure and format the text on the Web page.

SAVE A WEB PAGE

You must save a Web page before you can view the page in a Web browser.

Make sure you add the .html or .htm extension to the name of a Web page you save. Some text editors do not recognize the .html or .htm extension, so you may have to enclose the Web page name in quotation marks, such as "index.html". A Web page name can contain alphanumeric characters but should not contain spaces.

If you create a Web page in a word processor, you must save the page in a text only format. Otherwise, you will not be able to display the page in a Web browser.

After you save a Web page you have created, you can use the Web browser installed on your computer to see how the page will appear on the Web.

You can view and edit the HTML code for a Web page you have saved. You must save any changes you make before viewing the changes in a Web browser.

SAVE A WEB PAGE

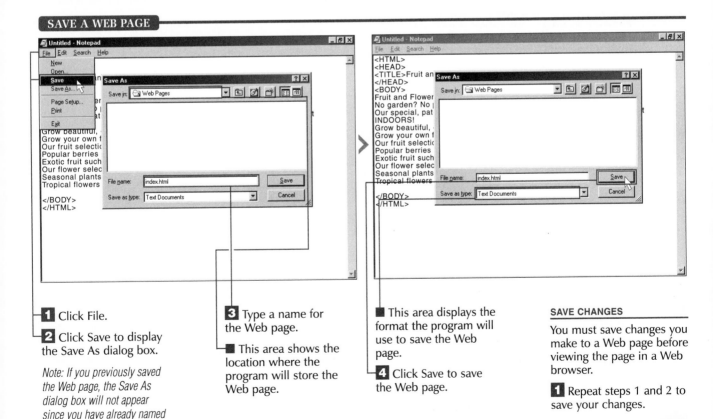

1 Click File.

2 Click Save to display the Save As dialog box.

Note: If you previously saved the Web page, the Save As dialog box will not appear since you have already named the page.

3 Type a name for the Web page.

■ This area shows the location where the program will store the Web page.

■ This area displays the format the program will use to save the Web page.

4 Click Save to save the Web page.

SAVE CHANGES

You must save changes you make to a Web page before viewing the page in a Web browser.

1 Repeat steps 1 and 2 to save your changes.

DISPLAY A WEB PAGE IN A WEB BROWSER

D isplaying your Web page in a Web browser allows you to see how your page will appear on the Web. The most popular Web browsers include Microsoft Internet Explorer and Netscape Navigator.

A Web browser reads the HTML code used to create a Web page and then displays the Web page in the Web browser window. As a Web browser reads each section of HTML code, the browser displays the resulting information on the screen. This means the Web browser will display the first part of a Web page before it has completely finished processing the page.

The most current Web browsers will be able to display Web pages created with the latest version of HTML, but older browsers may not be able to properly display Web pages created with a newer version of HTML.

If a Web page you want to view is saved on your own computer, you can locate the page and then display it in the Web browser. If a Web page you want to view is stored on a remote Web server, you can enter the URL of the Web page to display the page.

DISPLAY A WEB PAGE IN A WEB BROWSER

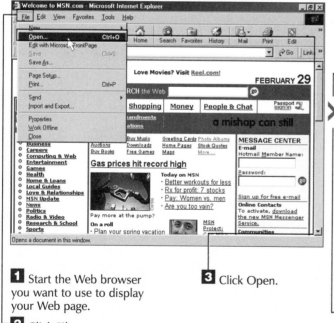

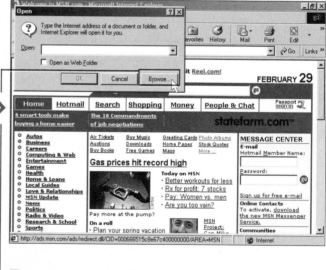

1 Start the Web browser you want to use to display your Web page.

2 Click File to open your Web page in the Web browser.

3 Click Open.

■ The Open dialog box appears.

4 Click Browse to locate the Web page on your computer.

■ A dialog box appears.

Extra

Even though you can display your Web page in a Web browser, other people on the Web cannot view your Web page. You must transfer the page to a server that makes Web pages available on the Web before other people can view the page.

If you cannot find the Web page you want to open, you may have saved the Web page incorrectly. When saving a Web page, you must save the page in a text only format and add the .html or .htm extension to the name of the page.

Your Web page will look different in different Web browsers because each type of browser displays Web pages in a slightly different way. You should display your Web page in several types of Web browsers so you can see how each browser will display your page. In addition to Microsoft Internet Explorer and Netscape Navigator, other Web browsers include Opera and Lynx. For information on Opera, visit the www.opera.com Web site. For information on Lynx, visit the lynx.browser.org Web site.

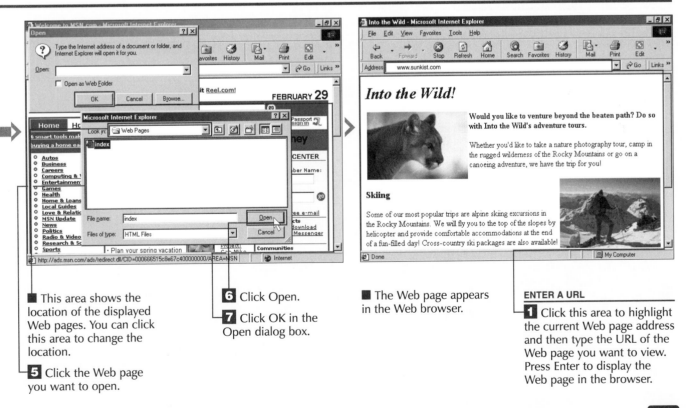

■ This area shows the location of the displayed Web pages. You can click this area to change the location.

5 Click the Web page you want to open.

6 Click Open.

7 Click OK in the Open dialog box.

■ The Web page appears in the Web browser.

ENTER A URL

1 Click this area to highlight the current Web page address and then type the URL of the Web page you want to view. Press Enter to display the Web page in the browser.

VIEW HTML CODE FOR A WEB PAGE

When you display a Web page, the Web server sends the HTML code used to create the page to your Web browser. Your Web browser reads the code and displays the page on the screen. While the page is displayed on your screen, you can view the HTML code used to create the page.

Viewing the HTML code you used to create a Web page can help you troubleshoot problems the page contains. For example, if a Web browser displays a blank screen when you display your Web page, you can view the HTML code for the page to determine if there is an error in the code.

When you view the HTML code for your Web page, you can make changes to the code. You must save any changes you make to apply the changes to the Web page.

You can also view the HTML code for a Web page you did not create. This is a good way to get ideas for creating your own Web pages. Keep in mind that Web page content, such as text, images and sounds, may be copyrighted, so you should not copy information from a Web page without first obtaining permission from the author of the page.

VIEW HTML CODE FOR A WEB PAGE

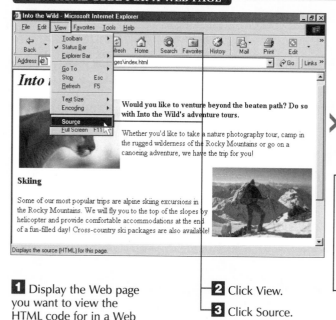

1 Display the Web page you want to view the HTML code for in a Web browser.

2 Click View.

3 Click Source.

■ A window appears, displaying the HTML code used to create the Web page.

■ If you are viewing the HTML code for a Web page you created, you can edit the code. If you edit the code, you must save your changes before redisplaying the page.

REFRESH A WEB PAGE

If you make changes to your Web page, you can display the changes in a Web browser to see how the updated page will appear on the Web.

Most Web browsers store the Web pages you display in a file or folder called a cache. This enables the browser to quickly redisplay a page you have recently viewed. Before a browser displays a page, the browser checks to see if the page is stored in the cache. If the page is stored in the cache, the browser reads the HTML code from the stored page rather than from the original document. This means

the browser may display an out-dated version of the page. You can refresh a page to have the browser read the HTML code from the original document and not from the cache.

If you have made changes to an image or other non-HTML element of a Web page, you may have to force the Web browser to reread all of the elements from the original document. If you are using Internet Explorer, you can hold down the Ctrl key as you refresh the page to reread all of the elements.

REFRESH A WEB PAGE

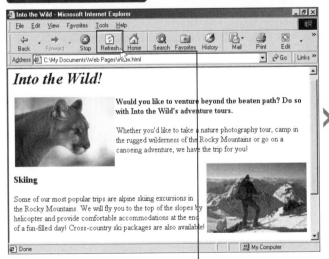

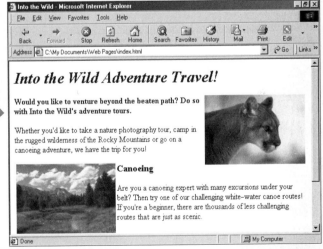

1 Display the Web page you want to refresh in a Web browser.

2 Click Refresh to display your changes in the Web browser.

■ The Web browser displays an up-to-date version of the Web page.

TRANSFER WEB PAGES TO WEB SERVER

Y ou must transfer your Web pages to a Web server to make the pages available on the Web.

You need a File Transfer Protocol (FTP) program to transfer your Web pages to a Web server. WS_FTP Pro for Windows is a popular FTP program. In the example below, we use WS_FTP Pro version 6.5.

Before you can transfer Web pages to a Web server, you must set up a connection to the server. You only need to set up a connection to a Web server once. After you set up a connection, you can connect to the server at any time.

To set up a connection to a Web server, you must know the address of the server, your user ID and your password. If you do not know this information, contact your Web presence provider.

Many FTP programs allow you to save your password, which saves you from having to retype your password each time you transfer Web pages to the Web server. When you save your password, anyone who uses your computer will be able to connect to the Web server, so you should not save your password if other people will have access to your computer.

SET UP A CONNECTION

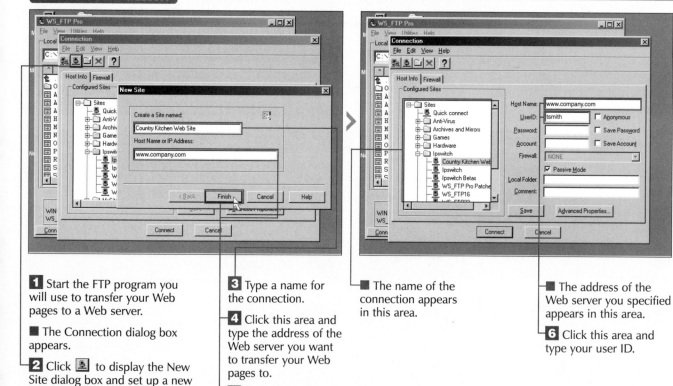

1 Start the FTP program you will use to transfer your Web pages to a Web server.

■ The Connection dialog box appears.

2 Click 🔳 to display the New Site dialog box and set up a new connection to the Web server.

3 Type a name for the connection.

4 Click this area and type the address of the Web server you want to transfer your Web pages to.

5 Click Finish to continue.

■ The name of the connection appears in this area.

■ The address of the Web server you specified appears in this area.

6 Click this area and type your user ID.

Extra

You can obtain the latest version of WS_FTP Pro at the www.ipswitch.com Web site.

You can create a new folder to store and organize your Web server connections. In the Configured Sites area of the Connection dialog box, click the folder you want to store the new subfolder. If you want to create a main folder, click the Sites folder. Then click 🗀 to create the folder. In the New Folder dialog box, type the name of the new folder and then click Finish.

FTP programs allow you to set up multiple connections. This is useful if you want to use one connection to transfer your Web pages to a Web server and another connection to download files from a different Web server. Perform steps 1 to 9 below for each connection you want to set up.

You can delete a connection you no longer need. Click the connection in the Configured Sites area of the Connection dialog box and then click ☒ to delete the connection. Click Yes in the dialog box that appears to confirm the deletion.

CONNECT TO WEB SERVER

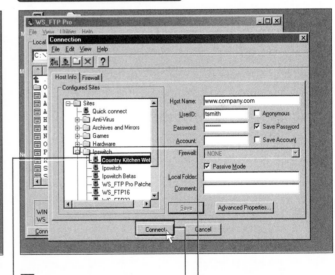

7 Click this area and type your password. A symbol (ˣ) appears for each character you type to prevent others from seeing your password.

8 To save your password so you will not need to retype the password again later, click this option (☐ changes to ☑).

9 Click Save to have the program store the information you entered for the connection.

1 Click the connection for the Web server you want to transfer your Web pages to.

■ If the connection you set up is not displayed, click the plus sign (➕) beside the Ipswitch folder (➕ changes to ➖).

2 Click Connect to connect to the Web server.

CONTINUED ▶

TRANSFER WEB PAGES TO WEB SERVER (CONTINUED)

O nce you have connected to a Web server, you can transfer information to the server.

You can transfer a single file, multiple files or an entire folder to the Web server at once. Before you transfer files and folders to a Web server, you must locate the folder on the server you want to transfer your files and folders to. This folder is often named "public." If you do not know the name of the folder, contact your Web presence provider.

If your connection to the Web server is idle for an extended period of time, the server may

automatically disconnect you. This helps ensure that the Web server's resources are available for other people who need to access the server.

If you later make changes to the Web pages stored on your computer, you must transfer the updated pages to the Web server. The updated Web pages will replace the old Web pages on the server. When you transfer updated pages, a message may appear, indicating that the updated pages will replace the old pages.

TRANSFER WEB PAGES TO WEB SERVER

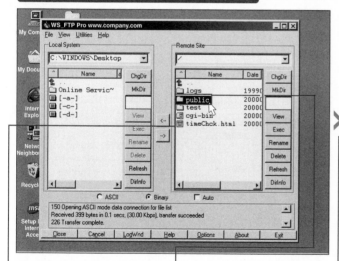

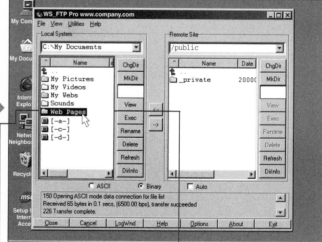

■ The WS_FTP Pro window appears.

■ This area displays the folders and files stored on the Web server.

1 Locate the folder you want to transfer your Web pages to. In many cases, the folder is named "public."

2 Double-click the folder to display the contents of the folder.

■ This area displays the folders and files stored on your computer.

3 Locate the folder that contains the Web page(s) you want to transfer to the Web server.

Note: You can double-click 🔼 *to move up one level in the folder structure.*

4 Double-click the folder to display the contents of the folder.

Extra

You should check all references to files on your Web pages before transferring the pages to a Web server. For example, if an image on a Web page is stored in the same folder as the Web page, make sure you specified just the name of the image (example: banner.gif). If the image is stored in a subfolder, make sure you specified the location and name of the image (example: images/banner.gif).

Before transferring your Web pages to a Web server, you should make sure the Web page file names all have the .html, .htm or .asp extension and do not include spaces or special characters, such as * or &. You should also check with your Web presence provider to ensure that you have used the correct name for your home page.

If you have accidentally transferred a file to the Web server, you should delete the file from the server. This helps save storage space on the Web server. To delete a file from the Web server, select the file in the right pane of the WS_FTP Pro window and then click the Delete button. Click Yes in the dialog box that appears to confirm the deletion.

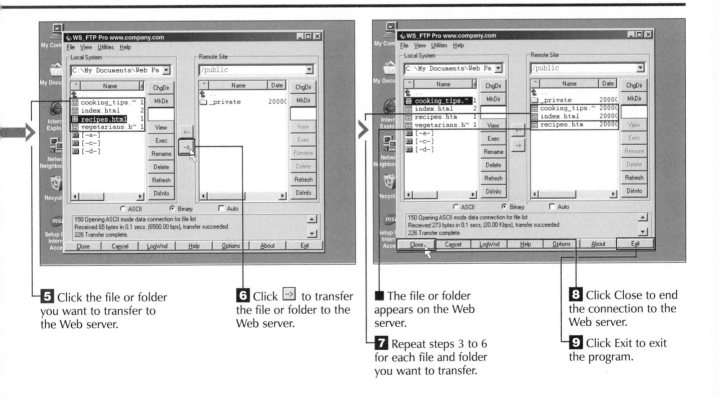

5 Click the file or folder you want to transfer to the Web server.

6 Click ⇥ to transfer the file or folder to the Web server.

■ The file or folder appears on the Web server.

7 Repeat steps 3 to 6 for each file and folder you want to transfer.

8 Click Close to end the connection to the Web server.

9 Click Exit to exit the program.

INTRODUCTION TO VBSCRIPT

V isual Basic Scripting Edition (VBScript) is a scripting language used with HTML to create interactive Web pages. A section of VBScript code in an HTML document is known as a script.

VBScript was developed by Microsoft and is based on the popular Microsoft Visual Basic and Visual Basic for Applications programming languages. If you are familiar with one of these programming languages, VBScript will be familiar to you.

SCRIPTING LANGUAGES

A scripting language instructs a computer to perform a specific task. You must be familiar with a scripting language, such as VBScript, in order to create Active Server Pages (ASP) code. Other examples of scripting languages include JavaScript and PerlScript. Each scripting language offers distinct features. Microsoft developed VBScript specifically to be used to create

documents for the World Wide Web. VBScript offers ease of use, versatility and Active Server Pages compatibility. JavaScript offers some advanced features other scripting languages do not and is useful if you are already familiar with Java, C or C++. PerlScript is most useful when you are creating code that processes or manipulates text or if you are familiar with Perl.

VBSCRIPT FEATURES

Easy to Learn

One of the major benefits of using VBScript is that it is easy to learn. VBScript shares many features with the BASIC programming language, which was developed specifically for novice programmers. Like BASIC, VBScript uses many easy-to-understand commands. For example, VBScript uses the `Document.Write` statement to display information on a Web page. These plain-language commands make it easy for you to read VBScript code and determine the purpose of the code.

Easy to Use

Compared to other scripting languages, VBScript is easy to use. Many scripting languages require you to follow strict syntax rules, such as including a semi-colon at the end of each line of code or using case-sensitive names. In these scripting languages, a simple typing error can cause code not to work. VBScript does not require you to abide by such strict syntax rules. This makes VBScript easier to use than other scripting languages; however, it may also make it more difficult to troubleshoot an error in a script.

Versatile

VBScript can be used on a computer running a Unix, Windows or Macintosh operating system. This makes VBScript a versatile scripting language. The computer must have a current version of Microsoft Internet Explorer installed.

VBSCRIPT FEATURES (CONTINUED)

Create Scripts

Many programming languages require you to use complicated software tools, such as compilers or development environments, in order to use the language effectively. VBScript does not require special software tools. You can create and edit scripts using the programs already installed on your computer, such as a simple text editor like Microsoft Notepad.

Run Scripts

You can run scripts you create using the latest version of Microsoft Internet Explorer. This allows you to view and test Web pages that include scripts on your own computer before transferring the pages to a Web server. If you are using Netscape Navigator, there may be plug-ins available that you can install to enable Netscape to process VBScript.

ActiveX Control Compatible

An ActiveX control is a small program you add to a Web page to add functionality to the page. For example, you can add an ActiveX text box to a Web page to allow users to enter a user name. VBScript enables your Web page to communicate with the ActiveX control and then access the information from the control, such as verifying that a user name was entered correctly.

Client-side Processing

A Web browser processes the HTML code used to create a Web page. When VBScript is included in HTML code, a browser will also process the VBScript code. This is known as client-side processing. The Web browser is considered a client of the Web server storing the Web page. The advantage of client-side processing is that a Web server does not have to use its resources to process the code used to create the page. The disadvantage of client-side processing is that it takes time to transfer the HTML and VBScript code from the server to the Web browser.

Active Server Pages Compatible

Active Server Pages (ASP) is technology developed by Microsoft that is used to create powerful and dynamic Web pages. You use a scripting language, such as VBScript, to access and use information from ASP objects. When ASP code contains VBScript, the code will work properly with any type of Web browser.

VBScript is the default scripting language for all Web servers that support ASP.

INTRODUCTION TO VBSCRIPT

VBSCRIPT CONCEPTS

VBScript shares many concepts with other programming and scripting languages, such as C, Visual Basic and JavaScript. While most programming and scripting languages use the same concepts, the names of items and coding syntax sometimes differ. For example, the command used to create a variable in VBScript is `Dim`, but in JavaScript, the command used to perform the same task is `var`.

The features of VBScript that you can use will change depending on where the VBScript code is processed. For example, when VBScript code is processed by a Web browser, the `Document.Write` statement can be used to display information on the screen. If the same statement is processed by a Web server, as is the case when VBScript is used to create ASP code, an error will occur. When using VBScript to create scripts, you must always consider where the code will be processed.

OBJECTS

Using objects is a way for Web page developers to organize VBScript code so it is easier to understand and use. An object is a self-contained section of code that performs a specific task. VBScript includes built-in objects that can be used in many different scripts to perform tasks such as accessing a storage system, reporting on errors and reading and writing to files. Instead of writing several lines of code to perform a task, one line of code can be used to access, or call, one of these built-in objects.

METHODS

A method refers to the way an object can be used in a script. A method typically instructs an object to perform a single task. For example, the `Document` object has a method called `Write` that writes information from the script to a Web page.

A method can also be used to specify one or more parameters that are passed to the object. The method then performs an action based on the value of the parameter(s). Objects are typically separated from methods by a period, with any parameters enclosed in parentheses, such as `Document.Write("This is a test.")`.

Most objects have at least one method. Some objects use the same methods, such as VBScript's `Dictionary` and `Folder` objects, which both use the `Add` method. The `Add` method is used to create values for the `Dictionary` object and create folders for the `Folder` object.

PROPERTIES

Properties are attributes associated with an object. Properties can be used to determine the status of an object, such as if the object is being used, and to determine and set the characteristics of an object. The name of a property usually indicates what value the property is used to access. For example, the `DriveLetter` property of the `Drive` object is used to indicate the letter assigned to a storage device. Objects are typically separated from properties by a period, such as `Drive.DriveLetter`.

The properties of some objects are read-only and cannot manually be changed. Many VBScript objects share the same properties, such as the `Path` property, which can be used with the `File`, `Drive` and `Folder` objects to determine the path of the object.

SUBROUTINES

Subroutines are sections of VBScript code you create that can be used repeatedly throughout a script without having to retype the section of code. Subroutines allow Web page developers to divide a script into several separate sections. Each subroutine usually performs a single task and should only contain code related to that specific task. Using subroutines in a script makes the script easier to update. Additionally, when an error occurs, using subroutines makes it easier to troubleshoot the error because you are working with small sections of code.

FUNCTIONS

A function is a procedure that performs a task and returns a result. VBScript includes many built-in functions that can be used for a wide variety of purposes, from generating message boxes to formatting the current date and time. Many functions require you to use a parameter to specify the information you want the function to process. For example, the `Len` function determines the length of a text string that you enter as a parameter.

Functions are the primary way that data is manipulated in VBScript. As well as the built-in functions of VBScript, you can also create your own functions to process information and return values.

PROGRAM FLOW STATEMENTS

As with most programming languages, VBScript can instruct a computer to process the lines of code that make up a script in a certain order. Program flow is manipulated by using two types of statements–conditional and looping. Conditional statements are used to enable scripts to process a specific section of code, depending on the outcome of a calculation. Looping statements are used to repeatedly process a section of VBScript code until a condition is met. Conditional and looping statements are often combined to create powerful and versatile scripts with a minimum of coding.

ADD VBSCRIPT TO HTML

B efore a Web browser can display a Web page, the browser must process the HTML code used to create the page. If the browser finds the `<SCRIPT>` tag in the HTML code, the browser sends the script that follows the tag to a *scripting engine*. A scripting engine is the part of a Web browser that processes scripts. Each scripting language has its own scripting engine. You use the LANGUAGE attribute for the `<SCRIPT>` tag to indicate that the VBScript engine must process the script.

Web browsers that do not recognize the `<SCRIPT>` tag will simply display the script as text on the Web page. You can use comment tags (`<!--` and `-->`) to make browsers that do not recognize the `<SCRIPT>` tag ignore the script.

Microsoft Internet Explorer is the only Web browser that can reliably interpret VBScript when it is included in HTML code. You can obtain the latest version of Microsoft Internet Explorer at the www.microsoft.com/windows/ie Web site.

ADD VBSCRIPT TO HTML

```
index - Notepad
File   Edit   Search   Help
<HTML>
<HEAD>
<TITLE>Add VBScript to HTML</TITLE>
</HEAD>
<BODY>

<SCRIPT LANGUAGE="VBScript">



</SCRIPT>

</BODY>
</HTML>
```

```
index - Notepad
File   Edit   Search   Help
<HTML>
<HEAD>
<TITLE>Add VBScript to HTML</TITLE>
</HEAD>
<BODY>

<SCRIPT LANGUAGE="VBScript">
<!--


-->
</SCRIPT>

</BODY>
</HTML>
```

ADD SCRIPT TAGS

1 Click where you want to include a script and type **<SCRIPT LANGUAGE="VBScript">**.

■ You can place scripts anywhere in the `<HEAD>` or `<BODY>` sections of an HTML document.

2 Click where you want to end the script and type **</SCRIPT>**.

ADD COMMENT TAGS

1 Click directly below the `<SCRIPT>` tag and type **<!--**.

2 Click directly above the `</SCRIPT>` tag and type **-->**.

■ You are now ready to create a script.

USE VBSCRIPT TO DISPLAY INFORMATION

VBScript uses the Document.Write statement to display information on a Web page. You can use this statement to display information such as a greeting or the result of a calculation.

If you want to use the Document.Write statement to display text, you must enclose the text in quotation marks. You can use HTML tags to format the text you want to display. When using HTML tags in a Document.Write statement, you must include the tags within the quotation marks.

If you want to display multiple items, such as a phrase followed by the value of a variable, you can display all the items using one Document.Write statement.

A Document.Write statement should contain only a small amount of data. This can help make your statements easier to read, understand and troubleshoot. You can use multiple Document.Write statements to display a large amount of data.

USE VBSCRIPT TO DISPLAY INFORMATION

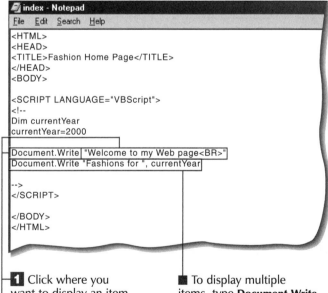

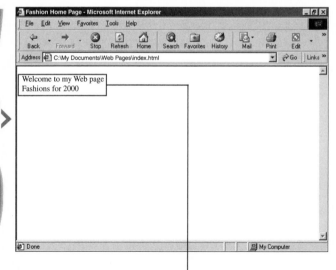

1 Click where you want to display an item on the Web page and type **Document.Write**.

2 Type the item you want to display and then press Enter.

■ To display multiple items, type **Document.Write** followed by each item you want to display, separated by a comma.

■ You must enclose text in quotation marks. Spaces you want to display must also be included within the quotation marks.

3 Display the Web page in a Web browser.

■ The Web browser displays the data you specified in each Document.Write statement.

DECLARE A VARIABLE

A variable is a name that represents a value. For example, you could have the variable myAge represent the value 29. You can use variables to perform many types of calculations in your scripts.

To declare a variable you want to use in your script, you enter a `Dim` statement that includes the name of the variable. You should choose a meaningful name so you will be able to recognize the variable in the future. Variable names can be up to 255 characters in length, must begin with a letter and cannot contain spaces or periods.

Variable names are not case sensitive. You can use multiple words to name a variable and capitalize each word except the first, such as myDateOfBirth.

After you declare a variable, you must assign an initial value to the variable, which is known as storing a value. A variable can store any alphanumeric value, such as 123 or "text". When you assign a text value to a variable, you must enclose the text in quotation marks.

DECLARE A VARIABLE

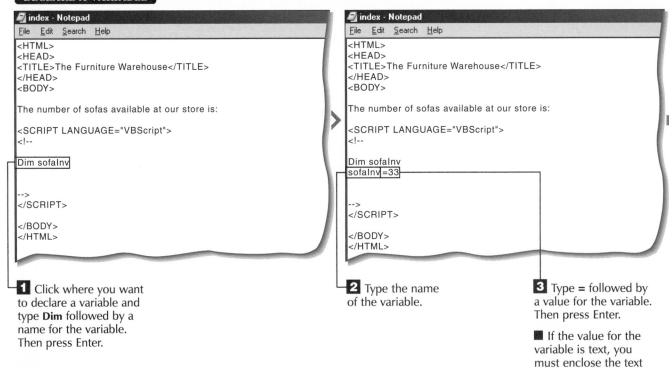

1 Click where you want to declare a variable and type **Dim** followed by a name for the variable. Then press Enter.

2 Type the name of the variable.

3 Type = followed by a value for the variable. Then press Enter.

■ If the value for the variable is text, you must enclose the text in quotation marks.

Extra

You can make a variable name easier to read by using the underscore character (_) to separate the words in the name. When you separate the words in a variable name, you should capitalize each word.

Example:
```
Dim My_Date_Of_Birth
```

You can use the OPTION EXPLICIT statement to ensure all the variables in a script are declared properly. If variables are not declared properly, the Web browser will display an error message stating that a variable is undefined. You should place the OPTION EXPLICIT statement below the <SCRIPT> tag.

Example:
```
<SCRIPT LANGUAGE="VBScript">
<!--
OPTION EXPLICIT
```

You can declare more than one variable at a time. In the Dim statement, enter the name of each variable you want to declare, separated by a comma. You can then assign a value to each variable.

Example:
```
Dim x,y
x=100
y=200
```

If the script containing the variable did not work properly, you may have made a typing mistake in the variable name. When using a variable throughout a long script, you should refer back to the Dim statement to confirm the spelling of the variable name.

Example:
```
Dim maxNumberOfUsers
maxNumberOfUsers=5
Document.Write maxNumberOUsers
```

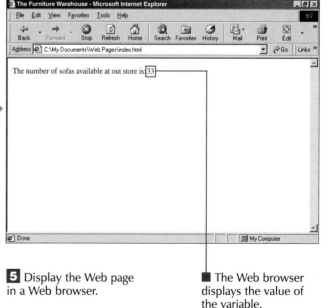

```
index - Notepad
File  Edit  Search  Help
<HTML>
<HEAD>
<TITLE>The Furniture Warehouse</TITLE>
</HEAD>
<BODY>

The number of sofas available at our store is:

<SCRIPT LANGUAGE="VBScript">
<!--

Dim sofaInv
sofaInv=33

Document.Write sofaInv

-->
</SCRIPT>

</BODY>
```

The Furniture Warehouse - Microsoft Internet Explorer

Address C:\My Documents\Web Pages\index.html

The number of sofas available at out store is: 33

4 Click where you want to type the code that displays the value of the variable on the Web page and type the code.

5 Display the Web page in a Web browser.

■ The Web browser displays the value of the variable.

USING VARIABLES IN A CALCULATION

O nce you have declared a variable, you can use the variable in a calculation.

You can use arithmetic operators, such as +, - and * to perform mathematical calculations using variables. You can also use comparison operators such as >, < and = to compare variables in your scripts. Logical operators, including And, Or and Not allow you to check if statements containing variables are true. If you use a calculation that contains more than one operator, you can use parentheses ( ) to make sure VBScript processes the variables

in the order you want. For more information about operators, see page 56.

A calculation can contain only variables, such as x+y-z, only numbers, such as 20-5*2, or a combination of variables and numbers, such as x/y+10.

After you use variables in a calculation, you can display the result of the calculation on your Web page or use the result in another calculation in your script.

USING VARIABLES IN A CALCULATION

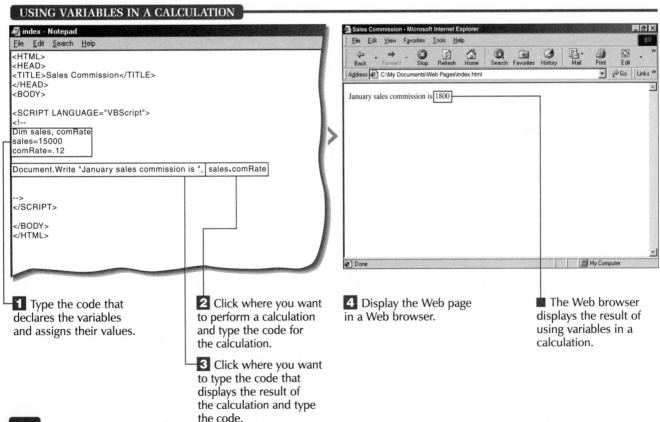

1 Type the code that declares the variables and assigns their values.

2 Click where you want to perform a calculation and type the code for the calculation.

3 Click where you want to type the code that displays the result of the calculation and type the code.

4 Display the Web page in a Web browser.

■ The Web browser displays the result of using variables in a calculation.

USING A VARIABLE TO STORE A CALCULATION

A calculation can determine the value of a variable. For example, the calculation 62+75+23 could determine the value of the milesTraveled variable. The calculation that determines the value of a variable can also contain variables, such as myAge = yearNow - yearOfBirth.

When you use a calculation to determine the value of a variable, VBScript processes the calculation and then stores the resulting value in the variable.

You can use the variable in the calculation that will determine its value. For example, in the calculation

counter=counter+1, the counter variable is used to determine its own value. Once you use a calculation to change the value of a variable, VBScript erases the value previously stored in the variable.

You must ensure the calculation you use to determine the value of a variable is valid. For example, an error occurs when you divide a number by a variable that stores a value of zero. This type of error is often difficult to troubleshoot.

USING A VARIABLE TO STORE A CALCULATION

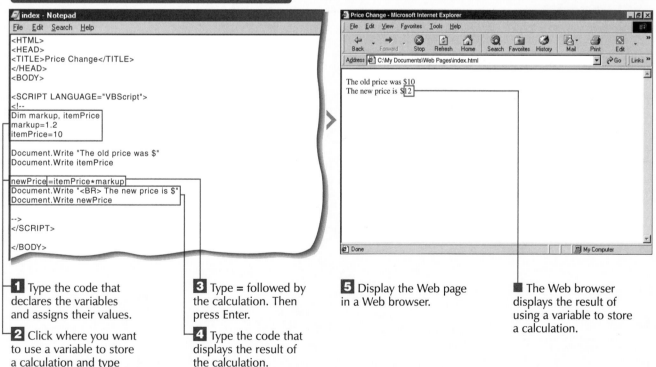

1 Type the code that declares the variables and assigns their values.

2 Click where you want to use a variable to store a calculation and type the name of the variable.

3 Type = followed by the calculation. Then press Enter.

4 Type the code that displays the result of the calculation.

5 Display the Web page in a Web browser.

■ The Web browser displays the result of using a variable to store a calculation.

USING CONSTANTS

A constant is a name that represents a value you want to remain the same throughout a script. For example, if the state sales tax is 10%, the constant SALES_TAX could represent the value .10. If the sales tax changes, you only need to change the value of the constant to update the script.

You use a `Const` statement to declare and name a constant in your script.

You should choose a meaningful name for a constant so you will be able to recognize the constant in the future. To help you distinguish constants from variables, you should use all uppercase letters to name a constant. If a constant name consists of multiple words, use the underscore character to separate each word, such as MAX_NUMBER_OF_USERS.

After you declare a constant, you must assign a value to the constant. A constant can store any alphanumeric value. You cannot use a calculation to determine the value of a constant, such as Const AGE=2000-1970. You also cannot assign the value of a variable to a constant, such as Const SALES_TAX=x.

You can use a constant in a calculation as you would use a variable.

USING CONSTANTS

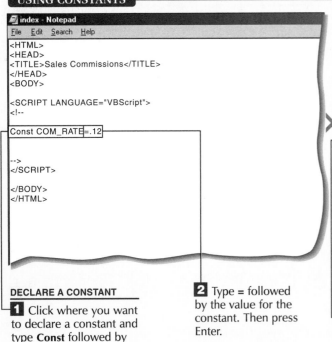

DECLARE A CONSTANT

1 Click where you want to declare a constant and type **Const** followed by the name of the constant.

2 Type = followed by the value for the constant. Then press Enter.

■ If the value for the constant is text, you must enclose the text in quotation marks.

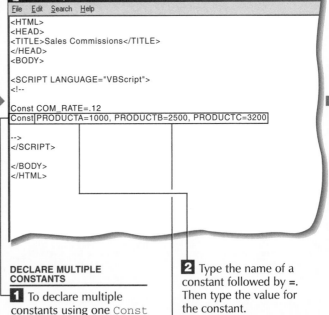

DECLARE MULTIPLE CONSTANTS

1 To declare multiple constants using one `Const` statement, type **Const**.

2 Type the name of a constant followed by =. Then type the value for the constant.

3 Repeat step 2, separating each constant with a comma, until you have declared all the constants you want to use.

Extra   If a script containing a constant did not work properly, you may have tried to declare the same constant more than once in the script. After you declare and assign a value to a constant, you cannot declare the same constant with a different value again in the script.

INVALID SCRIPT:

```
Const TAX=.10
Dim productAPrice, taxOnProduct, staTaxOnProduct
productAPrice=500
taxOnProduct=productAPrice*TAX
Document.Write "The tax on product A is $"
Document.Write taxOnProduct
Const TAX=.15
staTaxOnProduct=productAPrice*TAX
Document.Write "The state tax on product A is $"
Document.Write staTaxOnProduct
```

VALID SCRIPT:

```
Const TAX=.10
Dim productAPrice, taxOnProduct, staTaxOnProduct
productAPrice=500
taxOnProduct=productAPrice*TAX
Document.Write "The tax on product A is $"
Document.Write taxOnProduct
Const STA_TAX=.15
staTaxOnProduct=productAPrice*STA_TAX
Document.Write "The state tax on product A is $"
Document.Write staTaxOnProduct
```

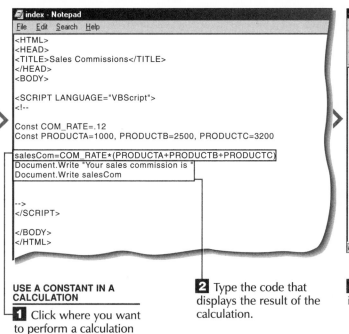

```
<HTML>
<HEAD>
<TITLE>Sales Commissions</TITLE>
</HEAD>
<BODY>

<SCRIPT LANGUAGE="VBScript">
<!--

Const COM_RATE=.12
Const PRODUCTA=1000, PRODUCTB=2500, PRODUCTC=3200

salesCom=COM_RATE*(PRODUCTA+PRODUCTB+PRODUCTC)
Document.Write "Your sales commission is "
Document.Write salesCom


-->
</SCRIPT>

</BODY>
</HTML>
```

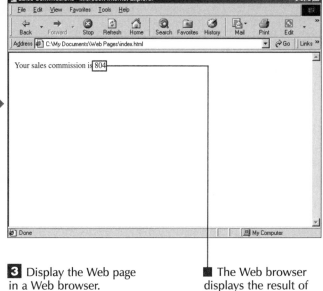

Your sales commission is 804

USE A CONSTANT IN A CALCULATION

1 Click where you want to perform a calculation and type the code for the calculation. Then press Enter.

2 Type the code that displays the result of the calculation.

3 Display the Web page in a Web browser.

■ The Web browser displays the result of using a constant in a calculation.

USING INTRINSIC CONSTANTS

VBScript comes with several intrinsic, or built-in, constants you can use in your scripts. A constant is a name that represents a value that does not change. Because VBScript sets the value of an intrinsic constant, these constants do not have to be declared and can be used in every script you create.

You can also create your own constants. This allows you to set the value of the constant. For information about declaring and using constants, see page 52.

The name of a VBScript constant usually describes the value the constant stores. For example, the vbBlack constant stores the hexadecimal value of the color black. Most VBScript constants begin with "vb", which makes an intrinsic constant easy to recognize when you are reading a script.

You cannot modify the value of an intrinsic VBScript constant. You also cannot use the name of an intrinsic constant as the name of a constant or a variable you create. If you attempt to do either of these tasks in a script, the script will generate an error.

USING INTRINSIC CONSTANTS

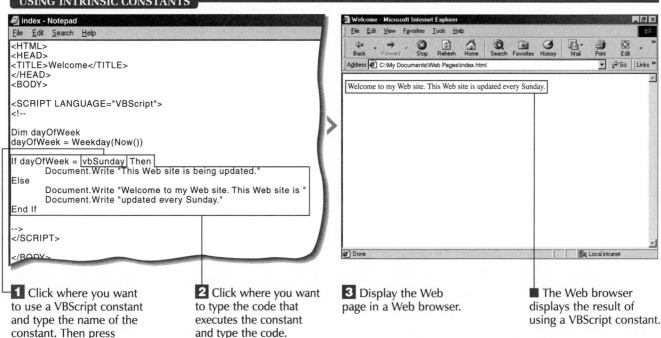

1 Click where you want to use a VBScript constant and type the name of the constant. Then press Enter.

2 Click where you want to type the code that executes the constant and type the code.

3 Display the Web page in a Web browser.

■ The Web browser displays the result of using a VBScript constant.

COMMON INTRINSIC CONSTANTS

Constant Name	Value	Description
vbSunday	1	Sunday
vbMonday	2	Monday
vbTuesday	3	Tuesday
vbWednesday	4	Wednesday
vbThursday	5	Thursday
vbFriday	6	Friday
vbSaturday	7	Saturday
vbFirstJan1	1	The week of January 1st
vbFirstFourDays	2	The first week to contain at least 4 days of the year
vbFirstFullWeek	3	The first full week of the year
vbUseSystem	0	Use the date format of the computer
vbUseSystemDayOfWeek	0	Use the first day of the week set for the computer

Constant Name	Value	Description
vbCr	Chr(13)	Carriage return
vbCrLf	Chr(13) & Chr(10)	Carriage return followed by a linefeed
vbLf	Chr(10)	Linefeed
vbNewLine	Chr(13) & Chr(10) or Chr(10)	New line
vbNullChar	Chr(0)	Character with a value of 0
vbNullString	String value of 0	String with a value of 0
vbTab	Chr(9)	Horizontal tab

Constant Name	Value	Description
vbBlack	&h00	Black
vbRed	&hFF	Red
vbGreen	&hFF00	Green
vbYellow	&hFFFF	Yellow
vbBlue	&hFF0000	Blue
vbMagenta	&hFF00FF	Magenta
vbCyan	&hFFFF00	Cyan
vbWhite	&hFFFFFF	White

USING OPERATORS

O perators allow you to manipulate data in your scripts. There are four types of operators—arithmetic, comparison, logical and concatenation.

ARITHMETIC OPERATORS

You can use arithmetic operators to perform mathematical calculations.

+ (Addition)	– (Subtraction)	* (Multiplication)
Finds the sum of two values.	Finds the difference between two values.	Multiplies two values.
`Document.Write 10 + 5`	`Document.Write 33 - 7`	`Document.Write 4 * 2`
Displays 15	Displays 26	Displays 8
/ (Division)	\ (Integer Division)	Mod (Modulus)	^ (Exponentiation)
Divides one value by another value.	Divides one value by another value and returns only a whole number in the result.	Divides one value by another value and returns only the remainder in the result.	Raises a value to the power of an exponent.
`Document.Write 6 / 4`	`Document.Write 6 \ 4`	`Document.Write 6 Mod 4`	`Document.Write 2 ^ 4`
Displays 1.5	Displays 1	Displays 2	Displays 16

COMPARISON OPERATORS

You can use comparison operators to compare values in your scripts.

> (Greater than)	>= (Greater than or equal to)	< (Less than)
Checks if one value is greater than another value.	Checks if one value is greater than or equal to another value.	Checks if one value is less than another value.

`Dim x,y`
`x=7`
`y=3`
`If x > y Then Document.Write x`
	`Dim x,y`
	`x=9`
	`y=7`
	`If x >= y Then Document.Write x`
		`Dim x,y`
		`x=7`
		`y=9`
		`If x < y Then Document.Write y`

Displays 7	Displays 9	Displays 9
<= (Less than or equal to)	<> (Not equal to)	= (Equal to)
Checks if one value is less than or equal to another value.	Checks if one value is not equal to another value.	Checks if one value is equal to another value.

`Dim x,y`
`x=9`
`y=9`
`If x <= y Then Document.Write y`
	`Dim x,y`
	`x=7`
	`y=3`
	`If x <> y Then`
	`Document.Write x, " is not equal to ", y`
	`End If`
		`Dim x,y`
		`x=7`
		`y=7`
		`If x = y Then`
		`Document.Write x, " is equal to ",y`
		`End If`

Displays 9	Displays 7 is not equal to 3	Displays 7 is equal to 7

LOGICAL OPERATORS

You can use logical operators to check if a statement in your script is true.

And

Checks if two or more statements are true.

```
Dim x,y
x=7
y=5
If x = 7 And y = 5 Then
Document.Write "True"
End If
```

Displays True

Or

Checks if one of two statements is true.

```
Dim x,y
x=7
y=5
If x = 7 Or y = 0 Then
Document.Write "True"
End If
```

Displays True

Not

Checks if a statement is not true.

```
Dim x
x=7
If Not x = 2 Then
Document.Write "True"
End If
```

Displays True

Eqv

Checks if the values of two statements are equal.

```
Dim x,y
x=7
y=5
If x - 1 Eqv y + 1 Then
Document.Write "True"
End If
```

Displays True

Xor

Checks if the values of two statements are not equal.

```
Dim x,y
x=7
y=3
If x - 1 Xor y + 1 Then
Document.Write "True"
End If
```

Displays True

CONCATENATION OPERATOR

You can use the concatenation operator (&) to combine two strings of text. This is useful when you want to combine text with a variable that has a text value.

& (Concatenation)

```
Dim currentTime, message
currentTime=Hour(Now)
If currentTime > 6 And currentTime < 12 Then
    message = "Morning!"
Else
    message = "Evening!"
End If
Document.Write "Good " & message
```

Displays Good Morning!
or
Displays Good Evening!

OPERATOR PRECEDENCE

When a statement contains more than one type of operator, VBScript processes the operators in a specific order, known as operator precedence. VBScript processes arithmetic operators first, then the concatenation operator, followed by comparison operators and logical operators.

When a calculation contains more than one arithmetic operator, VBScript processes exponentiation operators first, followed by multiplication, division, integer division and modulus operators. VBScript then processes addition and subtraction operators.

When a statement contains more than one logical operator, VBScript processes Not operators first, followed by And, Or, Xor and finally Eqv operators.

You can use parentheses ( ) to change the order in which VBScript processes operators. VBScript will process the data inside the parentheses first. For example, $10+5*2=20$ but $(10+5)*2=30$.

Comparison operators have no operator precedence. If a statement contains more than one comparison operator, VBScript processes the operators from left to right.

CREATE AN ARRAY

An array stores a set of related values. For example, an array could store the name of each day of the week. Using an array allows you to work with multiple values at the same time.

You use a `Dim` statement to declare an array. The `Dim` statement contains the name you want to use for the array. Array names are not case sensitive and cannot contain spaces.

Each element in an array is uniquely identified by an *index number*. When

you declare an array, you must specify the highest index number the array will contain. Index numbers in an array start at 0, not 1, so an array declared as daysOfWeek(6) can contain up to seven elements.

You must specify the alphanumeric value you want each element to store. A text value must be enclosed in quotation marks.

You can use an array element in a script as you would use a variable. Changing the value of an element does not affect the other elements in the array.

CREATE AN ARRAY

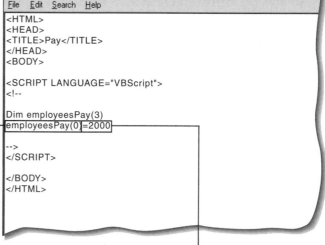

```
index - Notepad
File  Edit  Search  Help
<HTML>
<HEAD>
<TITLE>Pay</TITLE>
</HEAD>
<BODY>

<SCRIPT LANGUAGE="VBScript">
<!--

Dim employeesPay(3)

-->
</SCRIPT>

</BODY>
</HTML>
```

```
index - Notepad
File  Edit  Search  Help
<HTML>
<HEAD>
<TITLE>Pay</TITLE>
</HEAD>
<BODY>

<SCRIPT LANGUAGE="VBScript">
<!--

Dim employeesPay(3)
employeesPay(0)=2000

-->
</SCRIPT>

</BODY>
</HTML>
```

1 Click where you want to create an array and type **Dim** followed by the name of the array.

2 Type the highest index number the array will contain enclosed in parentheses ( ). Then press Enter.

3 To create an element in the array, type the name of the array, followed by the index number of the element enclosed in parentheses ( ).

4 Type = followed by the value for the element. Then press Enter.

■ If the value for the element is text, you must enclose the text in quotation marks.

Extra

When you do not know how many elements an array will contain, you can create a dynamic array. You do not have to specify the highest index number a dynamic array will contain in the `Dim` statement. Instead, you use a `Redim` statement to specify the initial highest index number. When you later want to add elements to the dynamic array, you use a `Redim Preserve` statement to change the highest index number.

Example:
```
Dim employee( )
Document.Write "ABC Corp Employees<BR>"
Redim employee(3)
employee(0)="Wanda"
employee(1)="Kelleigh"
employee(2)="Cathy"
employee(3)="James"
If employee(3)="James" Then
    Document.Write "James has been employed "
    Document.Write "by ABC Corp for 5 years."
End If
Redim Preserve employee(6)
employee(4)="Roxanne"
employee(5)="Janice"
employee(6)="Stacey"
```

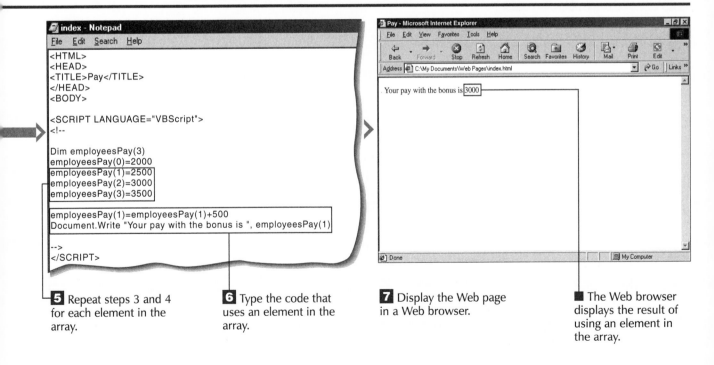

```
<HTML>
<HEAD>
<TITLE>Pay</TITLE>
</HEAD>
<BODY>

<SCRIPT LANGUAGE="VBScript">
<!--

Dim employeesPay(3)
employeesPay(0)=2000
employeesPay(1)=2500
employeesPay(2)=3000
employeesPay(3)=3500

employeesPay(1)=employeesPay(1)+500
Document.Write "Your pay with the bonus is ", employeesPay(1)

-->
</SCRIPT>
```

Your pay with the bonus is 3000

5 Repeat steps 3 and 4 for each element in the array.

6 Type the code that uses an element in the array.

7 Display the Web page in a Web browser.

■ The Web browser displays the result of using an element in the array.

USING THE ARRAY FUNCTION

U sing the Array function allows you to shorten the code needed to declare an array. For information on arrays, see page 58.

You may have to type many lines of code to create all the elements you want to store in an array, which can make the array difficult to read, understand and troubleshoot.

The Array function allows you to specify all the elements you want to store in an array in one line of code. When you use the Array function, you do not need to specify the highest *index number* the array will contain.

You use a Dim statement to declare and name an array. You then enter each value you want the array to store, separated by a comma. An array can store alphanumeric values, such as 123 or "text". A text value must be enclosed in quotation marks.

To use an array element in your script, you enter the name of the array followed by the index number of the element you want to use, such as productPr(0). Remember that VBScript numbers the elements in an array starting with 0, not 1.

USING THE ARRAY FUNCTION

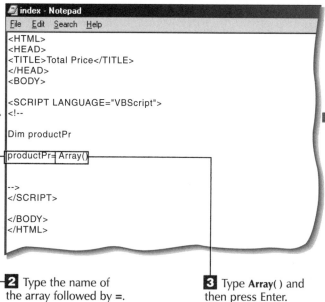

1 Click where you want to use the Array function and type **Dim** followed by the name of the array. Then press Enter.

2 Type the name of the array followed by **=**.

3 Type **Array( )** and then press Enter.

Apply It

You can use code that creates a loop, such as a `Do While` statement, to work with all the elements in an array at once.

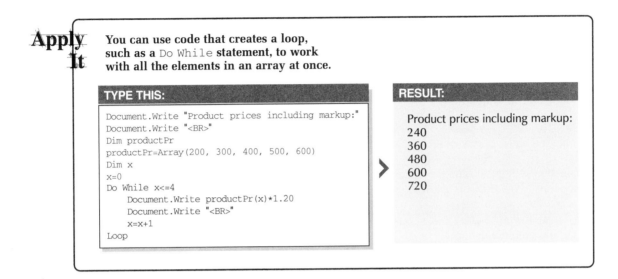

TYPE THIS:

```
Document.Write "Product prices including markup:"
Document.Write "<BR>"
Dim productPr
productPr=Array(200, 300, 400, 500, 600)
Dim x
x=0
Do While x<=4
    Document.Write productPr(x)*1.20
    Document.Write "<BR>"
    x=x+1
Loop
```

RESULT:

```
Product prices including markup:
240
360
480
600
720
```

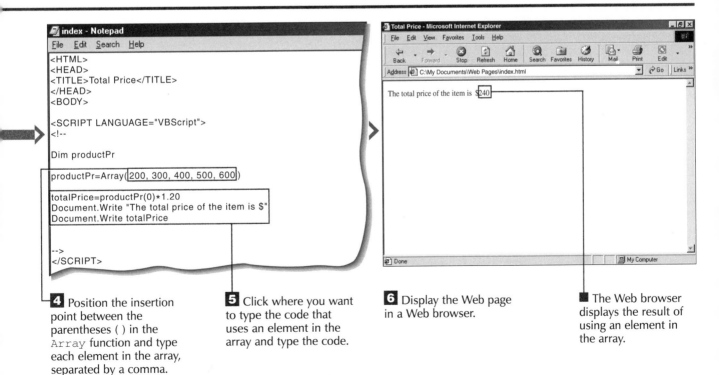

index - Notepad

File Edit Search Help

```
<HTML>
<HEAD>
<TITLE>Total Price</TITLE>
</HEAD>
<BODY>

<SCRIPT LANGUAGE="VBScript">
<!--

Dim productPr

productPr=Array(200, 300, 400, 500, 600)

totalPrice=productPr(0)*1.20
Document.Write "The total price of the item is $"
Document.Write totalPrice

-->
</SCRIPT>
```

Total Price - Microsoft Internet Explorer

File Edit View Favorites Tools Help

Address C:\My Documents\Web Pages\index.html

The total price of the item is $240

-4 Position the insertion point between the parentheses ( ) in the `Array` function and type each element in the array, separated by a comma.

-5 Click where you want to type the code that uses an element in the array and type the code.

-6 Display the Web page in a Web browser.

■ The Web browser displays the result of using an element in the array.

FIND THE SIZE OF AN ARRAY

T he UBound function finds the highest index number in an array.

When you create a dynamic array or an array using the Array function, you do not need to specify the highest index number the array will contain. This allows you to easily add elements to the array or remove elements from the array. For example, you could create a dynamic array that stores the names of individuals working in the marketing department.

The number of elements in the array will change depending on the number of people in the department. You can find the size of the dynamic array to determine the number of individuals currently working in the marketing department.

The UBound function can count elements that contain an alphanumeric value, such as 123 or "text", or no value at all, such as "".

FIND THE SIZE OF AN ARRAY

```
index - Notepad
File  Edit  Search  Help
<HTML>
<HEAD>
<TITLE>Employees</TITLE>
</HEAD>
<BODY>

<SCRIPT LANGUAGE="VBScript">
<!--

Dim marketingDept()
Redim marketingDept(4)
marketingDept(0)="Paul Whitehead"
marketingDept(1)="Janice Boyer"
marketingDept(2)="Cathy Benn"
marketingDept(3)="Jimmy Tam"
marketingDept(4)="Russ Marini"
Redim Preserve marketingDept(6)
marketingDept(5)="Kelleigh Wing"
marketingDept(6)="Wanda Lawrie"

-->
</SCRIPT>

</BODY>
```

```
index - Notepad
File  Edit  Search  Help
<HTML>
<HEAD>
<TITLE>Employees</TITLE>
</HEAD>
<BODY>

<SCRIPT LANGUAGE="VBScript">
<!--

Dim marketingDept()
Redim marketingDept(4)
marketingDept(0)="Paul Whitehead"
marketingDept(1)="Janice Boyer"
marketingDept(2)="Cathy Benn"
marketingDept(3)="Jimmy Tam"
marketingDept(4)="Russ Marini"
Redim Preserve marketingDept(6)
marketingDept(5)="Kelleigh Wing"
marketingDept(6)="Wanda Lawrie"

UBound(marketingDept)

-->
</SCRIPT>
```

1 Create a dynamic array or an array using the Array function. See the top of page 59 to create a dynamic array. See page 60 to use the Array function.

2 Click where you want to find the size of an array and type **UBound( )**.

3 Position the insertion point between the parentheses ( ) in the UBound function and type the name of the array you want to find the size of.

Extra

Since index numbers for the elements in an array start at 0, not 1, the UBound function reports one less element than there actually is in an array. For example, if an array contains three elements with the index numbers 0, 1, and 2, the UBound function will report that the array contains two elements, since the highest index number is 2. When you need to determine the exact size of the array, you can add one element to the UBound function code.

Example:
```
actualNumberOfElements=UBound(productPri) + 1
```

The UBound function can help you avoid changing code that uses an array. This is useful when the number of elements in an array is continually changing. In the following example, you can add as many elements as you need to the invoiceTotals array without having to change the code that displays the elements.

Example:
```
Dim invoiceTotals( )
Document.Write "Invoice Totals for ABC Corp","<BR>"
Redim invoiceTotals(2)
invoiceTotals(0)=500
invoiceTotals(1)=300
invoiceTotals(2)=480
Redim Preserve invoiceTotals(3)
invoiceTotals(3)=400
numberOfInvoices=UBound(invoiceTotals)+1
Dim x
x=0
Do While x<numberOfInvoices
    Document.Write invoiceTotals(x)
    Document.Write "<BR>"
    x=x+1
Loop
```

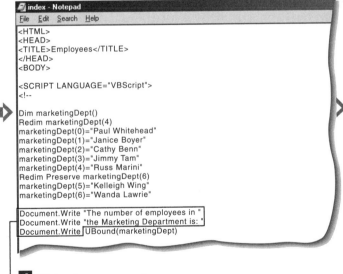

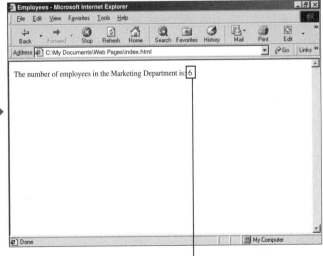

4 Click where you want to type the code that executes the UBound function and type the code.

5 Display the Web page in a Web browser.

■ The Web browser displays the result of using the UBound function.

USING THE IF...THEN STATEMENT

Using the If...Then statement creates a script that will execute a section of code if a condition is true. For example, you can create a script that displays a Good Morning message when a user views the Web page between 5:00 AM and 11:59 AM.

The If statement tests a condition you specify to determine if the condition is true. If the condition is true, VBScript will execute a section of code. You must specify the section of code you want

VBScript to execute. If the condition is not true, VBScript will skip the code and execute the code that follows the End If statement.

You should indent the section of code between the If statement and the End If statement. Indenting helps make the code easier to read and understand. There is no limit to the amount of code you can place between the If statement and the End If statement.

USING THE IF...THEN STATEMENT

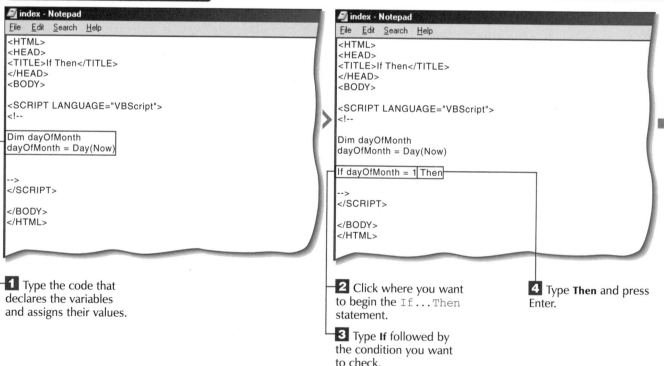

1 Type the code that declares the variables and assigns their values.

2 Click where you want to begin the If...Then statement.

3 Type **If** followed by the condition you want to check.

4 Type **Then** and press Enter.

Extra

Logical operators, such as And, Not or Eqv, allow you to combine multiple conditions in an If...Then statement. For example, you can create an If...Then statement that displays a message if two conditions are true.

Example:

```
Dim x,y
x=7
y=5
If x = 7 And y = 5 Then
    Document.Write "True"
End If
```

You can shorten an If...Then statement in a script. If you are going to execute only one line of code based on a condition being true, you can leave out the End If statement and place the code to be executed on the same line as the If statement.

Example:

```
If myCounter=999 Then
    myCounter=0
End If
```

Can be typed as:

```
If myCounter=999 Then myCounter=0
```

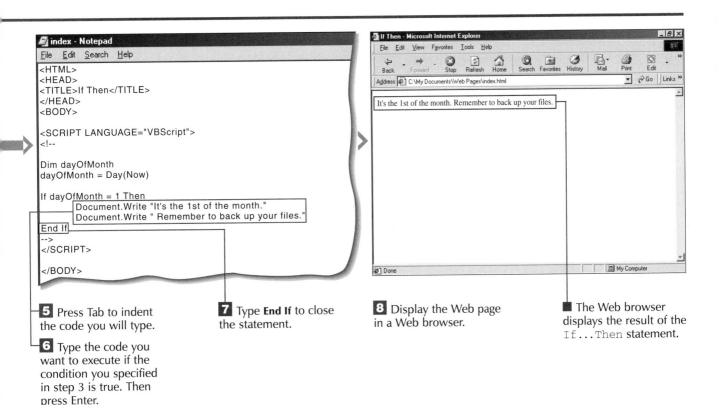

5 Press Tab to indent the code you will type.

6 Type the code you want to execute if the condition you specified in step 3 is true. Then press Enter.

7 Type **End If** to close the statement.

8 Display the Web page in a Web browser.

■ The Web browser displays the result of the If...Then statement.

USING THE IF...THEN...ELSE STATEMENT

An If...Then...Else statement allows you to execute one of two specific sections of code, depending on a condition you specify. For example, you may want to display a Good Morning message or a Good Evening message on a Web page, depending on the time set on a user's computer.

An If statement tests a condition to determine whether the condition is true or false. When a condition is true, the section of code between the If statement and the Else statement is executed. If the condition is false, the section

of code between the Else statement and the End If statement is executed.

Using an If...Then...Else statement ensures that a section of code is executed no matter what the outcome of the condition is.

If the code you want to execute in an If...Then...Else statement is long, the code may be difficult to read and troubleshoot. You may want to use *subroutines* within If...Then...Else statements for lengthy sections of code. For information on subroutines, see page 78.

USING THE IF...THEN...ELSE STATEMENT

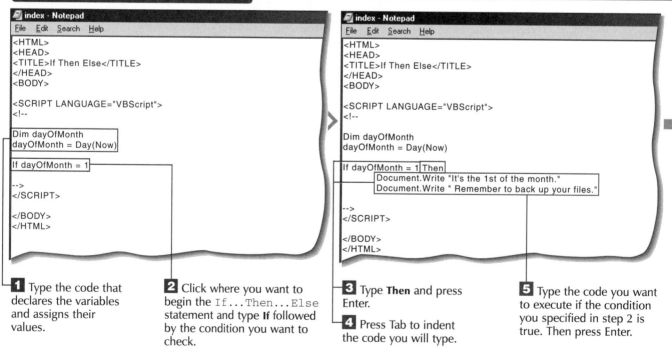

1 Type the code that declares the variables and assigns their values.

2 Click where you want to begin the If...Then...Else statement and type **If** followed by the condition you want to check.

3 Type **Then** and press Enter.

4 Press Tab to indent the code you will type.

5 Type the code you want to execute if the condition you specified in step 2 is true. Then press Enter.

Apply It

Nested If statements allow you to specify multiple conditions for an If...Then...Else statement. Each If statement will be evaluated only if the previous If statement is true. If all the If statements are true, the section of code is executed. If any of the If statements are false, the Else statement is executed. You must include an End If statement for each If statement you specify.

TYPE THIS:

```
Dim temp
temp=78
If temp > 65 Then
    If temp < 75 Then
        Document.Write "Temperature is normal."
    Else
        Document.Write "Temperature is too hot."
    End If
End If
```

RESULT:

Temperature is too hot.

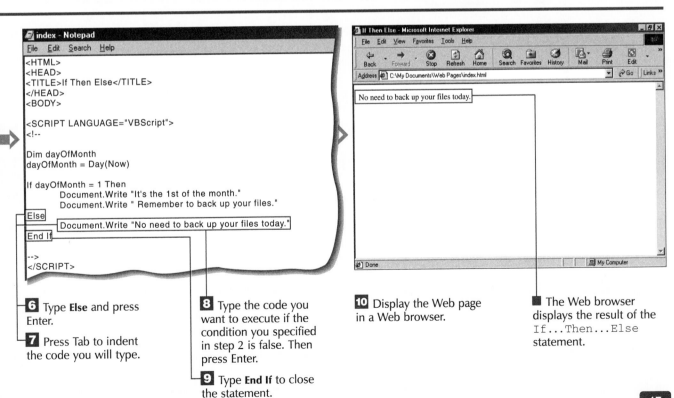

-6 Type **Else** and press Enter.

-7 Press Tab to indent the code you will type.

8 Type the code you want to execute if the condition you specified in step 2 is false. Then press Enter.

9 Type **End If** to close the statement.

10 Display the Web page in a Web browser.

■ The Web browser displays the result of the If...Then...Else statement.

USING THE IF...THEN...ELSEIF STATEMENT

The If...Then...ElseIf statement allows you to execute a section of code, depending on the result of testing multiple conditions. For example, you can have a Web page display Good Morning when the page is displayed between 6:00 AM and 12:00 PM, Good Afternoon when the page is displayed between 12:00 PM and 6:00 PM and Good Evening when the page is displayed before 10:00 PM.

An If...Then...ElseIf statement begins with an If statement and ends with an End If statement. The If statement tests a condition to determine whether the condition is true or false. If the condition

is true, the section of code between the If statement and the ElseIf statement will be executed.

If the condition is false, VBScript will test each ElseIf condition until a condition is true. VBScript will execute the code for the first true ElseIf statement.

An If...Then...ElseIf statement can be difficult to write correctly, particularly if it contains many ElseIf statements. To avoid errors in your scripts, you should carefully analyze and test the logical execution of an If...Then...ElseIf statement.

USING THE IF...THEN...ELSEIF STATEMENT

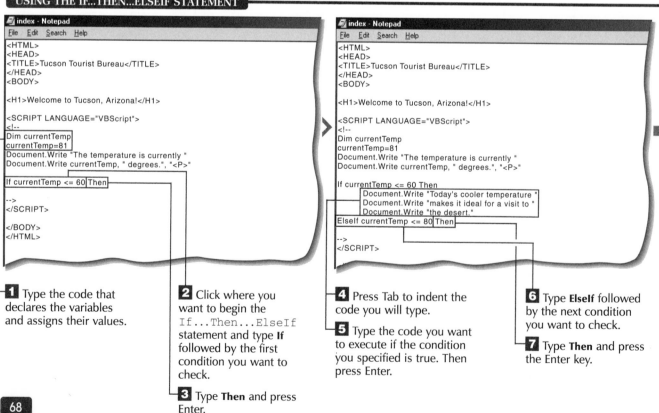

1 Type the code that declares the variables and assigns their values.

2 Click where you want to begin the If...Then...ElseIf statement and type **If** followed by the first condition you want to check.

3 Type **Then** and press Enter.

4 Press Tab to indent the code you will type.

5 Type the code you want to execute if the condition you specified is true. Then press Enter.

6 Type **ElseIf** followed by the next condition you want to check.

7 Type **Then** and press the Enter key.

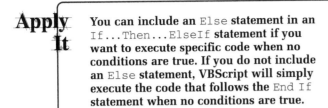

Apply It

You can include an `Else` statement in an `If...Then...ElseIf` statement if you want to execute specific code when no conditions are true. If you do not include an `Else` statement, VBScript will simply execute the code that follows the `End If` statement when no conditions are true.

TYPE THIS:

```
Dim currentHour, newTime
currentHour=Hour(Now)
newTime=Time()
Document.Write "The time is now "
Document.Write newTime, "<BR>"
If currentHour > 6 And currentHour < 12 Then
    Document.Write "Good Morning!"
ElseIf currentHour < 18 Then
    Document.Write "Good Afternoon!"
Else
    Document.Write "Good Evening!"
End If
```

RESULT:

The time is now
7:45:00 PM
Good Evening!

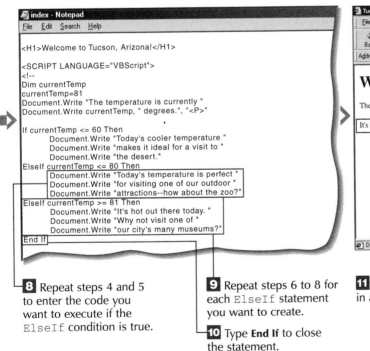

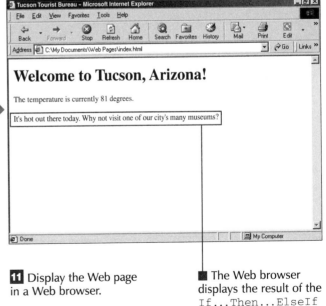

8 Repeat steps 4 and 5 to enter the code you want to execute if the `ElseIf` condition is true.

9 Repeat steps 6 to 8 for each `ElseIf` statement you want to create.

10 Type **End If** to close the statement.

11 Display the Web page in a Web browser.

■ The Web browser displays the result of the `If...Then...ElseIf` statement.

USING THE SELECT CASE STATEMENT

The Select Case statement executes a specific section of code, depending on the value of a variable. For example, you can create a script that displays a different message, depending on whether the shippingOption variable contains the Air, Land, Sea or Overnight value.

To create a Select Case statement, you must indicate the variable you want to check. You use Case statements to indicate the code you want to execute for each possible value of the variable. There is no limit to the number of Case statements you can create. The

End Select statement closes the Select Case statement.

When executing the script, VBScript checks the value of the variable against each Case statement. If VBScript finds a match, the code for the appropriate Case statement is executed. If no match is found, the code following the End Select statement is executed.

Select Case statements are case sensitive. The text value of the variable must exactly match the text values you specify in the Case statements.

USING THE SELECT CASE STATEMENT

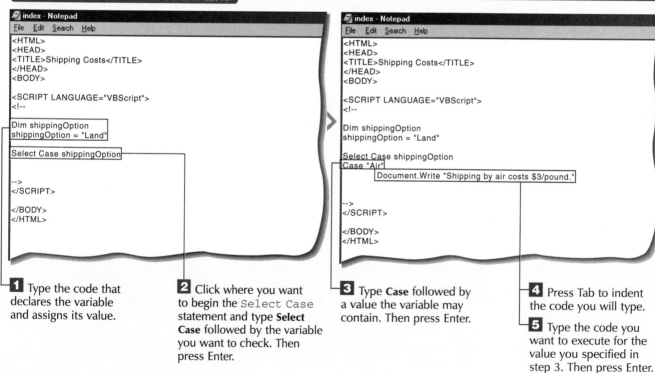

1 Type the code that declares the variable and assigns its value.

2 Click where you want to begin the Select Case statement and type **Select Case** followed by the variable you want to check. Then press Enter.

3 Type **Case** followed by a value the variable may contain. Then press Enter.

4 Press Tab to indent the code you will type.

5 Type the code you want to execute for the value you specified in step 3. Then press Enter.

Apply It

You can use a `Select Case` statement in an ASP page to process information a user enters into a form. For example, you can create a form that allows users to select a shipping method using a drop down list. When the form sends the shipping method to the ASP page, the page will display the cost of the selected shipping method.

FORM:	IN THE ASP PAGE, TYPE:	RESULT:

FORM:

ABC Corporation Shipping Form

IN THE ASP PAGE, TYPE:

```
<%
varShipMethod = Request.Form("shipMethod")
Select Case varShipMethod
Case "Air"
    Response.Write("Shipping by air costs $3/pound.")
Case "Land"
    Response.Write("Shipping by land costs $2/pound.")
Case "Sea"
    Response.Write("Shipping by sea costs $1/pound.")
End Select
%>
```

RESULT:

ABC Corporation Shipping Details

Shipping by land costs $2/pound.

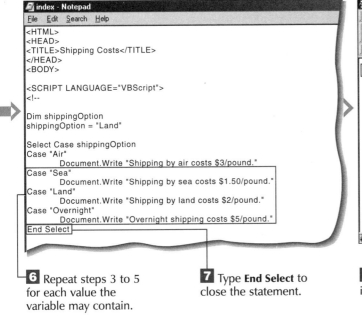

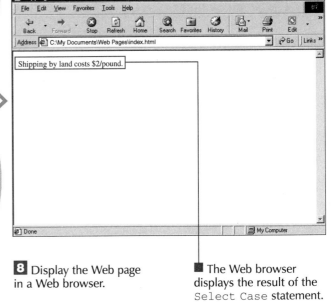

6 Repeat steps 3 to 5 for each value the variable may contain.

7 Type **End Select** to close the statement.

8 Display the Web page in a Web browser.

■ The Web browser displays the result of the `Select Case` statement.

USING THE FOR...NEXT STATEMENT

The For...Next statement allows you to repeat the execution of a section of code a specific number of times. For example, you may want to create five text boxes on a Web page. Instead of typing the code that creates a text box five times, you can create a loop that executes the code to create a text box and then repeats the loop until a counter reaches 5.

When creating a For...Next statement, you use a variable that acts as a counter for the loop. You then specify a starting value and an ending value for the counter variable.

VBScript increases, or increments, the value of the counter variable by one each time the Next statement is executed. When the value of the counter variable reaches the ending value, VBScript executes the code following the Next statement.

The Step keyword allows you to change the value of the counter variable by more than one. When you use the Step keyword, you specify the amount by which you want to increase the counter variable in each repetition of the loop.

USING THE FOR...NEXT STATEMENT

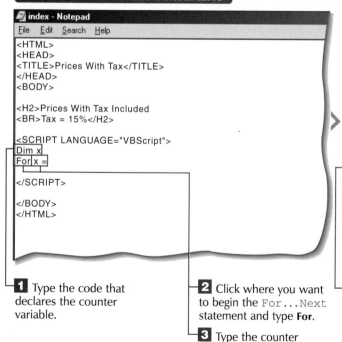

1 Type the code that declares the counter variable.

2 Click where you want to begin the For...Next statement and type **For**.

3 Type the counter variable followed by an equal sign (=).

4 Type the starting value of the counter variable. Then type **To** followed by the ending value of the counter variable.

5 To change the value of the counter variable by more than one in each loop, type **Step** followed by the amount by which you want to change the counter variable. Then press Enter.

Extra

You can use the Step keyword with a negative number to reduce, or decrement, the counter variable in a For...Next statement. When you are decrementing a counter variable, the starting value of the counter variable must be larger than the ending value.

Example:

```
Dim x
Document.Write "Even numbers<BR>"
For x = 10 To 2 Step -2
    Document.Write x, "<BR>"
Next
```

You can use variables instead of numbers for the starting and ending values of the counter variable to make a For...Next statement more versatile. This is useful when the starting or ending values will change. For example, if you want to display the name and department of each employee in a company, you can use the numberOfEmployees variable as the ending value in the loop.

Example:

```
For x = 1 To numberOfEmployees
    Document.Write name, ": " , department
    Document.Write "<BR>"
Next
```

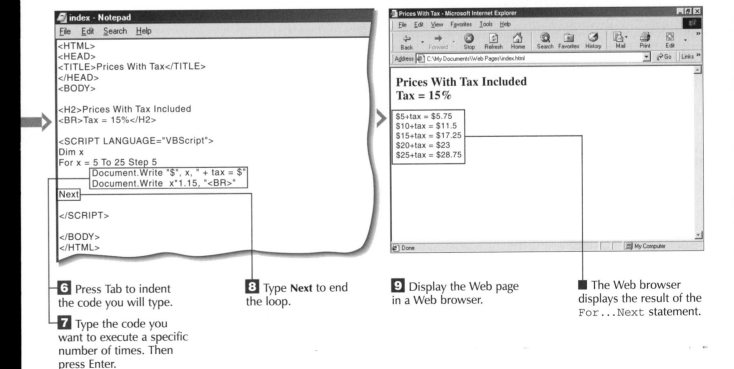

6 Press Tab to indent the code you will type.

7 Type the code you want to execute a specific number of times. Then press Enter.

8 Type **Next** to end the loop.

9 Display the Web page in a Web browser.

■ The Web browser displays the result of the For...Next statement.

USING THE FOR EACH...NEXT STATEMENT

The For Each...Next statement is used to access the items stored in a collection of information, such as an array. The For Each...Next statement creates a loop that accesses each item in a collection, regardless of the number of items the collection contains.

The For Each...Next statement is an effective way to access information when you do not know how many items a collection contains. For example, a For Each...Next statement can access each item in a *dynamic array*.

The For Each statement allows you to specify the variable you want to use to access each item

in a collection and the name of the collection that contains the items.

You then specify the code you want the For Each...Next statement to execute for each item in the collection. If no items exist in the collection, the code will not be executed.

As with other VBScript loops, the Next statement indicates the end of the loop. Once the For Each...Next statement has completed processing all the items in the collection, the line of code following the Next statement will be executed.

USING THE FOR EACH...NEXT STATEMENT

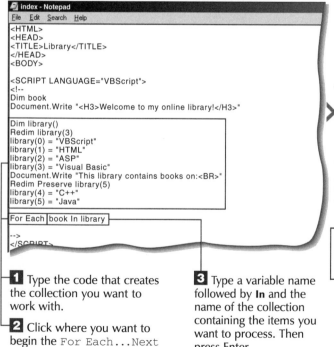

1 Type the code that creates the collection you want to work with.

2 Click where you want to begin the For Each...Next statement and type **For Each**.

3 Type a variable name followed by **In** and the name of the collection containing the items you want to process. Then press Enter.

4 Press Tab to indent the code you will type.

5 Type the code you want to execute to process each item in the collection. Then press Enter.

Extra

You can stop a `For Each...Next` statement from processing any more code and exit the loop by using the `Exit For` statement. For example, you can use an `If...Then` statement to test a condition within the `For Each...Next` statement. If the condition is true, VBScript will execute the `Exit For` statement. When the `Exit For` statement is executed, VBScript skips to the line of code following the `Next` statement.

TYPE THIS:

```
names=array("John","Jim","","Clive")
For Each x In names
    If x = "" Then
        Document.Write "Item has no data."
        Exit For
    End If
    Document.Write x, "<BR>"
Next
```

RESULT:

John
Jim
Item has no data.

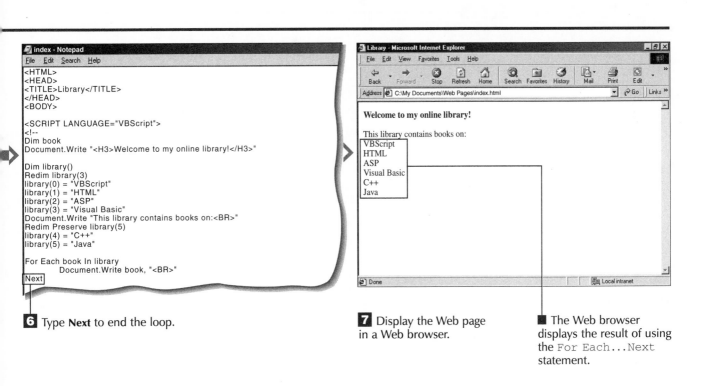

6 Type **Next** to end the loop.

7 Display the Web page in a Web browser.

■ The Web browser displays the result of using the `For Each...Next` statement.

USING THE DO WHILE STATEMENT

The Do While statement allows you to repeat the execution of a section of code as long as a condition is true. For example, you may want to process a pay statement for each of the 100 employees in a company. Instead of typing the code that will process a pay statement 100 times, you can create a loop to process the pay statement for one employee and then repeat the loop for each of the employees.

When creating a Do While statement, you specify a condition you want VBScript to evaluate. If the condition is true, the code for the statement is executed. When VBScript

reaches the Loop statement, the condition you specified is re-evaluated. If the condition is still true, the code is executed again. If the condition is false, VBScript executes the code following the Loop statement.

A Do While statement usually contains code to alter the condition. For example, if the condition tests the value of a counter, the Do While statement will contain code to increment the value of the counter each time the loop is executed. This ensures that the condition will not always be true. If a condition is always true, the code will be executed indefinitely.

USING THE DO WHILE STATEMENT

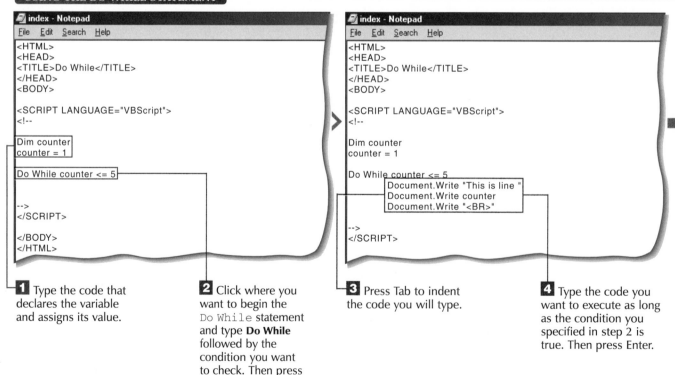

1 Type the code that declares the variable and assigns its value.

2 Click where you want to begin the Do While statement and type **Do While** followed by the condition you want to check. Then press Enter.

3 Press Tab to indent the code you will type.

4 Type the code you want to execute as long as the condition you specified in step 2 is true. Then press Enter.

Extra

The `Exit Do` statement stops a loop in a specific circumstance. For example, you can have a loop display the age of clients. If the age is greater than 120, you can have VBScript display an error message and then stop the loop.

Example:
```
Dim x
x=0
age=Array(35, 47, 23, 201, 52)
Do While x<=4
    If age(x) > 120 Then
        Document.Write "Invalid age"
        Exit Do
    End If
    Document.Write age(x), "<BR>"
    x=x+1
Loop
```

You can ensure the code for a `Do While` statement is executed at least once in your script. Type **While** and the condition you want to check in the `Loop` statement rather than the `Do` statement. In the following example, the `Document.Write` code will be executed once, even though x does not equal zero.

Example:
```
Dim x
x=1
Do
    Document.Write "Hello world"
Loop While x=0
```

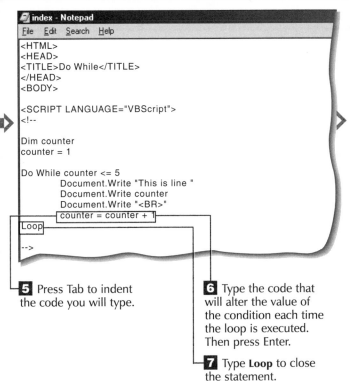

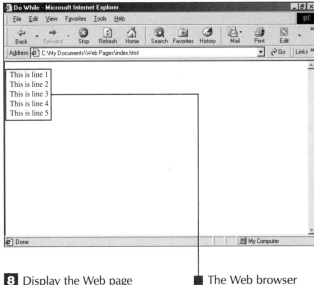

5 Press Tab to indent the code you will type.

6 Type the code that will alter the value of the condition each time the loop is executed. Then press Enter.

7 Type **Loop** to close the statement.

8 Display the Web page in a Web browser.

■ The Web browser displays the result of the `Do While` statement.

CREATE A SUBROUTINE

A subroutine contains lines of code that perform a specific task, such as displaying a message.

Using subroutines makes it easy to re-use sections of code. For example, you may have a subroutine that displays a warning message when a client enters invalid data into a form. Instead of retyping the section of code that displays the message for each field in the form, you can simply re-use the subroutine.

Subroutines also allow you to group lines of code into smaller, more manageable sections. This makes it easier for people to understand and troubleshoot the code.

A subroutine begins with a `Sub` statement and ends with an `End Sub` statement. The `Sub` statement includes the name of the subroutine, which must begin with a letter and cannot contain spaces or periods. Multiple capitalized words are often used to name a subroutine, such as ShowDateAndTime. You should also include parentheses ( ) at the end of the subroutine name.

You use a `Call` statement to tell VBScript to access the code in a subroutine. For information about calling a subroutine, see page 80.

A subroutine can be placed between the `<HEAD>` and `</HEAD>` tags or in the same script as the `Call` statement in a Web page.

CREATE A SUBROUTINE

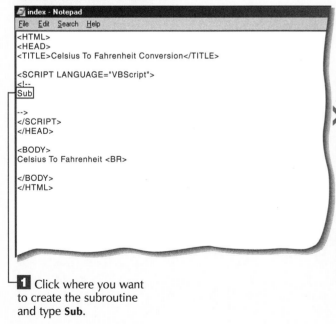

1 Click where you want to create the subroutine and type **Sub**.

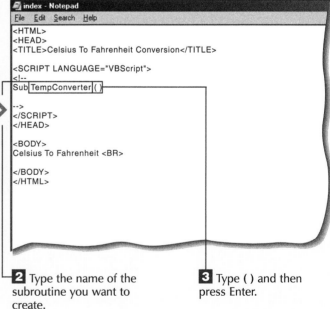

2 Type the name of the subroutine you want to create.

3 Type ( ) and then press Enter.

Extra

You can use comments to make your subroutines easier to understand. This is helpful when you or other people need to modify or troubleshoot your code. In VBScript, comments begin with an apostrophe (') and can help you quickly identify the purpose of a subroutine. You should also use indentation to help improve the readability of your scripts.

FOR EXAMPLE:

```
Dim userAge
userAge=34
Call CheckAge( )
Sub CheckAge( )
If userAge < 1 Or userAge > 120 Then
Exit Sub
Else
Document.Write "User's age is acceptable"
End If
End Sub
```

CAN BE TYPED AS:

```
Dim userAge
userAge=34
Call CheckAge( )
Sub CheckAge( )
' Subroutine checks if the age of a user is
' between 1 and 120 and then generates a message
' stating that the age is valid.
   If userAge < 1 Or userAge > 120 Then
        Exit Sub
        ' Checks if age is less than 1 or greater
        ' than 120. If so, the subroutine is ended.
   Else
        Document.Write "User's age is acceptable"
        ' Displays message indicating the age is valid.
   End If
End Sub
```

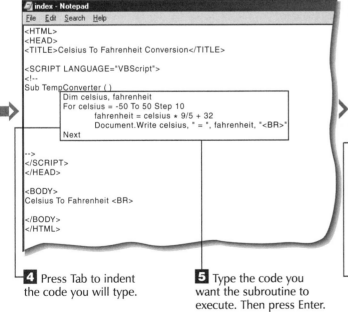

index - Notepad
File Edit Search Help

```
<HTML>
<HEAD>
<TITLE>Celsius To Fahrenheit Conversion</TITLE>

<SCRIPT LANGUAGE="VBScript">
<!--
Sub TempConverter ( )
        Dim celsius, fahrenheit
        For celsius = -50 To 50 Step 10
                fahrenheit = celsius * 9/5 + 32
                Document.Write celsius, " = ", fahrenheit, "<BR>"
        Next

-->
</SCRIPT>
</HEAD>

<BODY>
Celsius To Fahrenheit <BR>

</BODY>
</HTML>
```

index - Notepad
File Edit Search Help

```
<HTML>
<HEAD>
<TITLE>Celsius To Fahrenheit Conversion</TITLE>

<SCRIPT LANGUAGE="VBScript">
<!--
Sub TempConverter ( )
        Dim celsius, fahrenheit
        For celsius = -50 To 50 Step 10
                fahrenheit = celsius * 9/5 + 32
                Document.Write celsius, " = ", fahrenheit, "<BR>"
        Next
End Sub
-->
</SCRIPT>
</HEAD>

<BODY>
Celsius To Fahrenheit <BR>

</BODY>
</HTML>
```

4 Press Tab to indent the code you will type.

5 Type the code you want the subroutine to execute. Then press Enter.

6 Type **End Sub** to close the subroutine.

■ You can now call the subroutine in the script. See page 80 to call a subroutine.

CALL A SUBROUTINE

O nce you have created a subroutine, you need to call the subroutine to tell VBScript to access and execute the code in the subroutine. The code specified in a subroutine will not be executed until the subroutine is called.

You use a `Call` statement to call a subroutine in a script. The `Call` statement tells VBScript the name of the subroutine you want to execute. You must ensure the spelling of the subroutine name in the `Call` statement exactly matches the spelling of the name in the `Sub` statement.

When entering a subroutine name, you should include the parentheses at the end of the name. It is good programming practice to include the parentheses in all statements relating to subroutines.

When a subroutine is called, the code in the subroutine is executed as if it were typed in the location where you placed the `Call` statement. After VBScript finishes executing the code in the subroutine, VBScript executes the code in the line following the `Call` statement.

CALL A SUBROUTINE

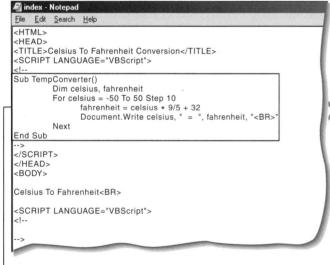

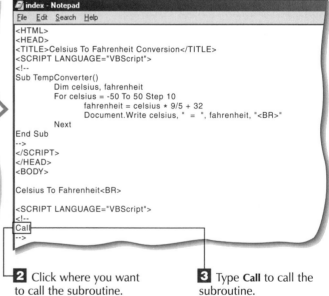

1 Create the subroutine you want to call. See page 78 to create a subroutine.

2 Click where you want to call the subroutine.

3 Type **Call** to call the subroutine.

Extra

You can call a subroutine from within another subroutine. When calling other subroutines from within a subroutine, be careful not to generate a loop that causes the subroutines to continuously call each other.

TYPE THIS:

```
<SCRIPT LANGUAGE="VBScript">
<!--
Document.Write "<H3>Result of System Check:</H3>"
Call ErrorMessage()

Sub ErrorMessage()
  Call FormatText()
  Document.Write "An error has been "
  Document.Write "detected.</FONT><BR>"
End Sub

Sub FormatText()
   Document.Write "<FONT SIZE=5 FACE=ARIAL>"
End Sub
-->
</SCRIPT>
```

RESULT:

Result of System Check:

An error has been detected.

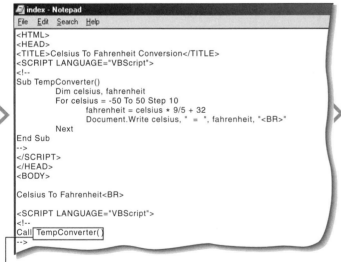

```
index - Notepad
File   Edit   Search   Help
<HTML>
<HEAD>
<TITLE>Celsius To Fahrenheit Conversion</TITLE>
<SCRIPT LANGUAGE="VBScript">
<!--
Sub TempConverter()
        Dim celsius, fahrenheit
        For celsius = -50 To 50 Step 10
                fahrenheit = celsius * 9/5 + 32
                Document.Write celsius, " = ", fahrenheit, "<BR>"
        Next
End Sub
-->
</SCRIPT>
</HEAD>
<BODY>

Celsius To Fahrenheit<BR>

<SCRIPT LANGUAGE="VBScript">
<!--
Call TempConverter()
-->
```

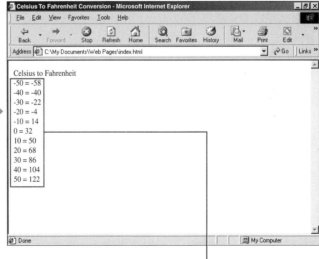

4 Type the name of the subroutine you want to call, including the parentheses ( ). Then press Enter.

5 Display the Web page in a Web browser.

■ The Web browser displays the result of the subroutine.

PASS VALUES TO A SUBROUTINE

Passing a value to a subroutine you have created can make the subroutine more powerful. You can pass one or more values to a subroutine.

To pass a value to a subroutine, you include a variable name in the parentheses ( ) at the end of the Sub statement. In the Call statement for the subroutine, you include the value you want to pass to the subroutine. When the subroutine is called, VBScript uses the value from the Call statement to execute the code in the subroutine.

The variable names and values included in the Sub and Call statements are referred to as *arguments*. The Sub statement and the Call statement must contain the same number of arguments and each argument must be separated by a comma.

You can pass any alphanumeric value to a subroutine, but the value must be appropriate for the purpose of the subroutine. For example, you cannot pass a text value to a subroutine if the value will be used in a mathematical calculation in the subroutine.

PASS VALUES TO A SUBROUTINE

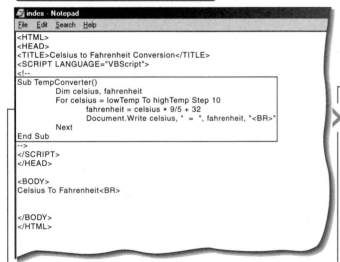

1 Create the subroutine you want to pass values to. See page 78 to create a subroutine.

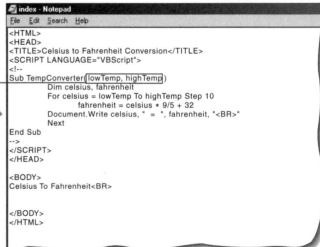

2 In the Sub statement, position the insertion point between the parentheses ( ) at the end of the subroutine name and type the variables you want to use in the subroutine, separated by commas.

Apply It

You can combine text, numbers and variables in the arguments you pass to a subroutine. Any text arguments you pass to a subroutine must be enclosed in quotation marks.

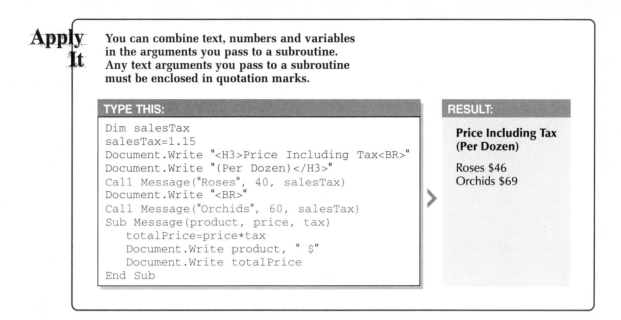

TYPE THIS:

```
Dim salesTax
salesTax=1.15
Document.Write "<H3>Price Including Tax<BR>"
Document.Write "(Per Dozen)</H3>"
Call Message("Roses", 40, salesTax)
Document.Write "<BR>"
Call Message("Orchids", 60, salesTax)
Sub Message(product, price, tax)
    totalPrice=price*tax
    Document.Write product, " $"
    Document.Write totalPrice
End Sub
```

RESULT:

**Price Including Tax
(Per Dozen)**

Roses $46
Orchids $69

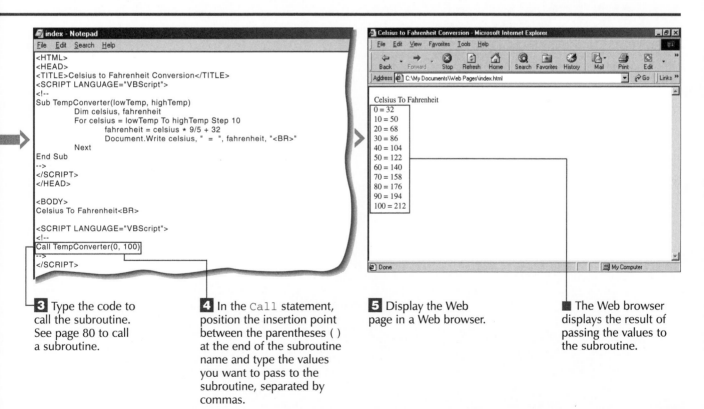

3 Type the code to call the subroutine. See page 80 to call a subroutine.

4 In the `Call` statement, position the insertion point between the parentheses ( ) at the end of the subroutine name and type the values you want to pass to the subroutine, separated by commas.

5 Display the Web page in a Web browser.

■ The Web browser displays the result of passing the values to the subroutine.

EXIT A SUBROUTINE

There may be cases in which you do not want to execute all of the code in a subroutine. In these cases, you can use the `Exit Sub` statement to stop the execution of the code. For example, you may have a subroutine that displays information from a database. If an error occurs while executing the subroutine code, you can display an error message in the user's Web browser and exit the subroutine.

When VBScript encounters the `Exit Sub` statement in a subroutine, VBScript stops

the execution of the subroutine and ignores the code following the `Exit Sub` statement within the subroutine. VBScript then returns to the line of code following the `Call` statement and executes that code.

If you exit a subroutine that is called from within another subroutine, VBScript will exit only the subroutine that contains the `Exit Sub` statement. The code in the other subroutine will be processed as normal.

EXIT A SUBROUTINE

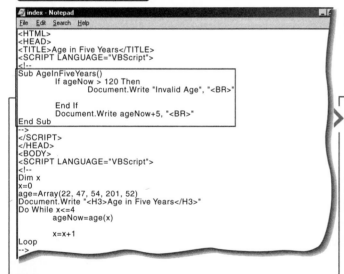

1 Create a subroutine that tests a condition. See page 78 to create a subroutine.

2 Position the insertion point below the condition you want to end the subroutine for and type **Exit Sub** to end the subroutine when the condition is true.

Apply It

Using multiple `Exit Sub` statements in a subroutine is useful when a subroutine contains an `If...Then` or `Select Case` statement.

TYPE THIS:

```
Call CheckAge(34)
Document.Write "<BR>"
Call CheckAge(170)
Document.Write "<BR>"

Sub CheckAge(userAge)
If userAge < 1 Then
        Document.Write "Please check user's age."
        Exit Sub
    ElseIf userAge > 120 Then
        Document.Write "Please check user's age."
        Exit Sub
    Else
        Document.Write "The user age "
        Document.Write userAge, " is acceptable."
    End If
End Sub
```

RESULT:

The user age 34 is acceptable. Please check user's age.

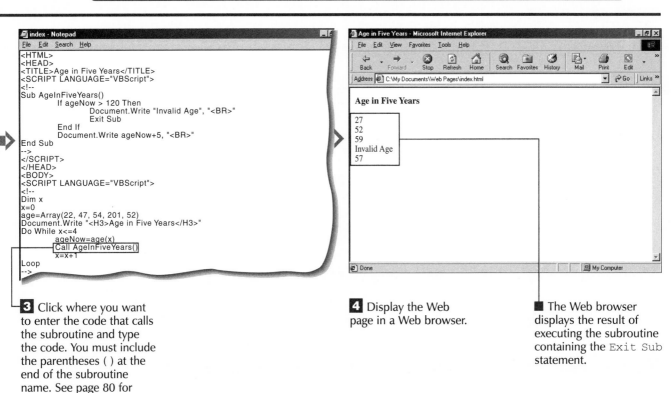

```
<HTML>
<HEAD>
<TITLE>Age in Five Years</TITLE>
<SCRIPT LANGUAGE="VBScript">
<!--
Sub AgeInFiveYears()
        If ageNow > 120 Then
                Document.Write "Invalid Age", "<BR>"
                Exit Sub
        End If
        Document.Write ageNow+5, "<BR>"
End Sub
-->
</SCRIPT>
</HEAD>
<BODY>
<SCRIPT LANGUAGE="VBScript">
<!--
Dim x
x=0
age=Array(22, 47, 54, 201, 52)
Document.Write "<H3>Age in Five Years</H3>"
Do While x<=4
        ageNow=age(x)
        Call AgeInFiveYears()
        x=x+1
Loop
-->
```

3 Click where you want to enter the code that calls the subroutine and type the code. You must include the parentheses ( ) at the end of the subroutine name. See page 80 for more information.

4 Display the Web page in a Web browser.

■ The Web browser displays the result of executing the subroutine containing the `Exit Sub` statement.

CREATE A FUNCTION

A function is often used to perform a calculation and generate a value for a script. Like a subroutine, a function allows you to re-use sections of code and can help organize a script.

The Function statement includes the name of the function followed by parentheses ( ). A function name must begin with a letter and cannot contain spaces. Multiple capitalized words are often used to name a function, such as CalculateInterest.

A function used to generate a value for a script must contain a variable which stores

the result of the calculation performed by the function. The name of the variable must be the same as the name of the function.

The code specified in a function will not be executed until you *call* the function in your script. To call a function, you type the name of the function, including the parentheses, where you want to execute the code specified in the function.

A function can be placed between the <HEAD> and </HEAD> tags or in the script where the function is called in a Web page.

CREATE A FUNCTION

```
index - Notepad
File  Edit  Search  Help
<HTML>
<HEAD>
<TITLE>Total Income</TITLE>
<SCRIPT LANGUAGE="VBScript">
<!--
Function NetIncome ()

-->
</SCRIPT>
</HEAD>

<BODY>
<SCRIPT LANGUAGE="VBScript">
<!--
Dim sales, commissionRate
sales=40000
commissionRate=0.04

Document.Write "My total income for 1999 is: $"

-->
</SCRIPT>

</BODY>
```

1 Click where you want to create the function and type **Function**.

2 Type the name of the function you want to create.

3 Type ( ) and then press Enter.

```
index - Notepad
File  Edit  Search  Help
<HTML>
<HEAD>
<TITLE>Total Income</TITLE>
<SCRIPT LANGUAGE="VBScript">
<!--
Function NetIncome()
    commission=sales*commissionRate
    NetIncome=base+commission
End Function

-->
</SCRIPT>
</HEAD>

<BODY>
<SCRIPT LANGUAGE="VBScript">
<!--
Dim sales, commissionRate
sales=40000
commissionRate=0.04

Document.Write "My total income for 1999 is: $"

-->
```

4 Press Tab to indent the code you will type.

5 Type the code you want the function to execute. Then press Enter.

6 Type **End Function** to close the function.

Extra

The `Exit Function` statement allows you to stop a function when you do not want to execute all of the code in the function. This is useful when an error is detected. In this example, the `Exit Function` statement is used to prevent the function from displaying the result of adding 5 to an age over 120.

TYPE THIS:

```
Dim x
x=0
age=Array(22, 47, 54, 201, 52)
Document.Write "<H3>Age in Five Years</H3>"
Do While x<=4
    ageNow=age(x)
    Document.Write AgeInFiveYears(), "<BR>"
    x=x+1
Loop

Function AgeInFiveYears()
    If ageNow > 120 Then
        Document.Write "Invalid Age"
        Exit Function
    End If
    AgeInFiveYears=ageNow+5
End Function
```

RESULT:

Age in Five Years

27
52
59
Invalid Age
57

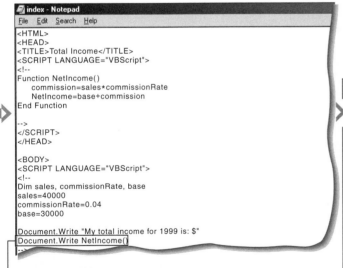

CALL A FUNCTION

7 Click where you want to call the function and type the code that calls the function. You must include the parentheses ( ) at the end of the function name.

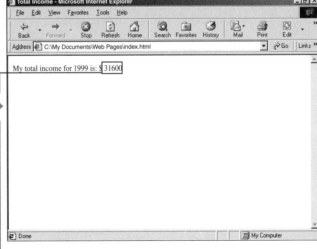

8 Display the Web page in a Web browser.

■ The Web browser displays the result of the function.

■ You can now pass values to the function. See page 88 to pass values to a function.

PASS VALUES TO A FUNCTION

Passing values to a function you have created allows you to use one function throughout a script to process different data and return a result. You can pass one or more values to a function.

In the Function statement, you define one or more variables. Each variable represents a value you will pass to the function. Each time you call the function in your script, you specify the values, called *arguments*, you want to use in the function.

A function can use the values you specify to perform a calculation and then send the result

back to the code you used to call the function. The result can be used in many ways in the script. For example, you can assign the result to another variable or display the result on the screen.

You can pass any alphanumeric value to a function, but the value must be appropriate for the purpose of the function. For example, you cannot pass a text value to a function if the value will be used in a mathematical calculation. Text values must be enclosed in quotation marks.

PASS VALUES TO A FUNCTION

```
index - Notepad
File   Edit   Search   Help
<HTML>
<HEAD>
<TITLE>Bill's Bargain House</TITLE>
<SCRIPT LANGUAGE="VBScript">
<!--
Function CalculatePrice()
    Document.Write itemName, " - $"
    CalculatePrice=itemPrice*tax
End Function
-->
</SCRIPT>
</HEAD>

<BODY>
<H1>Bill's Bargain House</H1>

<SCRIPT LANGUAGE="VBScript">
<!--
Document.Write "<H3>Prices With Tax</H3>"
Document.Write CalculatePrice()
Document.Write "<BR>"
Document.Write CalculatePrice()
Document.Write "<BR>"
Document.Write CalculatePrice()
-->
</SCRIPT>
```

1 Create and call the function you want to pass values to. See page 86 to create and call a function.

```
index - Notepad
File   Edit   Search   Help
<HTML>
<HEAD>
<TITLE>Bill's Bargain House</TITLE>
<SCRIPT LANGUAGE="VBScript">
<!--
Function CalculatePrice(itemPrice, tax, itemName)
    Document.Write itemName, " - $"
    CalculatePrice=itemPrice*tax
End Function
-->
</SCRIPT>
</HEAD>

<BODY>
<H1>Bill's Bargain House</H1>

<SCRIPT LANGUAGE="VBScript">
<!--
Document.Write "<H3>Prices With Tax</H3>"
Document.Write CalculatePrice()
Document.Write "<BR>"
Document.Write CalculatePrice()
Document.Write "<BR>"
Document.Write CalculatePrice()
-->
</SCRIPT>
```

2 In the Function statement, position the insertion point between the parentheses ( ) at the end of the function name and type the variables you want to use in the function, separated by commas.

Extra Using conditional statements to call and create a function can make the function more versatile. For example, you can use an `If...Then` statement to call a function, which allows you to test a condition before passing a value to the function. You can then use a `Select Case` statement to create the function, which allows you to perform a specific action depending on the value passed to the function.

TYPE THIS:

```
Dim temperature
temperature=65
If temperature <= 50 Then
    Document.Write Message(1)
ElseIf temperature >= 80 Then
    Document.Write Message(2)
Else
    Document.Write Message(3)
End If
Function Message(code)
    Select Case code
        Case 1 Message="Temperature is too low.<BR>"
        Case 2 Message="Temperature is too high.<BR>"
        Case 3 Message="Temperature is normal.<BR>"
    End Select
End Function
```

RESULT:

Temperature is normal.

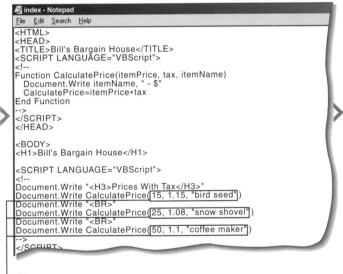

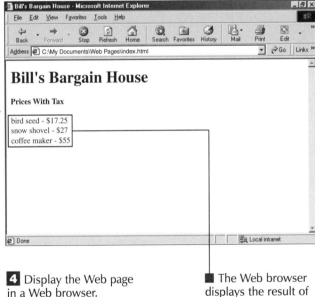

3 In the code you use to call the function, position the insertion point between the parentheses ( ) at the end of the function name and type the values you want to pass to the function, separated by commas.

4 Display the Web page in a Web browser.

■ The Web browser displays the result of passing the values to the function.

USING DATE AND TIME FUNCTIONS

V BScript includes a collection of functions that allow you to work with the date and time in a Web page. For example, you may need to display the current time on a Web page or perform a complex calculation, such as finding the number of days that have passed since a Web page was last updated.

Many date and time functions can be used with the Now() function, which can return the current date and time set on a computer. For example, to display the current hour, you use

the Hour() function in conjunction with the Now() function.

When date and time functions are included in scripts that will be processed by a user's Web browser, the functions use the date and time settings on the user's computer to retrieve and format the date and time. When VBScript is processed by a Web server, as is the case when VBScript is used in Active Server Pages code, the functions use the date and time settings on the Web server to retrieve and format the date and time.

USING DATE AND TIME FUNCTIONS

```
index - Notepad
File  Edit  Search  Help
<HTML>
<HEAD>
<TITLE>Using Date and Time Functions</TITLE>
</HEAD>
<BODY>

Welcome to my Web page.<P>

<SCRIPT LANGUAGE="VBScript">
<!--
Year()

-->
</SCRIPT>
</BODY>
</HTML>
```

```
index - Notepad
File  Edit  Search  Help
<HTML>
<HEAD>
<TITLE>Using Date and Time Functions</TITLE>
</HEAD>
<BODY>

Welcome to my Web page.<P>

<SCRIPT LANGUAGE="VBScript">
<!--
Year(Now())

-->
</SCRIPT>
</BODY>
</HTML>>
```

1 Click where you want to place a date or time function and type the name of the function you want to use. Then press Enter.

2 To execute the function based on the current date or time, position the insertion point between the parentheses ( ) in the function and type **Now( )**.

Note: The Date() *and* Time() *functions do not require the* Now() *function to return the current date or time.*

Extra

Common VBScript Date and Time Functions

EXAMPLE	DESCRIPTION
Date()	Returns the current date
DateAdd("d", 15, "20-May-00")	Adds a number of days to the date you specify
DateDiff("d", "20-May-00", "30-Jun-00")	Returns the number of days between two dates
Day(Now())	Returns the day of the month from 1 to 31
Month(Now())	Returns the month of the year from 1 to 12
MonthName(6)	Returns the name of the month
Weekday(Now())	Returns the day of the week from 1 to 7
Year(Now())	Returns the year
Time()	Returns the current time
Hour(Now())	Returns the hour in 24-hour format
Minute(Now())	Returns the minute from 0 to 59
Second(Now())	Returns the second from 0 to 59

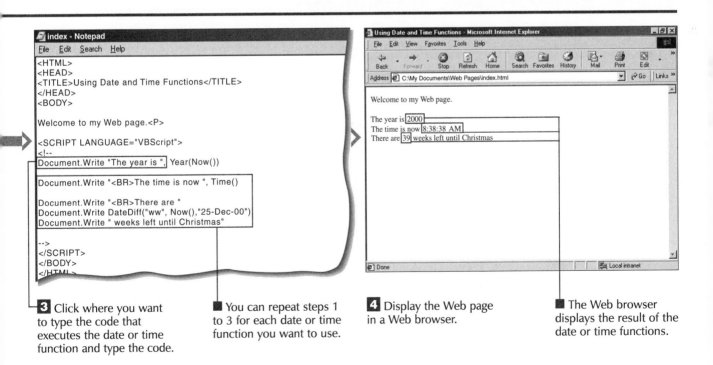

3 Click where you want to type the code that executes the date or time function and type the code.

■ You can repeat steps 1 to 3 for each date or time function you want to use.

4 Display the Web page in a Web browser.

■ The Web browser displays the result of the date or time functions.

MANIPULATE A STRING

A string can contain alphanumeric values and special characters commonly found on a keyboard, such as @, & and %. A string can also be empty or contain non-standard characters, such as the copyright symbol (©).

String functions allow you to manipulate the information that a string contains. For example, string functions can be used to check the length of data entered into a text element on a form or convert data to upper or lower case characters. You can also use a string function to extract data from an element on a form. Many of the string

functions available in VBScript are used to locate characters or phrases within a string. This is useful when you want to validate an e-mail address a user has entered by searching the string for the "@" symbol. You can also search for and remove strings containing offensive words or phrases before displaying strings on a Web page.

Using string functions saves time and bandwidth by allowing you to manipulate data a user enters into a Web page at the user's Web browser before submitting the data to the Web server.

USE STRING FUNCTION TO CHECK VALIDITY OF E-MAIL ADDRESS

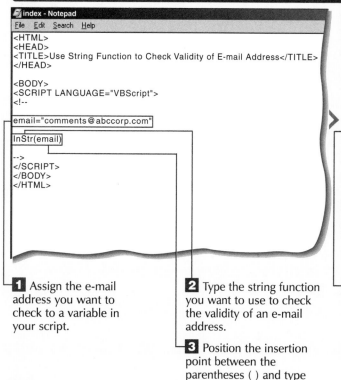

```
index - Notepad
File  Edit  Search  Help
<HTML>
<HEAD>
<TITLE>Use String Function to Check Validity of E-mail Address</TITLE>
</HEAD>

<BODY>
<SCRIPT LANGUAGE="VBScript">
<!--

email="comments@abccorp.com"

InStr(email)

-->
</SCRIPT>
</BODY>
</HTML>
```

```
index - Notepad
File  Edit  Search  Help
<HTML>
<HEAD>
<TITLE>Use String Function to Check Validity of E-mail Address</TITLE>
</HEAD>

<BODY>
<SCRIPT LANGUAGE="VBScript">
<!--

email="comments@abccorp.com"

If InStr(email, "@") = 0 Then
        Document.Write "The address appears invalid. Please re-try."
Else
        Document.Write "The address appears valid. Thank you."
End If

-->
</SCRIPT>
</BODY>
</HTML>
```

1 Assign the e-mail address you want to check to a variable in your script.

2 Type the string function you want to use to check the validity of an e-mail address.

3 Position the insertion point between the parentheses ( ) and type the name of the variable that stores the e-mail address.

4 Type a comma followed by the character you want to check for enclosed in quotation marks ("").

5 Click where you want to place the code that uses the string function and type the code.

■ In this example, when the page is displayed in a Web browser, the browser will display a message indicating that the e-mail address appears valid.

COMMON STRING FUNCTIONS

InStr Finds the position of one string in another, starting the search at the left end of a string. `InStr("Good wood","od")` Returns 3	**InStrRev** Finds the position of one string in another, starting the search at the right end of a string. `InStrRev("Good wood","od")` Returns 8	**LCase** Converts text to lowercase. `LCase("GoodBye")` Returns goodbye
UCase Converts text to uppercase. `UCase("GoodBye")` Returns GOODBYE	**Left** Extracts a specific number of characters, starting at the left end of a string. `Left("John Smith",4)` Returns John	**Right** Extracts a specific number of characters, starting at the right end of a string. `Right("John Smith",5)` Returns Smith
Mid Extracts a specific number of characters, starting at a specific point. `Mid("John Paul Smith",6,4)` Returns Paul	**Len** Finds the length of a string. `Len("John Smith")` Returns 10	**Trim** Removes spaces from the beginning and end of a string. `Trim("      John Smith      ")` Returns John Smith
Replace Replaces one string with another string. `Replace("My chair", "My", "Your")` Returns Your chair	**Asc** Returns the ANSI code number of a character. `Asc("u")` Returns 117	**Chr** Returns the character value of a number between 0 and 255. `Chr(65)` Returns A

IsNumeric Checks if a string contains a numerical value. `IsNumeric("12")` Returns True	**IsDate** Checks if a string contains a valid date. `IsDate("3/27/00")` Returns True	**FormatCurrency** Formats a string value as currency. `FormatCurrency("10")` Returns $10.00	**FormatNumber** Formats a string value as a number. `FormatNumber("9")` Returns 9.00

ERROR HANDLING

An error is generated when a script that contains a mistake is processed. Common mistakes include trying to divide a number by 0 or attempting to access an array element that does not exist. When an error is generated, VBScript stops processing the script and displays an error message in the user's Web browser.

The `On Error Resume Next` statement allows you to handle an error in your script. This statement instructs VBScript to skip to the line of code following an error and continue processing the script. This prevents the script from simply stopping and allows the script to perform any clean up procedures, such as closing open files or saving information to a database.

An `On Error Resume Next` statement should be placed at the beginning of a script. You can also place an `On Error Resume Next` statement at the beginning of a subroutine where an error is likely to occur; however, the statement will only handle errors generated by the code in the subroutine.

Before you use the `On Error Resume Next` statement in a script, you should carefully test and troubleshoot the script. The `On Error Resume Next` statement should only be used to handle errors that you cannot avoid, such as mistakes in information entered into your Web page by a user.

GENERATE AN ERROR

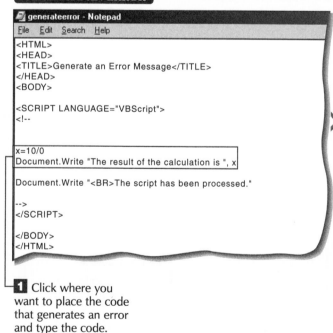

```
<HTML>
<HEAD>
<TITLE>Generate an Error Message</TITLE>
</HEAD>
<BODY>

<SCRIPT LANGUAGE="VBScript">
<!--


x=10/0
Document.Write "The result of the calculation is ", x

Document.Write "<BR>The script has been processed."

-->
</SCRIPT>

</BODY>
</HTML>
```

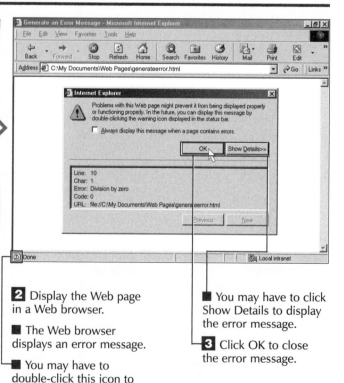

1 Click where you want to place the code that generates an error and type the code.

2 Display the Web page in a Web browser.

■ The Web browser displays an error message.

■ You may have to double-click this icon to display the error message.

■ You may have to click Show Details to display the error message.

3 Click OK to close the error message.

Extra VBScript allows you to access the number, description and source of an error to help you troubleshoot the error. You use the `Err.Number` statement to access the error number. A number greater than 0 indicates that an error has occurred. You use the `Err.Description` statement to access a description of the error. The `Err.Source` statement allows you to access the source of the error, which can help you find where the error occurred.

TYPE THIS:

```
On Error Resume Next
list=Array(apples, oranges)
Document.Write list(2)
If Err.Number > 0 Then
    Document.Write"<BR>An error has occurred."
    Document.Write"<BR>The error number is: "
    Document.Write Err.Number
    Document.Write"<BR>The description is: "
    Document.Write Err.Description
    Document.Write"<BR>The source of the error is: "
    Document.Write Err.Source
End If
```

RESULT:

An error has occurred.
The error number is: 9
The description is: Subscript out of range
The source of the error is: Microsoft VBScript runtime error

HANDLE AN ERROR

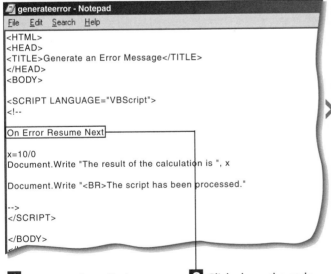

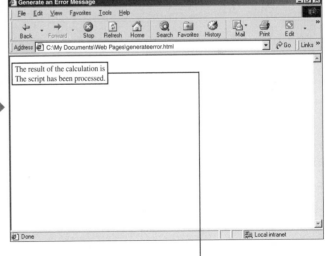

1 In a text editor, display the code you created to generate the error.

2 Click above the code that generates the error and type **On Error Resume Next**. Then press Enter.

3 Display the Web page in a Web browser.

■ The Web browser displays the result of using an `On Error Resume Next` statement to handle the error.

INSERT ASP CODE INTO A WEB PAGE

A dding ASP code to an HTML document allows you to create dynamic, interactive Web pages.

ASP code is inserted into HTML code using separator tags known as delimiters. The <% and %> delimiters tell the Web server where the ASP code begins and ends and help the server determine which parts of the Web page need to be processed before being sent to the user's Web browser.

ASP code can be inserted wherever you want to display the results of the code in a Web page. ASP code used to display information

on a user's browser must be inserted between the <BODY> and </BODY> tags.

When a user displays a Web page containing ASP code in a Web browser, the Web server first sends the HTML code used to create the Web page to the browser. The server then processes the ASP code found between the ASP delimiters and replaces the ASP code with the result generated by the code. The result of the ASP code is then sent to the Web browser as HTML code. The Web browser reads all the HTML code and displays the page on the user's screen.

INSERT ASP CODE INTO A WEB PAGE

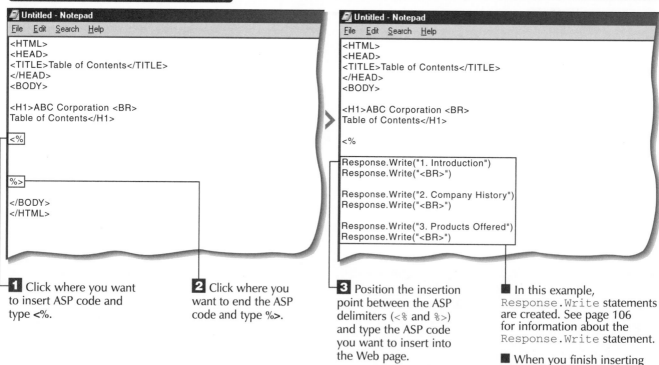

1 Click where you want to insert ASP code and type **<%**.

2 Click where you want to end the ASP code and type **%>**.

3 Position the insertion point between the ASP delimiters (<% and %>) and type the ASP code you want to insert into the Web page.

■ In this example, Response.Write statements are created. See page 106 for information about the Response.Write statement.

■ When you finish inserting ASP code into the Web page, you can save the page.

SAVE AN ASP PAGE

Saving an ASP page stores it for future use. You must save an ASP page on a computer running a Web server, such as Internet Information Server (IIS), before you can view the page. A Web server can run on the same computer you use to create ASP pages.

If your computer is not running a Web server, you must save the ASP page and then transfer the page to a Web server. For information on transferring pages to a Web server, see page 38.

After saving an ASP page on a Web server, you can view the page in a Web browser. See page 98 for more information.

You must ensure that the page is saved in a text only format. If the ASP page is not saved in a text only format, you will not be able to display the page in a Web browser.

An ASP page name can contain alphanumeric characters but should not contain spaces. You must add the .asp extension to the name of the ASP page.

You should frequently save changes made to an ASP page to avoid losing your work. You must also save any changes you have made before viewing the changes in a Web browser.

SAVE AN ASP PAGE

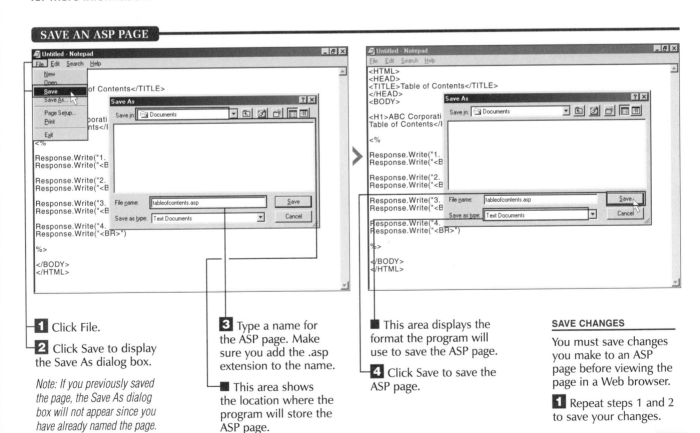

1 Click File.

2 Click Save to display the Save As dialog box.

Note: If you previously saved the page, the Save As dialog box will not appear since you have already named the page.

3 Type a name for the ASP page. Make sure you add the .asp extension to the name.

■ This area shows the location where the program will store the ASP page.

■ This area displays the format the program will use to save the ASP page.

4 Click Save to save the ASP page.

SAVE CHANGES

You must save changes you make to an ASP page before viewing the page in a Web browser.

1 Repeat steps 1 and 2 to save your changes.

VIEW AN ASP PAGE

O nce an ASP page has been saved to a Web server, you can use a Web browser to view the page. The Web server must be capable of processing ASP code.

You must know the address of the ASP page you want to display. The address must begin with http:// and contain the name of the Web server that stores the page. If you do not know the name of the Web server, you can use the IP number assigned to the Web server, such as 162.136.5.1.

If the Web server is running on your own computer, you can use the name of the

computer or the name localhost. If you wish to use an IP number, you can use 127.0.0.1, which is the IP number that computers using TCP/IP use to refer to themselves.

The file name of the ASP page must also be specified to view the page. If the page is stored in the home directory of the Web server, you do not need to specify the directory name. If the page is stored in a different directory, the name of the directory may be required in the address.

VIEW AN ASP PAGE

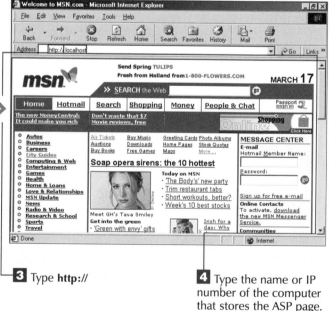

1 Start the Web browser you want to use to display your ASP page.

2 Click this area to highlight the current Web page address.

3 Type **http://**

4 Type the name or IP number of the computer that stores the ASP page.

Extra

ASP code is processed by the Web server and then sent to the Web browser as HTML code. People can view the HTML source code for the page, but they will not be able to view the Active Server Pages code. People who have access to the .asp file on the Web server will be able to open the file using a text editor such as Notepad and view the Active Server Pages code.

A person viewing the HTML source code sees:

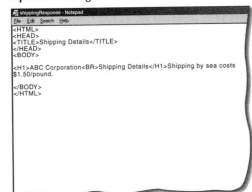

```
shippingResponse - Notepad
File  Edit  Search  Help
<HTML>
<HEAD>
<TITLE>Shipping Details</TITLE>
</HEAD>
<BODY>

<H1>ABC Corporation<BR>Shipping Details</H1>Shipping by sea costs
$1.50/pound.

</BODY>
</HTML>
```

A person viewing the .asp file on the Web server sees:

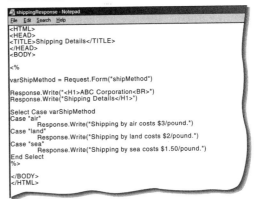

```
shippingResponse - Notepad
File  Edit  Search  Help
<HTML>
<HEAD>
<TITLE>Shipping Details</TITLE>
</HEAD>
<BODY>

<%

varShipMethod = Request.Form("shipMethod")

Response.Write("<H1>ABC Corporation<BR>")
Response.Write("Shipping Details</H1>")

Select Case varShipMethod
Case "air"
        Response.Write("Shipping by air costs $3/pound.")
Case "land"
        Response.Write("Shipping by land costs $2/pound.")
Case "sea"
        Response.Write("Shipping by sea costs $1.50/pound.")
End Select
%>

</BODY>
</HTML>
```

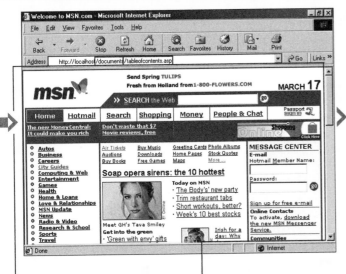

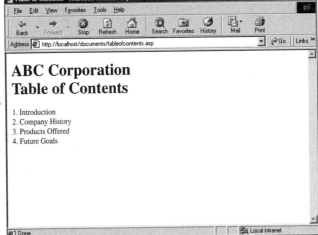

5 If the page is not stored in the home directory, type / followed by the name of the directory where the ASP page is located.

6 Type / followed by the file name of the ASP page.

7 Press Enter to view the ASP page.

■ The ASP page appears in the Web browser.

■ If you later make changes to the ASP page, you can display the updated page in the Web browser. See page 37 to refresh a page.

ADD A COMMENT

A dding a comment to HTML code or ASP code can help clarify the code. Comments you add to your code will not appear when a user views the page in a Web browser.

Adding comments to your code is good programming practice and can help make the code easier to understand. For example, you may use a variable named totalCost in your code. The variable could store the total cost of all the products in a database or only some of the products. You could use a comment to explain that the totalCost variable stores the total cost of all the products.

Besides describing the purpose of code, comments can contain information such as the author's name or the date the code was created. Comments can also be used as reminders to remove or update sections of code.

Comments do not have to be long, detailed explanations. The most effective comments are descriptive and concise.

You use comment tags (<!-- and -->) to add a comment to HTML code. To add a comment to ASP code, you place an apostrophe (') before the comment.

ADD A COMMENT

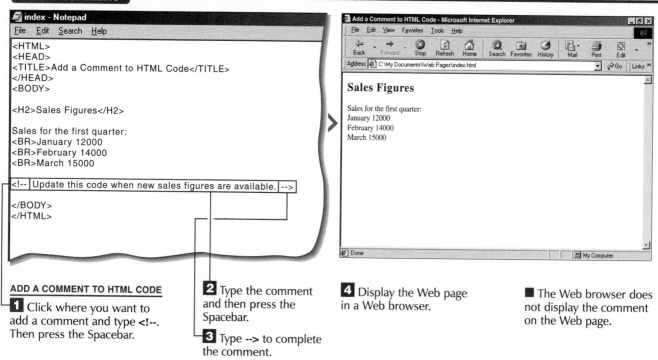

ADD A COMMENT TO HTML CODE

1 Click where you want to add a comment and type **<!--**. Then press the Spacebar.

2 Type the comment and then press the Spacebar.

3 Type **-->** to complete the comment.

4 Display the Web page in a Web browser.

■ The Web browser does not display the comment on the Web page.

Extra

When adding a comment to HTML code, you can type as many lines of text as you need between the comment tags.

Example:

```
<!--
This HTML code is for testing
purposes only and can be
deleted at any time.
-->
```

If the comment you add to ASP code requires more than one line, you must place an apostrophe at the beginning of each line.

Example:

```
' This ASP code is for testing
' purposes and can be deleted.
```

Adding comments to HTML code increases the time it will take for a Web server to transfer the code to a Web browser. Web servers ignore comments in ASP code, so adding comments to your ASP code will not significantly increase the amount of time a server requires to process the code.

You should avoid adding comments that contain private information to HTML code. If a user views the HTML code, they will be able to read any comments you added. Users will not be able to read comments you add to ASP code.

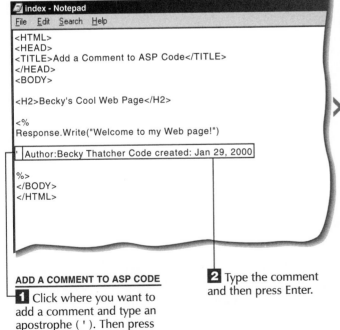

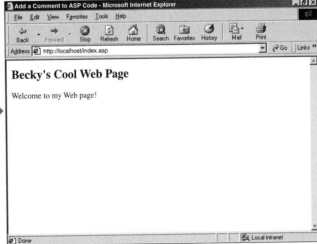

ADD A COMMENT TO ASP CODE

1 Click where you want to add a comment and type an apostrophe ('). Then press the Spacebar.

2 Type the comment and then press Enter.

3 Display the ASP page in a Web browser.

■ The Web browser does not display the comment on the ASP page.

CREATE A FORM

A dding a form to a Web page allows you to gather data from users who visit the page.

A form can be placed anywhere between the <BODY> and </BODY> tags in an HTML document. The body of your Web page can include as many forms as you need.

You use the <FORM> tag to create a form and the ACTION attribute to specify the name of the ASP page that will process the data entered into the form. If the ASP page is not stored on the same

Web server as the form, you must specify the full URL of the ASP page.

You must also specify which method the form will use to pass data to the ASP page. There are two methods the form can use—GET and POST. The GET method sends data to the ASP page by appending the data to the URL of the page. The POST method sends the data and the URL separately. The GET method is faster than the POST method and is suitable for small forms. The POST method is suitable for large forms that will send more than 2000 characters to the ASP page.

CREATE A FORM

```
createform - Notepad
File  Edit  Search  Help
<HTML>
<HEAD>
<TITLE>Create a Form</TITLE>
</HEAD>
<BODY>

<FORM ACTION="survey.asp"  METHOD="GET">

</BODY>
</HTML>
```

```
createform - Notepad
File  Edit  Search  Help
<HTML>
<HEAD>
<TITLE>Create a Form</TITLE>
</HEAD>
<BODY>

<FORM ACTION="survey.asp" METHOD="GET">

</FORM>

</BODY>
</HTML>
```

1 Click where you want to create a form and type **<FORM ACTION=** followed by the name of the ASP page, enclosed in quotation marks, that will process the data entered into the form.

2 Press the Spacebar and type **METHOD=** followed by the method, enclosed in quotation marks, that the form will use to pass data to the ASP page. Then type **>**.

3 Press Enter twice to leave space for the form elements and type **</FORM>** to complete the form.

■ You can now add elements to the form.

ADD ELEMENTS TO A FORM

E lements are areas in a form where users can enter data and select options. The most commonly used element is a text box, which allows users to enter a single line of data into a form.

You must add elements between the <FORM> and </FORM> tags. Your form can contain as many elements as you need.

There are many different types of elements you can add to a form, including text areas, check boxes and buttons. Each element has attributes, such as TYPE, NAME and SIZE, which offer

options for the element. For information about commonly used elements and attributes, see page 104.

You must add a submit button to every form you create. The submit button allows users to send the data they entered into the form to the Web server. When the Web server receives data from a form, the server transfers the data to the ASP page that will process the data. The ASP page can then perform an action with the data, such as storing the data in a database.

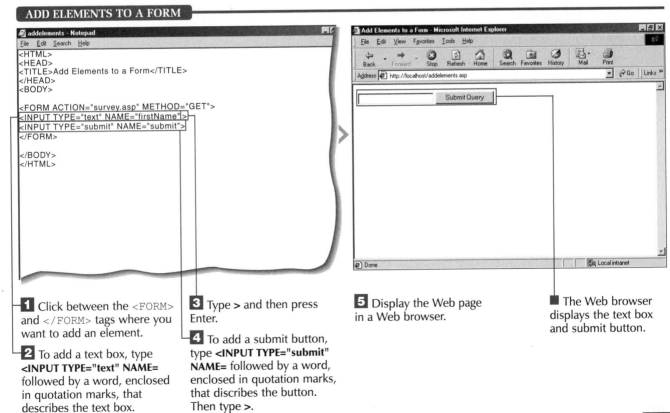

ADD ELEMENTS TO A FORM

1 Click between the <FORM> and </FORM> tags where you want to add an element.

2 To add a text box, type **<INPUT TYPE="text" NAME=** followed by a word, enclosed in quotation marks, that describes the text box.

3 Type **>** and then press Enter.

4 To add a submit button, type **<INPUT TYPE="submit" NAME=** followed by a word, enclosed in quotation marks, that discribes the button. Then type **>**.

5 Display the Web page in a Web browser.

■ The Web browser displays the text box and submit button.

FORM ELEMENTS

An element is an area in a form where users can enter data or select options. There are several different types of elements you can add to a form. For information on adding an element to a form, see page 103.

Most elements require you to specify attributes that determine how the element will appear on a Web page. You can find more information about form elements and attributes at the www.w3.org/TR/1999/REC-html401-19991224/interact/forms Web site.

COMMONLY USED ATTRIBUTES

TYPE
The TYPE attribute allows you to specify the kind of element you want to use.

NAME
The NAME attribute allows you to specify a name for an element. Element names can contain more than one word, but should not contain spaces or special characters. The ASP page that will process data from the element uses the NAME attribute to identify the data.

VALUE
The VALUE attribute allows you to specify a value for an element. If an element displays a button, you can use the VALUE attribute to specify the text that will appear on the button.

MAXLENGTH
The MAXLENGTH attribute allows you to restrict the number of characters a user can enter into an element.

SIZE
The SIZE attribute allows you to specify the width of an element.

CHECKED
The CHECKED attribute allows an element to display a selected option by default.

COMMONLY USED ELEMENTS

PASSWORD BOX
A password box allows users to enter private data. When a user types data into a password box, an asterisk (*) appears for each character, which prevents others from viewing the data on the screen. A password box does not protect the data from being accessed as it is transferred over the Internet. You must set the TYPE attribute to password and use the NAME attribute to create a password box. You may also want to use the VALUE, MAXLENGTH and SIZE attributes.

```
Password Please <INPUT TYPE="password"
NAME="secretWord" VALUE="password" MAXLENGTH="20">
```

Password Please ********

DROP DOWN LIST
The SELECT element displays a drop down list that allows users to select an option from a list of several options. For example, a drop down list can be used to allow users to select one of three shipping methods. You must use the NAME attribute to create a drop down list. You use the <OPTION> tag with the VALUE attribute to add options to the list.

```
How would you like your products shipped?
<SELECT NAME="shipMethod">
<OPTION VALUE="air">Air</OPTION>
<OPTION VALUE="land">Land</OPTION>
<OPTION VALUE="sea">Sea</OPTION>
</SELECT>
```

How would you like your products shipped?

Air
Land
Sea

TEXT BOX

A text box allows users to enter a single line of text, such as a name or telephone number. You must set the TYPE attribute to text and use the NAME attribute to create a text box. You may also want to use the MAXLENGTH and SIZE attributes.

```
First Name <INPUT TYPE="text" NAME="firstName" MAXLENGTH="20">
```

First Name

TEXT AREA

The TEXTAREA element displays a large text area that allows users to enter several lines or paragraphs of text. A large text area is ideal for gathering comments or questions from users. You must use the NAME attribute to create a text area.

```
Questions? <TEXTAREA NAME="userQuestions"></TEXTAREA>
```

Questions?

CHECK BOX

Check boxes allow users to select one or more options. For example, check boxes can be used to allow users to specify which states they have visited. You must set the TYPE attribute to checkbox and use the NAME and VALUE attributes to create a check box. You may also want to use the CHECKED attribute.

```
Which states have you visited in the past year?<BR>
New York <INPUT TYPE="checkbox" NAME="states" VALUE="New York" CHECKED>
California <INPUT TYPE="checkbox" NAME="states" VALUE="California">
Texas <INPUT TYPE="checkbox" NAME="states" VALUE="Texas">
```

Which states have you visited in the past year?
New York ☑ California ☐ Texas ☐

RADIO BUTTON

Radio buttons allow users to select only one of several options. For example, radio buttons can be used to allow users to specify if they are male or female. You must set the TYPE attribute to radio and use the NAME and VALUE attributes to create a radio button. You may also want to use the CHECKED attribute.

```
What is your gender?
Female <INPUT TYPE="radio" NAME="gender" VALUE="female">
Male <INPUT TYPE="radio" NAME="gender" VALUE="male" CHECKED>
```

What is your gender?
Female ○ Male ◉

SUBMIT BUTTON

A submit button allows users to send data in the form to the ASP page that will process the data. You must add a submit button to each form you create. You must set the TYPE attribute to submit to create a submit button. You may also want to use the NAME and VALUE attributes.

```
<INPUT TYPE="submit" NAME="submit" VALUE="Submit Now">
```

Submit Now

RESET BUTTON

A reset button allows users to clear the data they entered into a form. Once a user has cleared the data, they cannot redisplay the data. Reset buttons are commonly used in forms that have many text boxes. You must set the TYPE attribute to reset to create a reset button. You may also want to use the VALUE attribute.

```
<INPUT TYPE="reset" VALUE="Click to Reset">
```

Click to Reset

SEND DATA TO A WEB BROWSER

ASP uses the `Response.Write` statement to send data to a Web browser. The Web browser can then display the data.

You should enclose the data for a `Response.Write` statement in parentheses ( ). Consistently using parentheses will make your ASP code easier to read and troubleshoot.

A `Response.Write` statement can display data such as alphanumeric characters or the value of a variable. Text you want to display on an ASP page must be enclosed in quotation marks. You can use HTML tags to format the text in a `Response.Write` statement. HTML tags and any spaces you want to display must be included within the quotation marks.

If you want to use the `%>` symbols in a `Response.Write` statement, you must separate the symbols with a backslash (`%\>`). The `%>` symbols signify the end of a section of ASP code. If you do not separate the symbols with a backslash, the Web server will not properly process the `Response.Write` statement.

If you want to display multiple items, such as a phrase followed by the value of a variable, you can display all the items using one `Response.Write` statement. You must use the ampersand (&) symbol to separate each item.

SEND DATA TO A WEB BROWSER

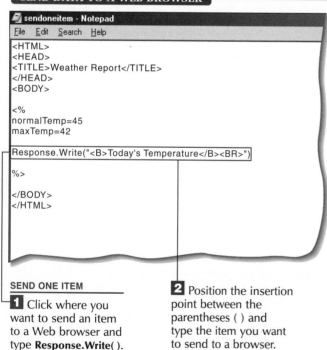

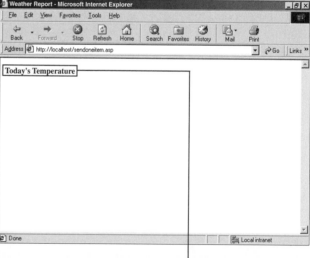

SEND ONE ITEM

1 Click where you want to send an item to a Web browser and type **Response.Write( )**. Then press Enter.

2 Position the insertion point between the parentheses ( ) and type the item you want to send to a browser.

■ You must enclose text in quotation marks. Spaces you want to display must also be included within the quotation marks.

3 Display the ASP page in a Web browser.

■ The Web browser displays the item you specified in the `Response.Write` statement.

Extra

When you have only a small amount of ASP code to include in an HTML document, you can use the `<%=` and `%>` delimiters, rather than a `Response.Write` statement. Using the `<%=` and `%>` delimiters reduces the amount of code you have to type and can make your scripts easier to read. Text you want to display using these delimiters must be enclosed in quotation marks. Using the `<%=` and `%>` delimiters does not affect how data appears on a page.

FOR EXAMPLE:

```
<HTML>
<BODY>
The current time is:<BR>
<%
Response.Write(Time)
%>
</BODY>
</HTML>
```

RESULT:

The current time is:
9:00:55 AM

CAN BE TYPED AS:

```
<HTML>
<BODY>
The current time is:<BR>
<%=Time%>
</BODY>
</HTML>
```

RESULT:

The current time is:
9:00:55 AM

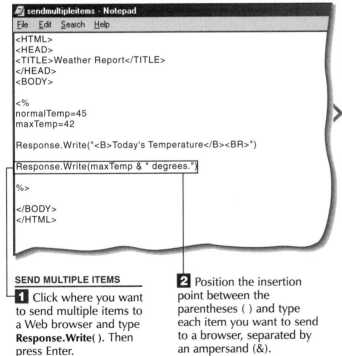

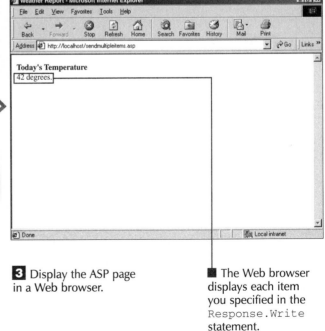

SEND MULTIPLE ITEMS

1 Click where you want to send multiple items to a Web browser and type **Response.Write( )**. Then press Enter.

2 Position the insertion point between the parentheses ( ) and type each item you want to send to a browser, separated by an ampersand (&).

3 Display the ASP page in a Web browser.

■ The Web browser displays each item you specified in the `Response.Write` statement.

TURN THE BUFFER ON OR OFF

The buffer is a section of the Web server's memory where an ASP page can be stored temporarily. Using the buffer allows you to tell the Web server when you want to send the information generated from ASP code to a user's Web browser. If you turn the buffer off, the Web server will send information to a user's Web browser as the information is generated from the ASP code.

You may want to turn off the buffer for ASP pages that require a small amount of processing. However, if an ASP page requires a large amount of processing, a user will have to wait until all the processing is complete before any information is displayed

in the Web browser. This may cause users to view a blank page for an extended period of time before the results of the ASP page are displayed.

The `Response.Buffer` statement should be placed before any HTML code in an ASP page. If HTML code is placed before the statement, the Web browser may display an error message.

The `Response.Buffer` statement can only be used on Web servers running Microsoft Internet Information Server (IIS). The buffer is turned on by default on Web servers running IIS version 5.

TURN THE BUFFER ON OR OFF

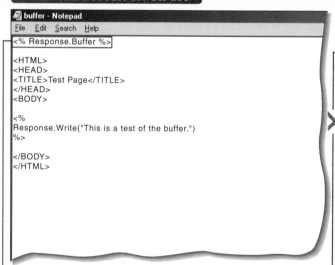

1 Position the insertion point in front of the first line of code in the ASP page and type **<% Response.Buffer %>**. Then press Enter.

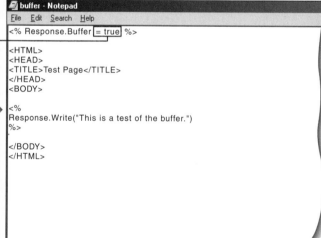

2 In the `Response.Buffer` statement, type **= true** to turn on the buffer.

■ You can type **= false** to turn off the buffer.

SEND CONTENTS OF BUFFER TO WEB BROWSER

The `Response.Flush` statement forces the Web server to send the contents of the buffer to a Web browser. Using this statement allows you to control when a user will see information from your ASP page.

You should use a `Response.Flush` statement to send data to a user's browser just before the ASP page performs a lengthy process such as a loop, a complex calculation or the retrieval of information from a database. For example, if your ASP page displays a banner image, such as an advertisement, followed by a large amount of data from a database, you should use a `Response.Flush` statement to force the

ASP page to display the banner first. This gives the user something to look at while the ASP page retrieves the information from the database.

When you use the `Response.Flush` statement, all the information in the buffer is immediately sent to the user's browser and the buffer is emptied. When the next `Response.Flush` statement is processed, the contents of the buffer will include only the information processed since the last `Response.Flush` statement.

The `Response.Flush` statement can only be used on Web servers running Microsoft Internet Information Server (IIS).

SEND CONTENTS OF BUFFER TO WEB BROWSER

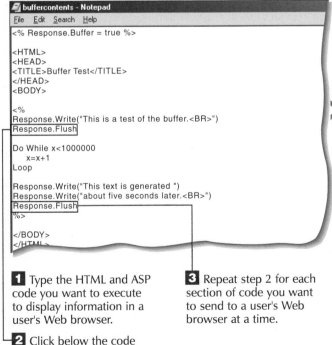

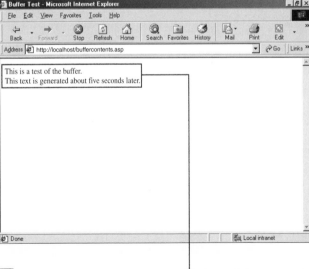

1 Type the HTML and ASP code you want to execute to display information in a user's Web browser.

2 Click below the code you want to send to a user's Web browser and type **Response.Flush**. Then press Enter.

3 Repeat step 2 for each section of code you want to send to a user's Web browser at a time.

4 Display the ASP page in a Web browser.

■ The Web browser displays the result of using `Response.Flush` statements.

DELETE BUFFER CONTENTS

The Response.Clear statement clears information from the buffer before the information is sent to a user's Web browser. The buffer must be turned on before you can delete the contents of the buffer.

When you use the Response.Clear statement, the Web server deletes any information that was processed and added to the buffer since the last Response.Flush statement or since the beginning of the ASP page.

Deleting the contents of the buffer is useful when an error occurs in an ASP page. For example, if there is information in the buffer and the ASP page detects

an error, such as an invalid value passed by a *query string*, you can clear the information in the buffer and display an error message in the user's Web browser.

In addition to using the Response.Clear statement, you may want to call *subroutines* to tie up any loose ends in an ASP page after an error has occurred. For example, you could call subroutines that close an open file and end the ASP page's connection to a database.

The Response.Clear statement can only be used on Web servers running Microsoft Internet Information Server (IIS).

DELETE BUFFER CONTENTS

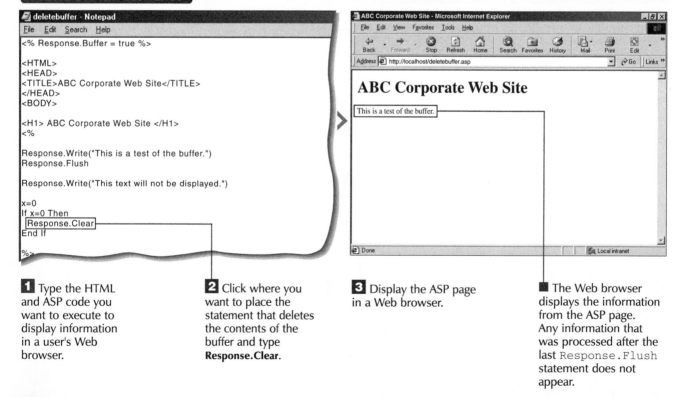

1 Type the HTML and ASP code you want to execute to display information in a user's Web browser.

2 Click where you want to place the statement that deletes the contents of the buffer and type **Response.Clear**.

3 Display the ASP page in a Web browser.

■ The Web browser displays the information from the ASP page. Any information that was processed after the last Response.Flush statement does not appear.

TERMINATE AN ASP PAGE

The `Response.End` statement allows you to stop processing code and immediately stop an ASP page from generating any further output.

The `Response.End` statement is commonly used to terminate the processing of code when an error or other unusual event is detected. For example, you may want to allow only registered users to access your Web site. You could have your ASP code validate user names and passwords and use the `Response.End` statement to end further processing of the page when an invalid name or password is detected.

When the buffer is turned on, any information in the buffer will be sent to the user's Web browser when

the ASP page executes the `Response.End` statement. The buffer contents will not be erased. If the buffer is turned off, the ASP page will not send any further data to the user's browser.

Using the `Response.End` statement stops the processing of all code. If the ASP code that contains the `Response.End` statement is followed by HTML code, the HTML code will not be sent to the user's browser.

Only the ASP page that contains the `Response.End` statement will stop processing code. If other ASP pages on the Web server are processing code, the other pages will not be affected.

TERMINATE AN ASP PAGE

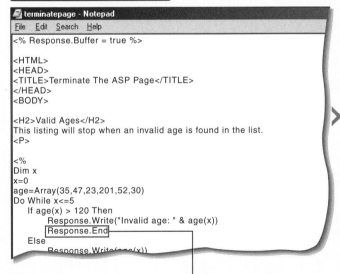

1 Type the HTML and ASP code you want to execute to display information in a user's Web browser.

2 Click where you want to place the statement that terminates the ASP page and type **Response.End**.

3 Display the ASP page in a Web browser.

■ The Web browser displays the result of terminating the ASP page.

SET EXPIRY TIME

The `Response.Expires` statement allows you to set the number of minutes that a Web browser stores your ASP page in its cache. The expiry time you should set depends on the content of the page.

All popular Web browsers use a cache to store the pages viewed by a user. When the user wishes to view the same page again, the browser checks to see if a copy of the page is stored in the cache. If a copy is in the cache, the Web browser checks to see if the expiry time set for the page has passed. If the expiry time has not passed, the browser will display the copy of the page.

Otherwise, the browser will retrieve the page from the Web server.

Caching saves the Web browser from retrieving an ASP page from the Web server each time the user views the page. However, caching may prevent users from seeing the latest version of a page that contains constantly changing information, such as stock quotes.

You must use the `Response.Expires` statement before any HTML code is sent to the user's Web browser. If HTML code is sent before the `Response.Expires` statement, the Web browser may display an error message.

SET EXPIRY TIME

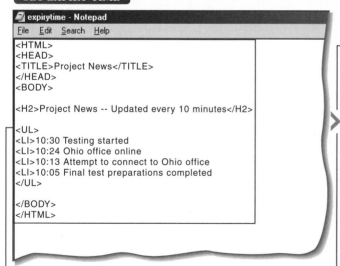

1 Type the HTML and ASP code you want to execute to display information in a client's Web browser.

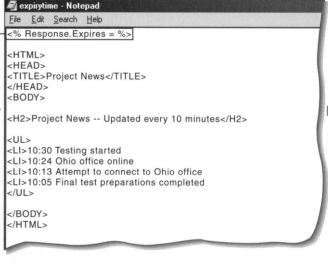

2 Position the insertion point in front of the first line of code in the ASP page and type **<% Response.Expires = %>**. Then press Enter.

Extra

Users may be able to disable the cache for their Web browser. Disabling the cache ensures that an ASP page will be transferred from the Web server each time the user views the page, regardless of the expiry time set for the page.

When no expiry time is set for an ASP page, a Web browser usually retrieves the page from the Web server once per browsing session. A browsing session begins each time the user starts the Web browser.

You can specify an expiry time of zero minutes for an ASP page you do not want to be placed in a Web browser's cache. This is useful for ASP pages that display constantly changing information, such as the current time.

Example:
```
<% Response.Expires = 0 %>
<HTML>
<BODY>
The current time is: <BR>
<%= Time() %>
</BODY>
</HTML>
```

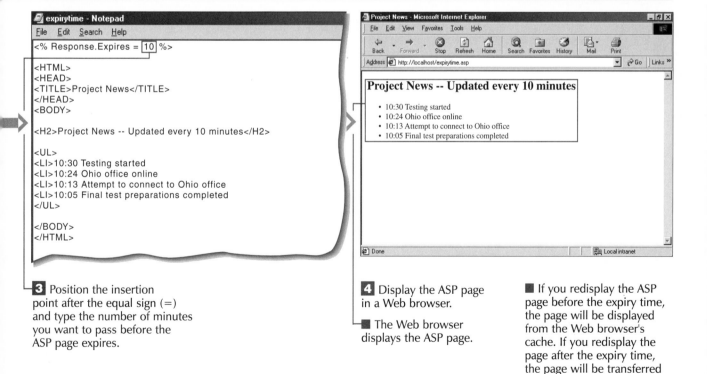

3 Position the insertion point after the equal sign (=) and type the number of minutes you want to pass before the ASP page expires.

4 Display the ASP page in a Web browser.

■ The Web browser displays the ASP page.

■ If you redisplay the ASP page before the expiry time, the page will be displayed from the Web browser's cache. If you redisplay the page after the expiry time, the page will be transferred from the Web server.

SET THE CONTENT TYPE

You can specify the type of content your ASP page contains. Setting the content type tells a Web browser what type of information to expect from the page and can help the browser correctly interpret the information. An ASP page can contain information such as text, audio or video.

The `Response.ContentType` statement sets the content type for an ASP page. In the `Response.ContentType` statement, you use a value to indicate the general category and the specific type of content an ASP page contains. For example, the `image/GIF` value

indicates that the ASP page contains an image, specifically a GIF image.

An ASP page can contain only one type of information. By default, the content type for ASP pages is `text/html`. You should specify a content type if your ASP page contains another type of information.

You must use the `Response.ContentType` statement before any HTML code is sent to the user's Web browser. If HTML code is sent before the `Response.ContentType` statement, the Web browser may display an error message.

SET THE CONTENT TYPE

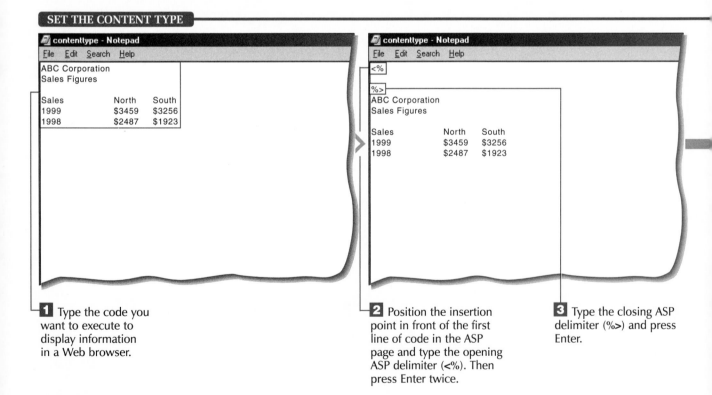

1 Type the code you want to execute to display information in a Web browser.

2 Position the insertion point in front of the first line of code in the ASP page and type the opening ASP delimiter (<%). Then press Enter twice.

3 Type the closing ASP delimiter (%>) and press Enter.

Extra

Some common content type values are:

CONTENT TYPE VALUES	DESCRIPTION
text/html	Page contains HTML code.
text/plain	Page contains only plain text.
audio/basic	Page contains an audio file.
video/MPEG	Page contains a video file.
image/GIF	Page contains a GIF image.
image/JPEG	Page contains a JPEG image.
application/x-pdf	Page contains a PDF file.
application/x-doc	Page contains a Word document.

Many Web browsers can be set up to automatically open a specific application, depending on the content type of a page. For example, if a user opens a page that has the content type set as application/x-pdf, the Web browser may be able to automatically open the Acrobat Reader program to display the PDF file.

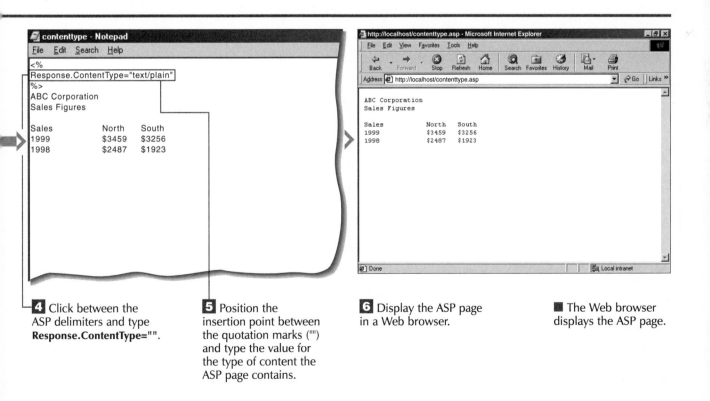

4 Click between the ASP delimiters and type **Response.ContentType=""**.

5 Position the insertion point between the quotation marks ("") and type the value for the type of content the ASP page contains.

6 Display the ASP page in a Web browser.

■ The Web browser displays the ASP page.

ADD A HEADER

Headers send information about your ASP page, such as the location of the page, to a Web browser. Information in headers is not displayed by a user's Web browser but is used by the browser to process the page. There are Web sites on the Internet that allow you to view information contained in the headers of a Web page.

The `Response.AddHeader` statement allows you to add a header to an ASP page. When you create a header, you must indicate the name of the header, such as `Last-Modified`. You must then include the information you want the header to contain, such as `Jan 01, 2000`.

Some Web servers automatically create commonly used headers for an ASP page. The `Response.AddHeader` statement also allows you to add custom headers to an ASP page. You may need to add custom headers to ASP pages used on your company's intranet.

You cannot use the `Response.AddHeader` statement to override headers that have already been created.

You must use the `Response.AddHeader` statement before any HTML code is sent to the user's Web browser. If HTML code is sent before the `Response.AddHeader` statement, the Web browser may display an error message.

ADD A HEADER

```
addheader - Notepad
File  Edit  Search  Help
<%
Response.AddHeader "", ""
%>
<HTML>
<HEAD>
<TITLE>ABC Corporation</TITLE>
</HEAD>
<BODY>

Welcome to our Web page.<BR>
This Web page uses the English language.

</BODY>
</HTML>
```

```
addheader - Notepad
File  Edit  Search  Help
<%
Response.AddHeader "Content-Language", "en"
%>
<HTML>
<HEAD>
<TITLE>ABC Corporation</TITLE>
</HEAD>
<BODY>

Welcome to our Web page.<BR>
This Web page uses the English language.

</BODY>
</HTML>
```

1 Position the insertion point in front of the first line of code in the ASP page and type the opening ASP delimiter (**<%**). Then press Enter twice.

2 Type the closing ASP delimiter (**%>**) and press Enter.

3 Click between the ASP delimiters and type **Response.AddHeader "", ""**.

4 Position the insertion point between the first set of quotation marks ("") and type the name of the header you want to create.

5 Position the insertion point between the second set of quotation marks ("") and type the information you want the header to contain.

116

Extra

There are many standard headers that most Web browsers can process. If a browser cannot process a header, the header will be ignored. You can find a comprehensive list of standard headers at the www.freesoft.org/CIE/RFC/2068/155.htm Web site.

Examples of Standard Headers

NAME	DESCRIPTION
Age	The amount of time that has passed since the Web server generated the ASP page.
Content-Language	The language used on the ASP page, such as English or French.
Content-Length	The number of characters in the ASP page.
Content-Type	The format of the ASP page, such as text/HTML.
Content-Base	The base URL used to determine relative URLs in the ASP page. For example, if the Content-Base header contains the base URL www.abccorp.com, you can use relative URLs, such as /sales-docs/1999.html, to create links to other pages in the Web site.
Server	The type and version of Web server software running on the server, such as Microsoft Internet Information Server, Version 5.0.

VIEW A HEADER

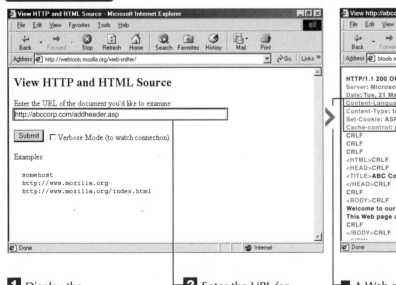

1 Display the http://webtools.mozilla.org/web-sniffer Web page in a Web browser.

2 Enter the URL for the ASP page you added a header to and then press Enter.

■ A Web page appears, displaying the header you added to the ASP page.

■ The Web page may also display other headers automatically created by the Web server.

117

SET PAGE STATUS

When a Web server sends a page to a Web browser, the server also sends headers that contain information about the page. One of the headers can include a status line, indicating the status of the user's request for the page.

A status line consists of a three-digit code and a description of the code. The status line may tell the Web browser that the server does not understand the request sent by the browser or that the user does not have permission to view the requested page. You can use the Response.Status statement to specify a status line for your ASP page.

There are several common status codes you can use. A list of common status codes is available at the following Web site: msdn.microsoft.com/workshop/networking/wininet/ reference/constants/statuscodes.asp

You can create your own custom status code, but the user's Web browser must be able to process the custom status code. Any status code a browser is unable to process will be ignored.

You must use the Response.Status statement before any HTML code is sent to the user's Web browser. If HTML code is sent before the Response.Status statement, the Web browser may display an error message.

SET PAGE STATUS

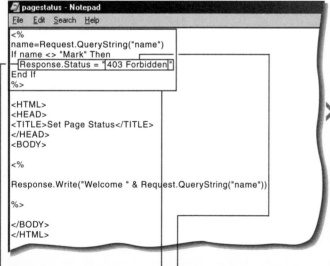

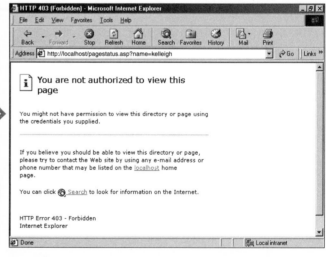

1 Click where you want to place the statement that sets the status of the ASP page and type **Response.Status = ""**. Then press Enter.

2 Position the insertion point between the quotation marks ("") and type the code and description of the status you want to set.

3 Click where you want to type the code that executes the Response.Status statement and type the code.

4 Display the ASP page in a Web browser.

■ The Web browser interprets the status code for the page and displays the appropriate information.

ADD A LOG ENTRY

M any Web servers generate a log file. The log file keeps track of the requests received by the Web server and can contain information such as the name of the Web pages accessed, the IP number of a client that is accessing the server and any messages or status codes sent to a user's Web browser. If your Web server uses the Microsoft IIS Log File Format to generate the log file, you can have your ASP page add an entry to the log file. The administrator of the Web server can view the log file.

Adding entries to the Web server's log file can be helpful if you need to find the source of an error

or if you need to find information about users who were accessing your ASP page at the time of a security breach.

You use the `Response.AppendToLog` statement to add a log entry. Each line in the log entry must not exceed 80 characters and must not contain commas. It is common programming practice to begin and end a message with special characters, such as the pound sign (#). Using special characters makes it easier to locate the entry you added when reviewing the log file.

ADD A LOG ENTRY

```
addlogentry - Notepad
File  Edit  Search  Help
<HTML>
<HEAD>
<TITLE>Add a Log Entry</TITLE>
</HEAD>

<BODY>
<H3>Add a Log Entry</H3>
This example adds the path of the Web page
to the log file on the Web server.

<%
Response.AppendToLog "######## Start Log ########"
%>
</BODY>
</HTML>
```

```
addlogentry - Notepad
File  Edit  Search  Help
<HTML>
<HEAD>
<TITLE>Add a Log Entry</TITLE>
</HEAD>

<BODY>
<H3>Add a Log Entry</H3>
This example adds the path of the Web page
to the log file on the Web server.

<%
Response.AppendToLog "######## Start Log ########"
Response.AppendToLog Server.MapPath(Request.ServerVariables("PATH_INFO"))
Response.AppendToLog "######## End Log ########"
%>
</BODY>
</HTML>
```

1 Click where you want to place the statement that adds a log entry and type **Response.AppendToLog**.

2 Type the information you want to add to the log file. Text you want to add to the log file must be enclosed in quotation marks ("").

3 Repeat steps 1 and 2 for each line you want to add to the log file.

■ When a user displays the ASP page in a Web browser, the information you specified is saved to the log file.

CHECK IF USER IS CONNECTED

Some ASP pages perform tasks, such as calculations or the retrieval of data, which take the Web server a long time to process. When creating an ASP page that may take a long time to process, you should include the `Response.IsClientConnected` statement to have the Web server check if a user is still connected before the Web server finishes processing and displaying the data for the page.

For example, if an ASP page requires information from two databases, you may want to have the Web server retrieve the information from the first database and then check if the user

is still connected before retrieving the information from the second database. This can help avoid wasting time and resources due to the unnecessary retrieval of data.

Users often disconnect because they request the wrong information or they cannot wait for the information to be displayed.

The `Response.IsClientConnected` statement does not work with some older versions of Web server software. Make sure the computer that stores your ASP page is running the latest version of the Web server software.

CHECK IF USER IS CONNECTED

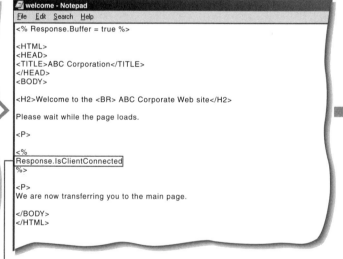

1 Type the HTML and ASP code you want to execute to display information in a user's Web browser.

2 Click where you want to place the statement that checks if the user is still connected to the Web server and type **Response.IsClientConnected**.

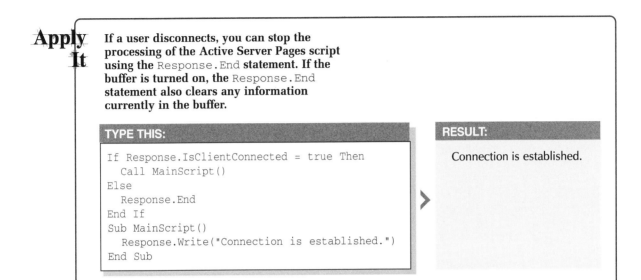

Apply It

If a user disconnects, you can stop the processing of the Active Server Pages script using the `Response.End` statement. If the buffer is turned on, the `Response.End` statement also clears any information currently in the buffer.

TYPE THIS:

```
If Response.IsClientConnected = true Then
  Call MainScript()
Else
  Response.End
End If
Sub MainScript()
  Response.Write("Connection is established.")
End Sub
```

RESULT:

Connection is established.

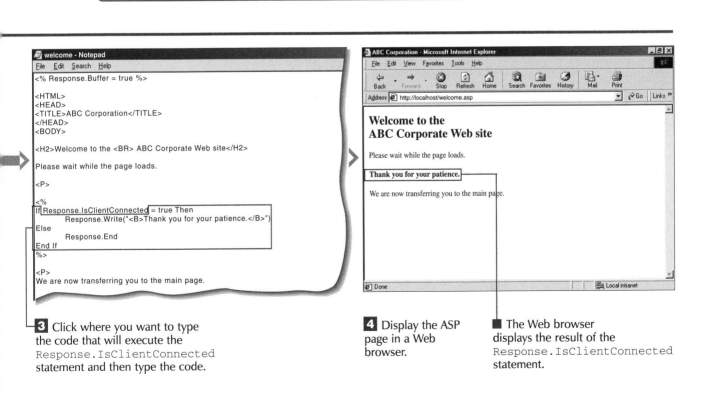

3 Click where you want to type the code that will execute the `Response.IsClientConnected` statement and then type the code.

4 Display the ASP page in a Web browser.

■ The Web browser displays the result of the `Response.IsClientConnected` statement.

CREATE A COOKIE

You can create a cookie on your ASP page. When a user views the page, the cookie is stored as a small text file on the user's computer. A cookie consists of a key, which indicates the name of the cookie, and a value, which is the information stored in the cookie.

Cookies are often used to personalize an ASP page. For example, a cookie can store a user's name. The next time the user accesses the ASP page, the page can use the value stored in the cookie to display the user's name.

When you create a cookie, you should specify when the cookie will expire. By default, a cookie will usually be deleted as soon as the user closes their Web browser. Setting an expiry date for a cookie allows the cookie to store information for longer periods of time.

You must use the `Response.Cookies` statement before any HTML code is sent to the user's Web browser. If HTML code is sent before the `Response.Cookies` statement, the Web browser may display an error message.

After creating a cookie, you can have an ASP page read the cookie. For information about reading a cookie, see page 136.

CREATE A COOKIE

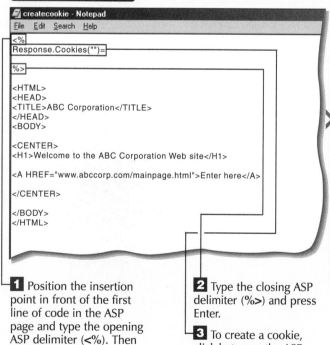

1 Position the insertion point in front of the first line of code in the ASP page and type the opening ASP delimiter (<%). Then press Enter twice.

2 Type the closing ASP delimiter (%>) and press Enter.

3 To create a cookie, click between the ASP delimiters and type **Response.Cookies("")=**. Then press Enter.

4 Position the insertion point between the quotation marks ("") and type a name for the cookie.

5 Position the insertion point after the equal sign (=) and type the value you want to assign to the cookie. Text values must be enclosed in quotation marks ("").

Extra

You can create many cookies on your ASP page to store a user's personalized information. However, all the cookies on your page should not exceed 4 kilobytes (KB) in size.

To prevent unauthorized pages from reading a cookie you have placed on a user's computer, you can specify a domain and path for the cookie. Only pages stored in the specified domain and directory will be able to read the cookie.

Example:

```
<%
Response.Cookies("Accessed")="Yes"
Response.Cookies("Accessed").Expires=#May 20, 2000#
    Response.Cookies("Accessed").Domain="abccorp.com"
        Response.Cookies("Accessed").Path="/Applications/pages"
%>
```

Instead of having a cookie expire on a specific date, you can use a relative date to have the cookie expire a certain number of days after the cookie is saved on the user's computer. When you use a relative date, the cookie will be reset for the number of days you specify each time the user accesses the ASP page. You do not need to add pound symbols (#) to a relative date.

Example:

```
<%
Response.Cookies("Accessed")="Yes"
Response.Cookies("Accessed").Expires=Date+30
%>
```

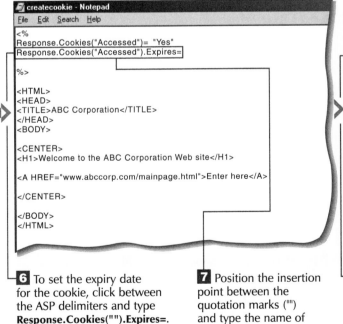

6 To set the expiry date for the cookie, click between the ASP delimiters and type **Response.Cookies("").Expires=**. Then press Enter.

7 Position the insertion point between the quotation marks ("") and type the name of the cookie.

8 Position the insertion point after the equal sign (=) and type the date you want the cookie to expire. Dates must begin and end with the pound symbol (#).

■ When a user accesses the ASP page, the cookie will be stored on the user's computer.

USING QUERY STRINGS

U sing a query string allows you to pass information, such as a user name, to an ASP page. You must first set up the ASP page to process the information from a query string.

Adding a `Request.QueryString` statement to an ASP page allows the page to process a value from a query string. The statement contains the name of the variable that will store the value passed by a query string. You can set up an ASP page to process more than one value.

Once you have set up the ASP page, you can enter a query string to pass information to the

page. In a Web browser, you enter the URL of the ASP page followed by a question mark (?). You then enter the name of the variable followed by an equal sign (=) and a value for the variable, such as www.abccorp.com?name=Jane. The variable name you enter in the query string and the variable name you specified in the `Request.QueryString` statement must be the same.

The ASP page can use the information provided in a query string to perform a task. For example, the ASP page can store the information in a database or use the information to determine the data to be displayed on the page.

USING QUERY STRINGS

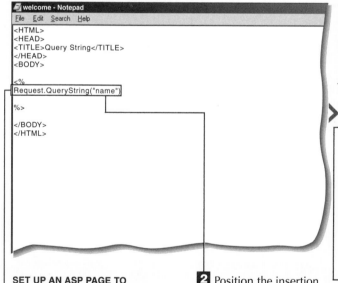

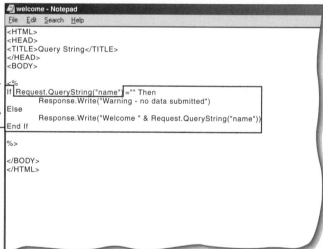

SET UP AN ASP PAGE TO PROCESS A QUERY STRING

1 Click where you want the ASP page to process a value from a query string and type **Request.QueryString("")**. Then press Enter.

2 Position the insertion point between the quotation marks ("") and type a name for the variable that will store the value.

■ You can repeat steps 1 and 2 for each `Request.QueryString` statement you want to add to the ASP page.

3 Click where you want to type the code that executes when a value for the variable is received by the ASP page and then type the code.

■ You can now enter a query string to pass a value to the ASP page.

Extra

The ampersand symbol (&) allows you to enter more than one variable and value in a query string.

Example:

```
http://www.abccorp.com/page.asp
?name=John&email=john@abccorp.com
```

If your query string contains a space, some Web browsers will truncate the query string at the space. This could cause an error when you try to pass information to an ASP page. Depending on the Web browser you are using, you may have to replace a space in your query string with %20. Some Web browsers automatically add the %20 for you.

Example:

```
http://www.abccorp.com/page.asp
?name=John%20Smith
```

A query string is displayed in the address bar of the Web browser. If the query string contains data you want to keep private, such as a password, you should ensure that other people cannot view the contents of your screen.

Example:

```
http://www.abccorp.com/page.asp
?name=John&password=abc123
```

You can use a query string with the HTML <A> tag to create a link to an ASP page. When you select the link, the information in the query string is passed to the ASP page. A query string included in a link often contains information needed to access the page, such as a user name.

Example:

```
<A HREF="http://www.abccorp.com/page.asp
?userName=John">John's page</A>
```

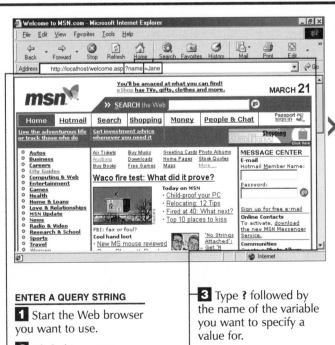

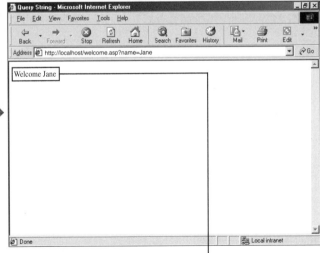

ENTER A QUERY STRING

1 Start the Web browser you want to use.

2 Click this area to highlight the current Web page address and type the URL of the ASP page you want to pass a value to.

3 Type ? followed by the name of the variable you want to specify a value for.

4 Type = followed by a value for the variable.

5 Press Enter to pass the query string to the ASP page.

■ The ASP page you set up appears.

■ The Web browser displays the result of passing a value to the ASP page in a query string.

ACCESS INFORMATION PASSED BY A QUERY STRING

When an ASP page receives information from a query string, the page can access the information and then perform an action, such as displaying the information on the screen. A query string is information you add to the URL of an ASP page to pass information to the page.

An ASP page can also access information passed by a form that uses the GET method. The GET method creates a query string by appending the information in the form to the URL of the ASP

page that will process the information. To have an ASP page access information passed by a form that uses the POST method, see page 132.

You may want to access information passed by a query string to analyze the information. For example, you can check to make sure variable names and values contain only alphanumeric characters. Accessing the information passed by a query string is also useful if you want to make sure your Web server is not losing information.

ACCESS INFORMATION PASSED BY A QUERY STRING

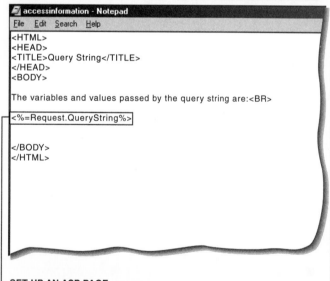

SET UP AN ASP PAGE TO ACCESS A QUERY STRING

1 Click where you want to access and display the information passed by a query string and type **<%= Request.QueryString%>**. Then press Enter.

ACCESS INFORMATION PASSED BY A QUERY STRING

1 Perform steps 1 to 4 on page 125 to enter a query string.

2 To enter another variable and value, type **&** followed by the next variable and value.

3 Press Enter to pass the variables and values in the query string to the ASP page.

■ The Web browser displays the variables and values passed by the query string.

Extra

In addition to accessing the variables and values passed by a query string, you can access information about where the ASP page is stored. You use the `Request.ServerVariables` statement with the `LOCAL_ADDR` variable to access the IP number of the Web server. Using the `Request.ServerVariables` statement with the `URL` variable allows you to access the file name of the ASP page.

TYPE THIS:

```
<%
servAddress=Request.ServerVariables("LOCAL_ADDR")
url=Request.ServerVariables("URL")
qstring=Request.QueryString
Response.Write(servAddress & url & "?" & qstring)
%>
```

RESULT:

172.17.235.34/accessquerystring.asp?password=abc123

The `Len` function allows you to determine the length of a query string you access. This can help you make sure information passed to your ASP page is valid. For example, you can have your ASP page automatically reject any query string longer than 100 characters.

Example:

```
<%
stringLength=Len(Request.QueryString)
If stringLength>100 Then
    Call RejectQuerystring()
End If
%>
```

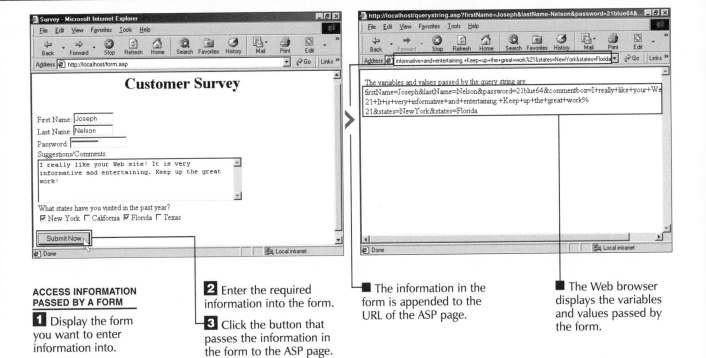

ACCESS INFORMATION PASSED BY A FORM

1 Display the form you want to enter information into.

2 Enter the required information into the form.

3 Click the button that passes the information in the form to the ASP page.

■ The information in the form is appended to the URL of the ASP page.

■ The Web browser displays the variables and values passed by the form.

ACCESS A VALUE PASSED BY A QUERY STRING

A query string can use one variable to pass multiple values to an ASP page. The ASP page can then access any one of the values.

An ASP page can also access a value passed by a form that uses the GET method. The GET method creates a query string by appending the information in a form to the URL of the ASP page that will process the information. Forms often use one variable to store multiple values in elements such as check boxes. For information about accessing a value passed by a form that uses the POST method, see page 132.

To access a specific value in a variable, you include the name of the variable and the value's *index number* in the Request.QueryString statement. Index numbers start at 1 and uniquely identify each value stored in a variable. For example, to access the second value in the invoice variable, you use the Request.QueryString("invoice")(2) statement. If you do not include the index number in the statement, the ASP page will display all the values stored in the variable, separated by a comma.

ACCESS A VALUE PASSED BY A QUERY STRING

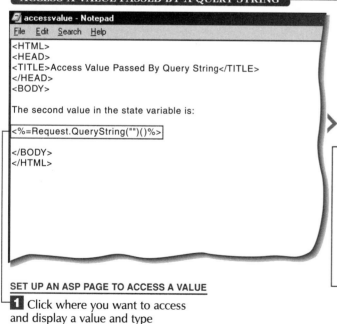

SET UP AN ASP PAGE TO ACCESS A VALUE

1 Click where you want to access and display a value and type **<%=Request.QueryString("")( )%>**. Then press Enter.

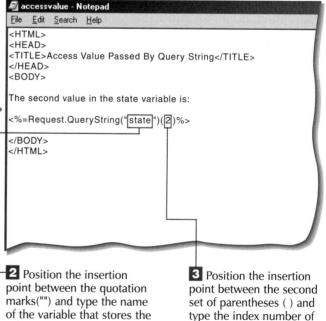

2 Position the insertion point between the quotation marks("") and type the name of the variable that stores the value you want to access.

3 Position the insertion point between the second set of parentheses ( ) and type the index number of the value you want to access.

Extra

Including a variable name in the `Request.QueryString.Count` statement allows you to count the number of values stored in the variable. Counting values is useful when you want to check if information passed to your ASP page is valid.

TYPE THIS:

```
<%
Response.Write("The query string is:<BR>")
Response.Write(Request.QueryString&"<BR>")
Response.Write("There are ")
Response.Write(Request.QueryString("name").Count)
Response.Write(" values in the name variable.")
%>
```

RESULT:

The query string is:
name=Teri&name=Bob
There are 2 values in the name variable.

A `Request.QueryString` statement can be used with a `For...Next` loop to work with all the values stored in a variable.

TYPE THIS:

```
<%
Response.Write("The query string is:<BR>")
Response.Write(Request.QueryString&"<BR>")
Response.Write("The values are:<BR>")
For x=1 to Request.QueryString("name").Count
    Response.Write(Request.QueryString("name")(x))
    Response.Write("<BR>")
Next
%>
```

RESULT:

The query string is:
name=Teri&name=Bob
The values are:
Teri
Bob

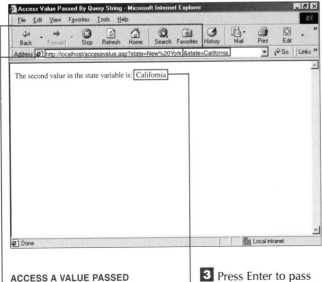

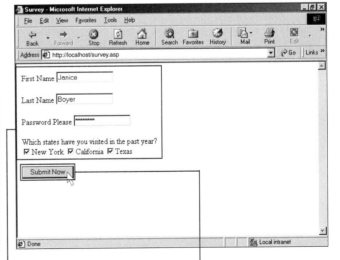

ACCESS A VALUE PASSED BY A QUERY STRING

1 Perform steps 1 to 4 on page 125 to enter a query string.

2 To enter another value for the variable, type & followed by the variable and next value.

3 Press Enter to pass the values in the query string to the ASP page.

■ The Web browser displays the result of accessing a value in the query string.

ACCESS A VALUE PASSED BY A FORM

1 Display the form you want to enter information into.

2 Enter the required information into the form.

3 Click the button that passes the information in the form to the ASP page.

■ The Web browser will display the result of accessing a value in the form.

COUNT VARIABLES PASSED BY A QUERY STRING

You can determine the number of variables passed to an ASP page by a query string. The number of variables passed to an ASP page may vary depending on the information included in the query string. For example, a user may enter their phone number, and if available, their fax number. You can count the variables and then have the ASP page perform an action depending on the number of variables.

To count variables, you add the Count keyword to a Request.QueryString statement.

ASP counts all the variables passed by a query string, even if a variable does not contain a value.

Counting variables is useful when you want to determine if information passed to your ASP page is valid. For example, if a user is supposed to pass three variables in a query string, you can count the variables and have the ASP page display an error message when a user tries to pass a number of variables that does not equal three.

COUNT VARIABLES PASSED BY A QUERY STRING

```
countvariables - Notepad
File  Edit  Search  Help
<HTML>
<HEAD>
<TITLE>Count Variables Passed by Query String</TITLE>
</HEAD>
<BODY>

<%

Request.QueryString.Count

%>
</BODY>
</HTML>
```

```
countvariables - Notepad
File  Edit  Search  Help
<HTML>
<HEAD>
<TITLE>Count Variables Passed by Query String</TITLE>
</HEAD>
<BODY>

<%

If Request.QueryString.Count <> 3 Then
        Response.Write("Error! Incorrect information has been entered.")
Else
        Response.Write("Thank you for entering your information.")
End If

%>
</BODY>
</HTML>
```

SET UP AN ASP PAGE TO COUNT VARIABLES

■1 Click where you want to count the variables passed to the ASP page and type **Request.QueryString.Count**. Then press Enter.

■2 Click where you want to type the code that executes the Request.QueryString.Count statement and type the code.

Extra

You can perform the steps on page 130 to set up an ASP page to count the variables passed by a form that uses the GET method. The GET method creates a query string by appending the information submitted by the form to the URL of the ASP page that will process the information. ASP considers each element in a form to be a variable, including buttons. To count variables passed by a form that uses the POST method, see page 132.

Example:

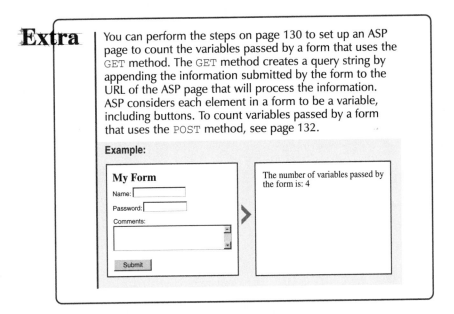

COUNT VARIABLES PASSED BY A QUERY STRING

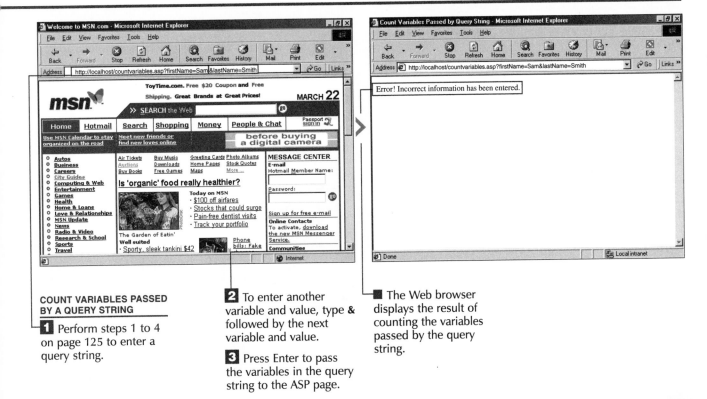

COUNT VARIABLES PASSED BY A QUERY STRING

■ Perform steps 1 to 4 on page 125 to enter a query string.

■ To enter another variable and value, type & followed by the next variable and value.

■ Press Enter to pass the variables in the query string to the ASP page.

■ The Web browser displays the result of counting the variables passed by the query string.

ACCESS INFORMATION PASSED BY A FORM

The `Request.Form` statement allows you to access information passed by a form that uses the POST method. This is useful when you want to display the information entered into a form or analyze the information to ensure it is valid.

When creating a form, you specify the method the form will use to pass information to an ASP page. The POST method passes the information in the form and the URL of the ASP page that will process the information separately. You must use a `Request.Form` statement to process information

passed using the POST method. The GET method adds the information in a form to the URL of the ASP page that will process the information. See pages 126 to 129 for information about accessing information passed by a form that uses the GET method.

You can also include the name of a variable in a `Request.Form` statement to access the value stored in the variable. If the variable stores more than one value, the ASP page will access all the values.

ACCESS INFORMATION PASSED BY A FORM

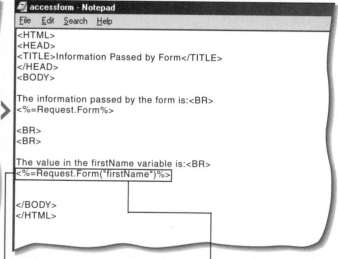

```
accessform - Notepad
File  Edit  Search  Help
<HTML>
<HEAD>
<TITLE>Information Passed by Form</TITLE>
</HEAD>
<BODY>

The information passed by the form is:<BR>
<%=Request.Form%>

<BR>
<BR>

The value in the firstName variable is:<BR>


</BODY>
</HTML>
```

```
accessform - Notepad
File  Edit  Search  Help
<HTML>
<HEAD>
<TITLE>Information Passed by Form</TITLE>
</HEAD>
<BODY>

The information passed by the form is:<BR>
<%=Request.Form%>

<BR>
<BR>

The value in the firstName variable is:<BR>
<%=Request.Form("firstName")%>


</BODY>
</HTML>
```

SET UP AN ASP PAGE TO ACCESS INFORMATION PASSED BY A FORM

1 Click where you want to access and display information passed by a form that uses the POST method and type `<%=Request.Form%>`. Then press Enter.

SET UP AN ASP PAGE TO ACCESS A VALUE PASSED BY A FORM

1 Click where you want to access and display a value passed by a form that uses the POST method and type `<%=Request.Form("")%>`. Then press Enter.

2 Position the insertion point between the quotation marks ("") and type the name of the variable that stores the value you want to access.

Extra

When a form uses one variable to store multiple values, you can use an *index number* to access a specific value stored in the variable. Index numbers start at 1 and uniquely identify each value stored in a variable. Forms often use one variable to store multiple values in elements such as check boxes.

TYPE THIS:

```
<%
Response.Write("The third value stored ")
Response.Write("in the wine variable is ")
Response.Write(Request.Form("wine")(3))
%>
```

▼

RESULT:

The third value stored in the wine variable is Merlot

You can determine the number of variables passed to an ASP page by a form that uses the POST method. Counting variables is useful when you want to determine if the form has been tampered with. For example, if you create a form to pass six variables and the form passes eight variables, you know the form has been changed and the information passed by the form may be compromised.

Example:

```
<%
If Request.Form.Count>6 Then
    Response.Write("The form has been changed! ")
    Response.Write("Your information will ")
    Response.Write("not be accepted.")
Else
    Response.Write("Thank you for ")
    Response.Write("completing the form.")
End If
%>
```

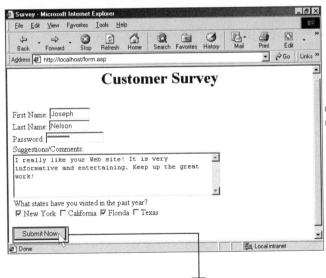

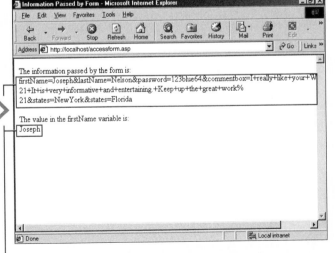

ACCESS INFORMATION PASSED BY A FORM

1 Display the form you want to enter information into.

2 Enter the required information into the form.

3 Click the button that passes the information in the form to the ASP page.

■ The Web browser displays the information and the value you accessed.

DISPLAY SERVER VARIABLES

An ASP page can access variables that contain information about the Web server and the client computer.

The `Request.ServerVariables` statement allows you to access a list of all the server variables available. You can then access the information stored in a variable of interest. The available server variables depend on the Web server you are using.

Variables containing information about the Web server include `SERVER_NAME`, which stores the name of the server, `LOCAL_ADDR`, which stores the IP number of the server and

`SERVER_SOFTWARE`, which stores the type of software used by the server.

Variables storing client information are often used to verify the identity of a client. For example, the `REMOTE_ADDR` variable can find the IP number of a client computer. You can then use this information to grant or deny the client access to your ASP page. Other variables you can use to access information about the client include `HTTP_USER_AGENT`, which stores the type of Web browser a client is using and `ALL_HTTP`, which contains all the information sent by a client to the Web server when the client requests an ASP page.

DISPLAY A LIST OF SERVER VARIABLES

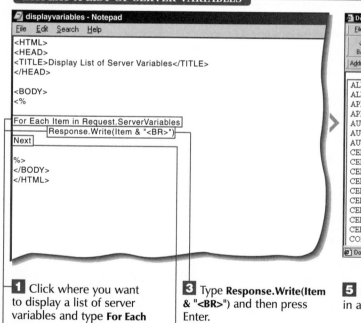

1 Click where you want to display a list of server variables and type **For Each Item in Request.ServerVariables**. Then press Enter.

2 Press Tab to indent the code you will type.

3 Type **Response.Write(Item & "<BR>")** and then press Enter.

4 Type **Next** and then press Enter.

5 Display the ASP page in a Web browser.

■ The Web browser displays a list of server variables. The variables displayed depend on the type of Web server that stores the ASP page.

Extra

The setup of the Web server or the client determines the information contained in the server variables. You cannot change the information contained in a server variable unless you change the setup of the Web server or client. For example, if you want to change the information in the SERVER_NAME variable, you must change the name of the Web server itself.

Server variables are often called environment variables because they provide information about the environment where an ASP page is processed.

You can also use server variables to access information about an ASP page. For example, the SCRIPT_NAME and PATH_INFO variables store the name and location of an ASP page on the Web server.

Using the information stored in a server variable may not be the best method if you want to access a specific part of the information. For example, if you want to access a value in a query string, you should use a Request.QueryString statement instead of the QUERY_STRING variable. If you want to access a key in a cookie, you should use a Request.Cookies statement instead of the HTTP_COOKIE variable.

ACCESS INFORMATION IN A SERVER VARIABLE

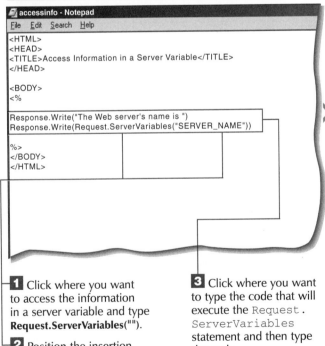

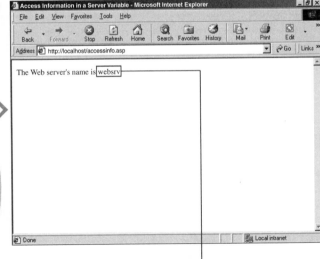

1 Click where you want to access the information in a server variable and type **Request.ServerVariables("")**.

2 Position the insertion point between the quotation marks ("") and type the name of the server variable that stores the information you want to access.

3 Click where you want to type the code that will execute the Request. ServerVariables statement and then type the code.

4 Display the ASP page in a Web browser.

■ The Web browser displays the result of accessing the information in a server variable.

READ A COOKIE

An ASP page can read a cookie stored on a user's computer. Reading a cookie allows the page to access the information in the cookie, such as the user's name and password.

When a user visits a Web page that sets a cookie, the cookie is stored as a small text file on the user's computer. The location where a cookie is stored depends on the type of Web browser the user has installed on their computer. Most Web browsers store all the cookies they receive in one folder.

A cookie consists of a key, which is the name of the cookie, and a value, which is the information stored in the cookie. After the ASP page finds the value of a cookie, you can have the page perform an action depending on the value.

A `Request.Cookies` statement allows you to read a cookie. You must know the name of the cookie you want to read. If the cookie you want to read does not exist on the user's computer, the value of the cookie will be empty.

READ A COOKIE

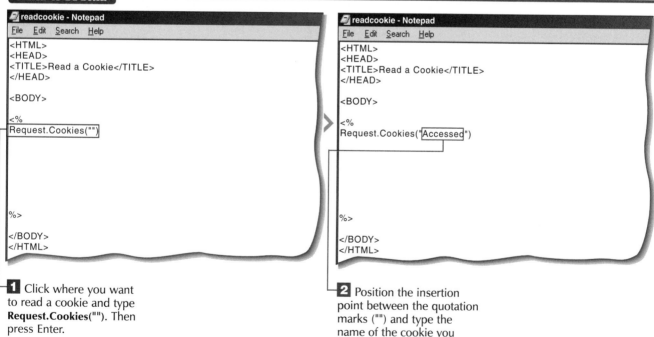

1 Click where you want to read a cookie and type **Request.Cookies("")**. Then press Enter.

2 Position the insertion point between the quotation marks ("") and type the name of the cookie you want to read.

Extra

A `Response.Redirect` statement allows you to automatically send a user to a specific page in your Web site, depending on the value of a cookie. For example, if your home page sets a cookie on the computer of every user who visits your site, you can redirect users who do not have the cookie to your home page from other pages in your site. This ensures that all visitors to your Web site access your home page and receive the cookie.

Example:

```
<%
If Request.Cookies("Accessed")="yes" Then
    Response.Write("Welcome Back")
Else
    Response.Redirect "HomePage.asp"
End If
%>
```

Although some people consider cookies to be a security risk, there has never been a report of a virus being transmitted by creating or reading a cookie. Cookies are text files, so unlike executable programs, they do not transmit viruses.

Some users change the setup of their Web browsers to disable the exchange of cookies. Some networks have a computer, called a firewall, which prevents the exchange of cookies with Web pages outside the network. You will not be able to create or read cookies on computers or networks that have disabled the exchange of cookies.

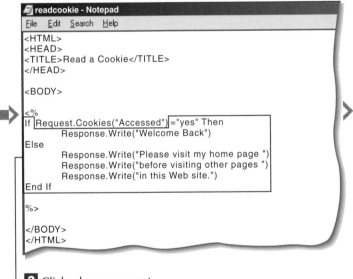

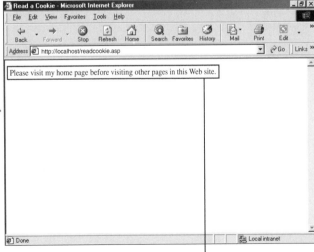

3 Click where you want to type the code that executes the value of the cookie and type the code.

4 Display the ASP page in a Web browser.

■ The Web browser displays the result of reading the cookie.

READ SUBKEYS IN A COOKIE

A cookie can use subkeys to store several related values. For example, a cookie called name could use subkeys called first and last to store the values John and Smith. An ASP page can read and access the information in one or more subkeys.

To read a subkey, you add the name of the subkey to the `Request.Cookies` statement. If you do not know the name of the subkey you want to read, you can use an index number to access the value of the subkey. For example, the `Request.Cookies("name")(1)` statement will access the value of the first subkey in the cookie called name.

After your ASP page has read the value in a subkey, you can have the page perform an action depending on the value. If the subkey you want to read does not exist on the user's computer, the value of the subkey will be empty.

While subkeys can be an effective method of storing multiple values, subkeys are not an efficient way to store large amounts of data. If you want to be able to access a large amount of data, you should store the data in a database on the Web server and use a cookie only to access the information.

READ SUBKEYS IN A COOKIE

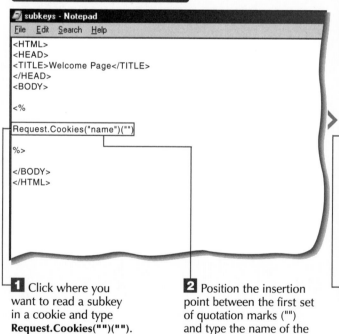

1 Click where you want to read a subkey in a cookie and type **Request.Cookies("")("")**. Then press Enter.

2 Position the insertion point between the first set of quotation marks ("") and type the name of the cookie you want to read.

3 Position the insertion point between the second set of quotation marks and type the name of the subkey you want to read.

■ If you do not know the name of the subkey, you can type the index number of the subkey.

■ You can repeat steps 1 to 3 for each subkey you want to read.

Extra

When creating a cookie, you can add subkeys to the cookie. To add a subkey, you must include the name of the subkey in the `Response.Cookies` statement. For information about creating a cookie, see page 122.

Example:
```
<%
Response.Cookies("name")("first")="John"
Response.Cookies("name")("last")="Smith"
Response.Cookies("name").Expires=Date+30
%>
```

The `HasKeys` property allows you to determine if a cookie contains subkeys.

Example:
```
<%
If Request.Cookies("name").HasKeys Then
    Response.Write("The cookie has subkeys.")
End If
%>
```

You can display the names and corresponding values of all the subkeys in a cookie.

Example:
```
<%=Request.Cookies("name")%>
```

Index numbers allow you to work with all subkeys in a cookie at once. For example, you can use a `For Each...Next` statement to display all the subkeys in a cookie.

Example:
```
<%
For Each x in Request.Cookies("name")
    Response.Write(Request.Cookies("name")(x))
    Response.Write("<BR>")
Next
%>
```

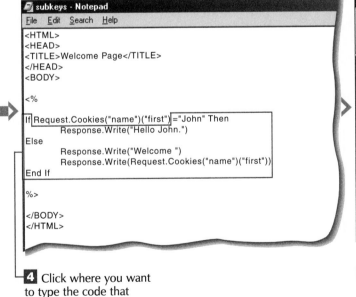

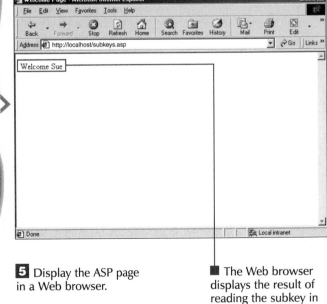

■4 Click where you want to type the code that executes the value of the subkey and type the code.

■5 Display the ASP page in a Web browser.

■ The Web browser displays the result of reading the subkey in the cookie.

139

SET SCRIPT TIMEOUT

I f an ASP page contains a script that will take a long time to process, you can set the timeout property for the script. This allows you to specify the amount of time the Web server will spend processing the script. Setting the script timeout can help ensure the Web server does not terminate the script before the script has finished processing.

Web servers are set up to automatically stop processing a script after a certain amount of time has passed. This helps increase Web server performance by reducing the amount

of time wasted processing incorrectly written scripts. An incorrectly written script may create a loop that continues to process data indefinitely. Most Web servers automatically stop processing a script after 90 seconds.

The `Server.ScriptTimeout` statement allows you to specify the number of seconds the Web server should attempt to process your script. If the Web server is unable to finish processing the script in the amount of time you specify, the server will send an error message to the Web browser.

SET SCRIPT TIMEOUT

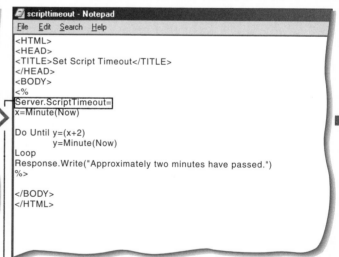

```
scripttimeout - Notepad
File  Edit  Search  Help

<HTML>
<HEAD>
<TITLE>Set Script Timeout</TITLE>
</HEAD>
<BODY>
<%

x=Minute(Now)

Do Until y=(x+2)
          y=Minute(Now)
Loop
Response.Write("Approximately two minutes have passed.")
%>

</BODY>
</HTML>
```

```
scripttimeout - Notepad
File  Edit  Search  Help

<HTML>
<HEAD>
<TITLE>Set Script Timeout</TITLE>
</HEAD>
<BODY>
<%
Server.ScriptTimeout=
x=Minute(Now)

Do Until y=(x+2)
          y=Minute(Now)
Loop
Response.Write("Approximately two minutes have passed.")
%>

</BODY>
</HTML>
```

1 Type the code that will take the Web server a long time to process. In this example, we create a loop that may take up to two minutes for the Web server to process.

2 Click where you want to set the script timeout and type **Server.ScriptTimeout =**.

Apply It

You cannot specify a lower script timeout setting than the timeout set for the Web server. For example, if you set the script timeout to 60 seconds and the Web server is set to stop processing a script after 90 seconds, the Web server's timeout setting will override the script timeout you set and the server will process the script for 90 seconds. You can use the `Server.ScriptTimeout` statement to determine the timeout set for the Web server.

TYPE THIS:

```
<%
Response.Write("The timeout set for the Web server is ")
Response.Write(Server.ScriptTimeout)
Response.Write(" seconds.")
%>
```

RESULT:

The timeout set for the Web server is 90 seconds.

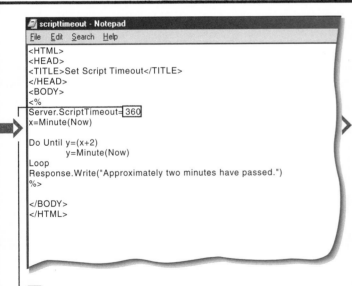

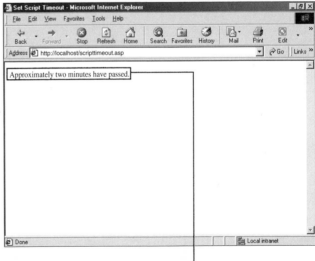

3 Type the number of seconds you want the Web server to process the script before terminating the script and then press Enter.

4 Display the ASP page in a Web browser.

■ The Web browser displays the result of setting the script timeout. The ASP page appears after approximately two minutes.

DISPLAY HTML CODE ON AN ASP PAGE

When a Web browser encounters HTML code in a Web page, the browser automatically attempts to interpret and process the code. You can prevent a Web browser from trying to process HTML code when you want to display the code as plain text on an ASP page.

Web browsers interpret the less than symbol (<) and greater than symbol (>) as the beginning and end of an HTML tag, such as <TABLE>. When a Web browser encounters these symbols, the browser attempts to process the symbols and any information between the symbols.

When you want to display HTML tags or data that contains the less than or greater than symbols as text on your ASP page, you should use a `Server.HTMLEncode` statement. The `Server.HTMLEncode` statement translates the symbols into a format that can be displayed as text on an ASP page. If you do not use the `Server.HTMLEncode` statement, the data you want to display may not appear properly or may not appear at all on the ASP page.

DISPLAY HTML CODE ON AN ASP PAGE

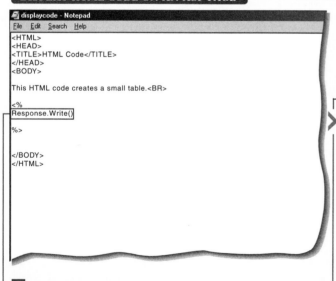

1 Click where you want to display HTML code on the ASP page and type **Response.Write( )**. Then press Enter.

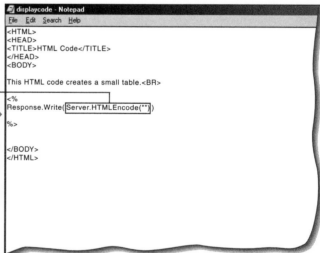

2 Position the insertion point between the parentheses ( ) and type **Server.HTMLEncode("")**.

Apply It

Even when you use a `Server.HTMLEncode` statement, a Web browser will automatically attempt to process data enclosed in quotation marks ("") in HTML code. To display quotation marks in HTML code on your ASP page, you must use double quotation marks.

TYPE THIS:

```
<%
Response.Write("You can use the COLOR attribute ")
Response.Write("to change the color of text.")
Response.Write("<BR>" & "For example: ")
Response.Write(Server.HTMLEncode("<FONT COLOR=""red"">"))
%>
```

RESULT:

You can use the COLOR attribute to change the color of text.
For example: <FONT COLOR="red">

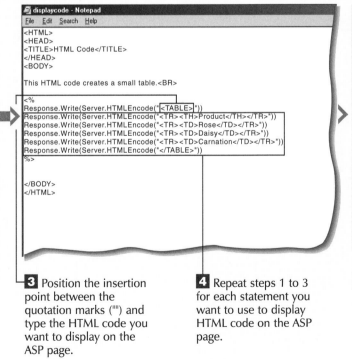

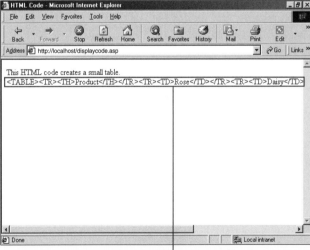

3 Position the insertion point between the quotation marks ("") and type the HTML code you want to display on the ASP page.

4 Repeat steps 1 to 3 for each statement you want to use to display HTML code on the ASP page.

5 Display the ASP page in a Web browser.

■ The Web browser displays the result of using the `Server.HTMLEncode` statement to display HTML code on an ASP page.

ENCODE A URL

A URL can be passed from one ASP page to another ASP page for processing. For example, you could create a form that allows users to enter the URLs of their favorite Web pages. The form could pass the URLs to another page for storage in a database. You should encode a URL passed from an ASP page to make sure a Web browser does not misinterpret the URL.

URLs, particularly those that include query strings, can contain blank spaces and special characters such as /, ? and &. When a Web browser encounters a blank space or special character in a URL, the

browser may truncate the URL or display an error message. The Server.URLEncode statement allows you to encode a URL to ensure these types of problems do not occur.

The Server.URLEncode statement replaces a blank space with a plus sign (+) and replaces a special character with a percent symbol (%) followed by the hexadecimal number for the character. For example, the Server.URLEncode statement replaces the ampersand symbol (&) with %26.

ENCODE A URL

```
encodeurl - Notepad
File  Edit  Search  Help
<HTML>
<HEAD>
<TITLE>Encode URL</TITLE>
</HEAD>
<BODY>

The URL
<I>http://www.abccorp.com?name=Tom Smith&age=35</I>
is encoded as:
<BR>
<BR>
<%
Server.URLEncode("")

%>

</BODY>
</HTML>
```

```
encodeurl - Notepad
File  Edit  Search  Help
<HTML>
<HEAD>
<TITLE>Encode URL</TITLE>
</HEAD>
<BODY>

The URL
<I>http://www.abccorp.com?name=Tom Smith&age=35</I>
is encoded as:
<BR>
<BR>
<%
Server.URLEncode("http://www.abccorp.com?name=Tom Smith&age=35")

%>

</BODY>
</HTML>
```

1 Click where you want to encode a URL and type **Server.URLEncode("")**. Then press Enter.

2 Position the insertion point between the quotation marks ("") and type the URL you want to encode.

Extra

A variable can store the `Server.URLEncode` statement.
Storing a statement in a variable is common programming
practice and can help make your code easier to read and use.

Example:
```
<%
encodedPageAddress=Server.URLEncode("http://www.abccorp.com?id=879")
Response.Write(encodedPageAddress)
%>
```

When you use ASP code to create a link to another page,
you should use the `Server.URLEncode` statement to
encode the URL in the link.

Example:
```
<%
encodedPageAddress=Server.URLEncode("www.abccorp.com?page=Jan Sales")
Response.Write("<A HREF='http://" & encodedPageAddress & "'>ABC
Corporation Web site</A>")
%>
```

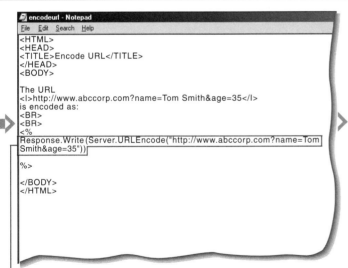

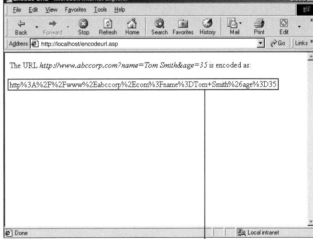

3 Click where
you want to type the
code that executes the
`Server.URLEncode`
statement and type
the code.

4 Display the ASP page
in a Web browser.

■ The Web browser
displays the result
of encoding a URL.

DETERMINE THE PATH OF A FILE

The `Server.MapPath` statement allows you to identify where a file, such as a Web page or ASP page, is stored on the Web server.

A Web server can store files in many different directories. The directory that stores a page is not always apparent in the URL of the page. For example, an ASP page named test.asp stored in the directory c:\inetpub\wwwroot\files, could have the URL http://www.abccorp.com/files/test.asp. When an ASP page needs to access a page on the Web server, the ASP page must know the exact location of the page, not the URL of the page.

To identify the path of a page, you must know the name used to display the page. If the name begins with a slash (/) or backslash (\), such as /files/test.asp, the `Server.MapPath` statement will find the directory that stores the page. If the page name does not begin with a slash or backslash, the `Server.MapPath` statement will find the path of the page relative to the current ASP page.

The `Server.MapPath` statement shows where a page is located on the Web server, but does not verify that the page or directories actually exist.

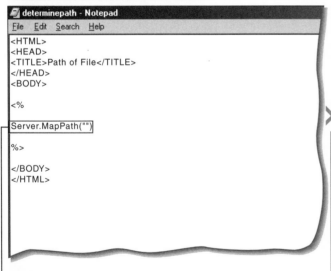

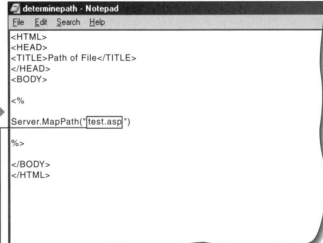

1 Click where you want to find the path of a file and type **Server.MapPath("")**. Then press Enter.

2 Position the insertion point between the quotation marks ("") and type the name of the file whose path you want to find.

Extra The server variable PATH_TRANSLATED allows
you to find the path of the current ASP page.

TYPE THIS:

```
<%
Response.Write("The location of this ASP page is:<BR>")
Response.Write(Request.ServerVariables("PATH_TRANSLATED"))
%>
```

RESULT:

The location of this ASP page is:
c:\inetpub\wwwroot\directory\filename.asp

You can use a Server.MapPath statement
with a slash (/) or backslash (\) to identify
the home directory of the Web server.

TYPE THIS:

```
<%
Response.Write(Server.MapPath("\"))
%>
```

RESULT:

c:\inetpub\wwwroot

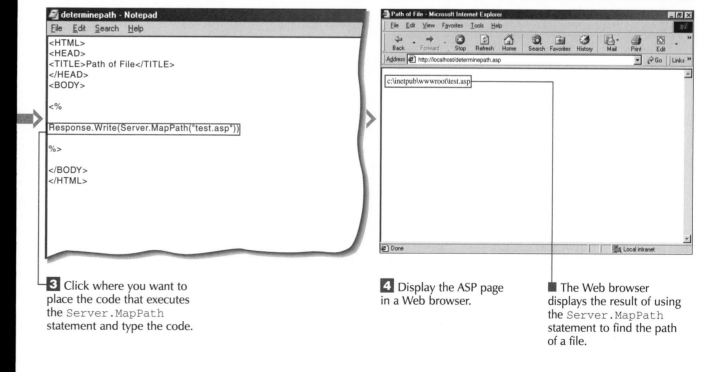

3 Click where you want to
place the code that executes
the Server.MapPath
statement and type the code.

4 Display the ASP page
in a Web browser.

■ The Web browser
displays the result of using
the Server.MapPath
statement to find the path
of a file.

CREATE SESSION INFORMATION

As a user moves through the pages in your Web site, the user may be asked to enter information such as a user name, password or preferences to display each page. Creating session variables allows you to store this information and make the information available to all the pages viewed by the user in your Web site. This saves the user from having to repeatedly enter the same information to display each page during a session.

A session starts when a user requests an ASP page from your Web site. The session ends when the user does not make another request

for a specific amount of time, usually twenty minutes, or the session is *abandoned*.

Session variables can only be used with Web browsers that support cookies. If a user has an older browser or has turned off support for cookies, the information stored in a session variable will be lost when the user requests another page.

There are other methods you can use to enable your Web pages to exchange information, such as creating cookies or using hidden elements in forms. However, these methods can be awkward to use.

CREATE SESSION INFORMATION

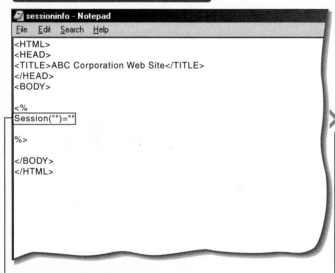

1 Click where you want to create a session variable and type **Session("")=""**. Then press Enter.

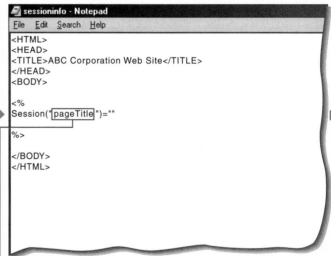

2 Position the insertion point between the first set of quotation marks ("") and type the name of the session variable.

You can create a form that sends information entered
by a user to an ASP page. The ASP page can then store
the information in a session variable. In this example,
the information entered by a user is a user name and
the ASP page that stores this information in a session
variable is called sessionvar.asp.

IN THE FORM, TYPE:

```
Please enter your user name.
<FORM ACTION="www.abccorp.com/sessionvar.asp" METHOD="POST">
<INPUT TYPE="text" NAME="userNameFromForm">
<INPUT TYPE="submit" VALUE="Submit">
</FORM>
```

IN THE ASP PAGE, TYPE:

```
<%
Session("userName")=Request.Form("userNameFromForm")
%>
```

---

sessioninfo - Notepad
File   Edit   Search   Help

```
<HTML>
<HEAD>
<TITLE>ABC Corporation Web Site</TITLE>
</HEAD>
<BODY>

<%
Session("pageTitle")="ABC Corporation Web Site"

%>

</BODY>
</HTML>
```

■3 Position the insertion
point between the
second set of quotation
marks and type a value
for the session variable.

sessioninfo - Notepad
File   Edit   Search   Help

```
<HTML>
<HEAD>
<TITLE>ABC Corporation Web Site</TITLE>
</HEAD>
<BODY>

<%
Session("pageTitle")="ABC Corporation Web Site"
Session("userName")="Joe"
Session("password")="cats"

%>

</BODY>
</HTML>
```

■4 Repeat steps 1 to 3
for each session variable
you want to create.

■ You can now read the
information stored in the
session variables. See
page 150 to read session
information.

READ SESSION INFORMATION

I f an ASP page in your Web site creates session variables for a user, other ASP pages viewed by the user in the Web site can read and process the values in the session variables. For information on creating session information, see page 148.

A Web server can personalize each ASP page in a Web site according to the user information saved in session variables. For example, if a user prefers not to view images on Web pages, each page that the user visits in the Web site will read the session information for the user and display only text.

You can use a session variable as you would use any other variable. You can display the value of the variable on the screen or use the variable to perform a more complex action, such as locating information in a database.

The session variables created for a user are available to all the ASP pages in a Web site until the session times out or is *abandoned*. Users visiting your Web site cannot access the session variables created for another user.

READ SESSION INFORMATION

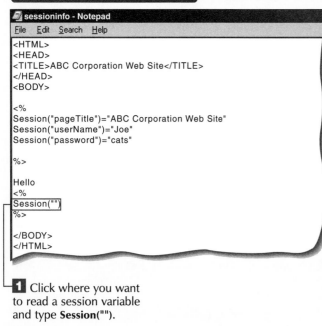

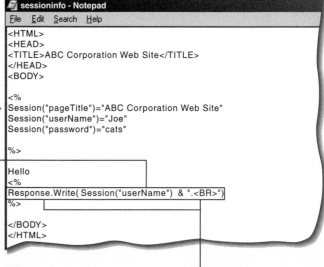

1 Click where you want to read a session variable and type **Session("")**.

2 Position the insertion point between the quotation marks ("") and type the name of the session variable you want to read.

3 Click where you want to place the code that executes the Session statement and type the code.

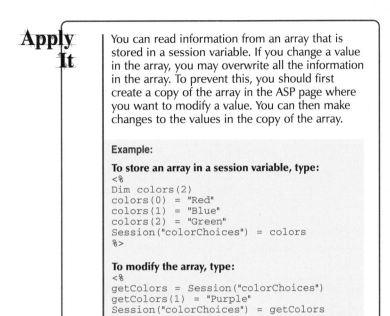

Apply It

You can read information from an array that is stored in a session variable. If you change a value in the array, you may overwrite all the information in the array. To prevent this, you should first create a copy of the array in the ASP page where you want to modify a value. You can then make changes to the values in the copy of the array.

Example:

To store an array in a session variable, type:
```
<%
Dim colors(2)
colors(0) = "Red"
colors(1) = "Blue"
colors(2) = "Green"
Session("colorChoices") = colors
%>
```

To modify the array, type:
```
<%
getColors = Session("colorChoices")
getColors(1) = "Purple"
Session("colorChoices") = getColors
%>
```

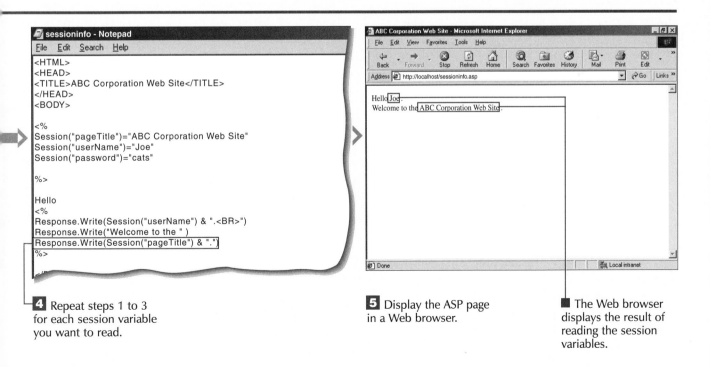

```
sessioninfo - Notepad
File  Edit  Search  Help

<HTML>
<HEAD>
<TITLE>ABC Corporation Web Site</TITLE>
</HEAD>
<BODY>

<%
Session("pageTitle")="ABC Corporation Web Site"
Session("userName")="Joe"
Session("password")="cats"

%>

Hello
<%
Response.Write(Session("userName") & ".<BR>")
Response.Write("Welcome to the " )
Response.Write(Session("pageTitle") & ".")
%>
```

4 Repeat steps 1 to 3 for each session variable you want to read.

5 Display the ASP page in a Web browser.

■ The Web browser displays the result of reading the session variables.

ADJUST THE SESSION TIMEOUT

The Session.Timeout statement allows you to specify, in minutes, the length of time a user's *session information* is stored on the Web server after the user last refreshes a page or requests a page in your Web site. For information about session information, see pages 148 to 151.

By default, a user's session information is stored on the Web server for 20 minutes and is available to the ASP pages that the user views in your Web site. The session information created for a user will be available to the

ASP pages even if the user visits another Web site and then returns to your site within the timeout period. If the user returns to your Web site after the timeout period, the session information for the user will no longer be available.

Using the Session.Timeout statement can help make your Web site more secure. For example, if you have a Web site that requires a user to log in, a short timeout period will help to prevent other users from accessing your site if the user leaves the computer while logged in.

ADJUST THE SESSION TIMEOUT

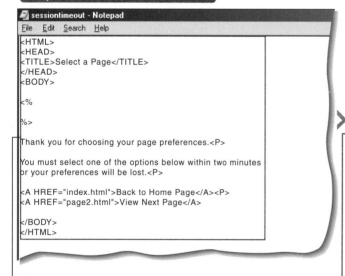

1 Type the code you want to execute to display information in a Web browser.

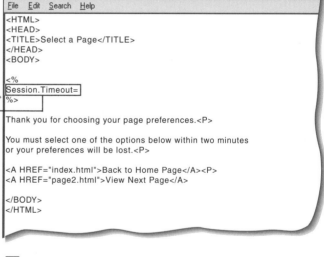

2 Click where you want to adjust the session timeout period for the ASP page and type **Session.Timeout=**.

Extra

The timeout period that you set for an ASP page will apply to every user who accesses the ASP page. You should set the timeout period carefully. If the session times out too quickly, the ASP page may time out before users are able to log into the site and access the page. If the timeout period is too long, session information may be stored in the Web server's memory long after users leave the Web site, which can decrease the efficiency of the server.

The `Session.Timeout` statement allows you to find the current timeout period set for your Web server.

TYPE THIS:

```
<%
Response.Write("The session timeout is currently ")
Response.Write(Session.Timeout & " minutes.")
%>
```

RESULT:

The session timeout is currently 20 minutes.

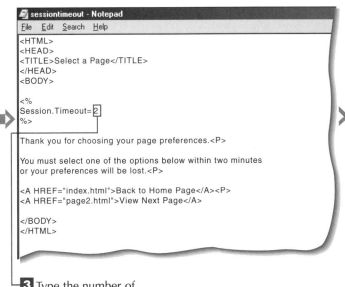

3 Type the number of minutes in which you want the session to end.

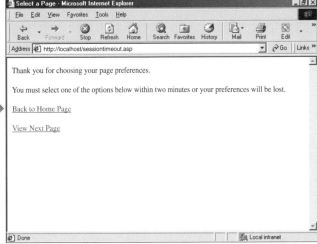

4 Display the ASP page in a Web browser.

■ The Web browser displays the ASP page in which the session timeout is adjusted.

■ If you do not request a new page or refresh a page within the new timeout period, the Web server will erase your session information.

ACCESS THE SESSION ID

A session is started for each user who requests an ASP page from your Web site. A session ID identifies each current user to the Web server.

When a user requests an ASP page from your Web site, the Web server stores a session ID as a cookie on the user's computer. When the user requests another page from the site, the user's Web browser sends the session ID to the Web server to identify the user.

You should not use the session ID as the *primary key* in a database, as the session ID may not always be unique. The session ID

is unique only until either the Web server or the user's Web browser is restarted. For example, if the Web server is restarted, the server may assign a user a session ID that was previously assigned to a different user.

A Web server can assign session IDs only to Web browsers that support cookies. If a user has an older browser or has turned off support for cookies, the server will not be able to assign a session ID.

You use the `Session.SessionID` statement to access a session ID. You cannot change a session ID you access.

ACCESS THE SESSION ID

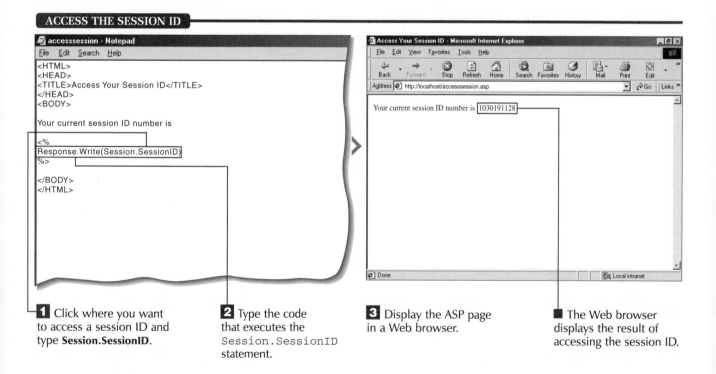

1 Click where you want to access a session ID and type **Session.SessionID**.

2 Type the code that executes the `Session.SessionID` statement.

3 Display the ASP page in a Web browser.

■ The Web browser displays the result of accessing the session ID.

ABANDON A SESSION

The `Session.Abandon` statement allows you to immediately end a session for one user and erase the information associated with the session, such as session variables. This frees up memory and resources on the Web server, which increases the efficiency of the server.

Abandoning a session is useful when an error occurs or when a user performs an action that indicates they no longer need the session information, such as logging out of the Web site. If the session was not abandoned, the Web server would keep the session information in memory until the session times out. Abandoning a session also allows users to perform tasks such as clearing

their preferences or logging into your Web site using a different user name.

Using the `Session.Abandon` statement does not stop the Web server from processing the ASP page. However, if you attempt to read a session variable after the session is abandoned, the value of the session variable will be null.

The `Session.Abandon` statement usually does not erase the *session ID* the Web server stored on the user's computer. If the user requests another page from your Web site after abandoning the session, the server may attempt to use the session ID previously stored on the user's computer.

ABANDON A SESSION

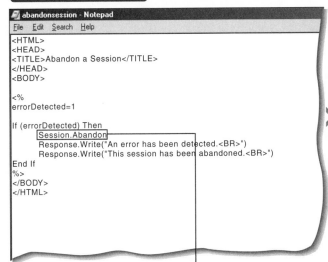

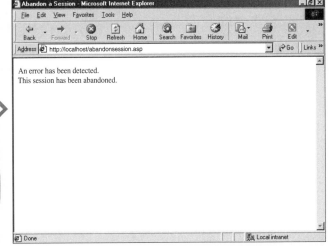

1 Type the HTML and ASP code you want to execute to display information in a user's Web browser.

2 Click where you want to abandon a session and type **Session.Abandon**.

3 Display the ASP page in a Web browser.

■ The Web server abandons the session.

USING APPLICATION INFORMATION

Active Server Pages allows you to define a Web site or a part of a Web site as an application.

An application is a collection of ASP pages stored in a specific directory and its subdirectories on the Web server. For example, if you have 10 ASP pages stored in the same directory, those pages would make up an application.

All the ASP pages in an application must be stored in the same *virtual* directory on the Web server. The type of Web server you use will determine how the virtual directory is created.

You can create variables to store information for the application, such as a counter or a welcome message. All the ASP pages in an application can access the information stored in an application variable. For example, if you create an application variable that stores a counter, the number of people who have used your application could be displayed at the bottom of each page in the application.

An application starts when the first user requests an ASP page from the application and ends when the Web server shuts down or restarts.

CREATE APPLICATION INFORMATION

```
applicationinfo - Notepad
File   Edit   Search   Help
<HTML>
<HEAD>
<TITLE>Time of Last Visit</TITLE>
</HEAD>
<BODY>

<%
Application("timeOfLastVisit")=

%>

The time of your visit has been logged.
</BODY>
</HTML>
```

```
applicationinfo - Notepad
File   Edit   Search   Help
<HTML>
<HEAD>
<TITLE>Time of Last Visit</TITLE>
</HEAD>
<BODY>

<%
Application("timeOfLastVisit")=Now( )

%>

The time of your visit has been logged.
</BODY>
</HTML> .
```

■1 Click where you want to create application information and type **Application("")=**. Then press Enter.

■2 Position the insertion point between the quotation marks ("") and type the name of the application variable you want to create.

■3 Position the insertion point after the equal sign (=) and type a value for the application variable.

■ You can repeat steps 1 to 3 for each application variable you want to create.

■ You can now access the information stored in an application variable.

Apply It

You can use an application variable to store and access an array. If you want to change a value in the array, you must first create a copy of the array in the ASP page where you want to modify the value. If you want to save your change, you must store the array with the new value in the application variable.

To store an array in an application variable, type:
```
<%
Dim message(2)
message(0) = "Welcome "
message(1) = "to my "
message(2) = "Web site"
Application("welcomeMessage") = message
%>
```

To modify the array and save the change, type:
```
<%
newMessage = Application("welcomeMessage")
newMessage(1) = "to my new and improved "
Application("welcomeMessage") = newMessage
%>
```

The value of an application variable can be changed. For example, you can use an application variable to create a simple counter that keeps track of the number of users who have visited your application.

Example:
```
<%
Response.Write("You are visitor number ")
numOfVisitors=Application("visitors")
Application("visitors") = numOfVisitors + 1
Response.Write(Application("visitors"))
Response.Write(" since this Web server ")
Response.Write("was last restarted.")
%>
```

ACCESS APPLICATION INFORMATION

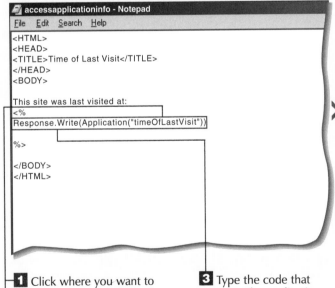

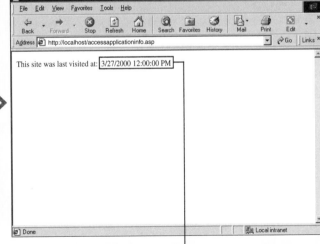

1 Click where you want to access application information and type **Application("")**. Then press Enter.

2 Position the insertion point between the quotation marks ("") and type the name of the application variable you want to access.

3 Type the code that accesses the application variable.

■ You can repeat steps 1 to 3 for each application variable you want to access.

4 Display the ASP page in a Web browser.

■ The Web browser displays the result of accessing the application information.

LOCK AND UNLOCK APPLICATION VARIABLES

Every ASP page in an application can access an application variable. This means that every user who displays an ASP page in an application may be able to modify the value of an application variable.

If several users attempt to modify the same application variable at the same time, only one of the user's modifications will be accepted. The other users' modifications may be ignored.

The `Application.Lock` statement allows you to lock all the variables in an application while a user modifies the value of a variable. If another user tries to access an application variable that

is locked, the Web server will pause the processing of the ASP page until the application variable is unlocked.

The `Application.Unlock` statement allows you to unlock application variables. If you do not use this statement, ASP will unlock the variables when the page is finished processing.

The `Application.Lock` and `Application.Unlock` statements should be placed directly around the code that accesses and modifies an application variable. Enclosing an entire ASP page in these statements will decrease the efficiency of the Web server.

LOCK AND UNLOCK APPLICATION VARIABLES

```
lock - Notepad
File  Edit  Search  Help
<HTML>
<HEAD>
<TITLE>Lock and Unlock Variables</TITLE>
</HEAD>
<BODY>

<H3>Thank you for browsing my Web site</H3>

<%
Application.Lock

Application("guests")=Application("guests") + 1

If Application("guests") = 1 Then
        strPeople=" person has "
Else
        strPeople=" people have "
End If
Response.Write(Application("guests") & strPeople)
Response.Write("signed the guest book.")
%
```

```
lock - Notepad
File  Edit  Search  Help
<HTML>
<HEAD>
<TITLE>Lock and Unlock Variables</TITLE>
</HEAD>
<BODY>

<H3>Thank you for browsing my Web site</H3>

<%
Application.Lock
Application("guests")=Application("guests") + 1
Application.Unlock

If Application("guests") = 1 Then
        strPeople=" person has "
Else
        strPeople=" people have "
End If
Response.Write(Application("guests") & strPeople)
Response.Write("signed the guest book.")
%
```

1 Type the code that accesses and modifies an application variable. See page 157 for information about accessing application information.

2 Position the insertion point in front of the code that accesses and modifies an application variable and type **Application.Lock**. Then press Enter.

3 Position the insertion point on the line after the code that accesses and modifies an application variable and type **Application.Unlock**. Then press Enter.

COUNT APPLICATION VARIABLES

After you have created application variables, you can use the `Application.Contents.Count` statement to count the number of variables that have been used by the application. Finding the number of variables in an application allows you to gather information about the application.

The number of variables being used in an application can change over time. For example, if you create an application that requires users to provide their location when they log in, you could have a different application variable store the number of users from each location. As users log into the application, the

number of variables used by the application will change. You could count the variables to determine the number of locations users are accessing your application from.

The `Application.Contents.Count` statement counts every application variable that has been used, even if the variable does not currently contain a value.

As you display the ASP page that counts application variables, the number of variables being used in the application may change.

COUNT APPLICATION VARIABLES

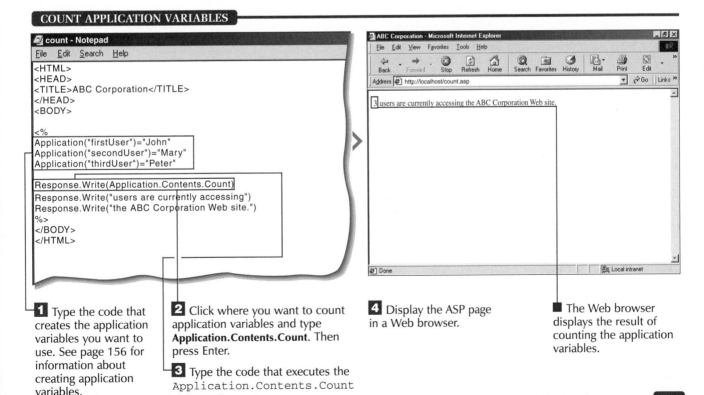

1 Type the code that creates the application variables you want to use. See page 156 for information about creating application variables.

2 Click where you want to count application variables and type **Application.Contents.Count**. Then press Enter.

3 Type the code that executes the `Application.Contents.Count` statement.

4 Display the ASP page in a Web browser.

■ The Web browser displays the result of counting the application variables.

REMOVE APPLICATION INFORMATION

Application variables store information for an application while the application is in use. You can remove one or all of the application variables. For information on application variables, see page 156.

Removing an application variable does not simply reset the value of the variable to null or 0. Removing an application variable clears the variable from the application until the variable is processed again.

The `Application.Contents.Remove` statement allows you to remove one variable from an application. You can also remove all

the variables created for an application using the `Application.Contents.RemoveAll` statement. This is useful if you want to clear all the application variables to perform an administrative task without having to restart the Web server.

It is common programming practice to create all the variables you want to use in an application in the *Global.asa* file. If you remove application variables that are created only in the Global.asa file, the variables are cleared from the application until the Web server is restarted and the Global.asa file is processed again. For more information about the Global.asa file, see page 162.

REMOVE ONE APPLICATION VARIABLE

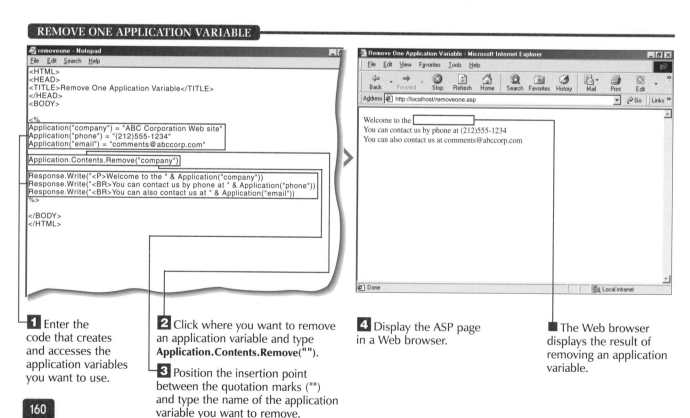

1 Enter the code that creates and accesses the application variables you want to use.

2 Click where you want to remove an application variable and type **Application.Contents.Remove("")**.

3 Position the insertion point between the quotation marks ("") and type the name of the application variable you want to remove.

4 Display the ASP page in a Web browser.

■ The Web browser displays the result of removing an application variable.

Extra

The `Application.Contents.Remove` statement can be used with an index number to remove a specific application variable. This is useful if the application variables are created dynamically and you do not know the name of the variable you want to remove. When you use an index number, ASP counts the number of variables in the application starting at 1 and removes the variable with the index number you specified.

TYPE THIS:

```
Welcome to my Web page. This information has been logged.
<%
Application("name")="Paul"
Application("password")="abc123"
Application("location")="California"
Application.Contents.Remove(3)

Response.Write("<BR>Username: " & Application("name"))
Response.Write("<BR>Password: " & Application("password"))
Response.Write("<BR>Location: " & Application("location"))
%>
```

RESULT:

Welcome to my Web page. This information has been logged.
Username: Paul
Password: abc123
Location:

REMOVE ALL APPLICATION INFORMATION

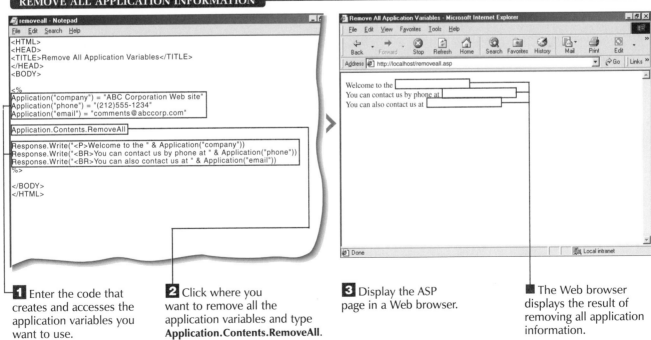

1 Enter the code that creates and accesses the application variables you want to use.

2 Click where you want to remove all the application variables and type **Application.Contents.RemoveAll**.

3 Display the ASP page in a Web browser.

■ The Web browser displays the result of removing all application information.

CREATE THE GLOBAL.ASA FILE

You can create the Global.asa file to store subroutines that are processed by the Web server when an application starts and ends. For information about applications, see page 156.

An application can have only one Global.asa file. The file must be named Global.asa and must be stored in the root directory of the application. The .asa extension stands for *Active Server Application*.

The subroutines for the Global.asa file must be enclosed within the <SCRIPT> and </SCRIPT> tags. The RUNAT attribute for the <SCRIPT> tag allows you to specify that the script will be run on the Web server.

The Global.asa file can include the Application_OnStart and Application_OnEnd

subroutines. Code included in the Application_OnStart subroutine is processed when an application starts, which occurs when the first user accesses a page in the application. You may want to use the Application_OnStart subroutine to create application variables that will be used throughout the application.

Code created in the Application_OnEnd subroutine is executed when an application ends, which usually occurs when the Web server is shut down. You may want to include code in the Application_OnEnd subroutine to tie up any loose ends in the application, such as removing application variables and writing information to log files.

CREATE APPLICATION_ONSTART AND APPLICATION_ONEND

```
<SCRIPT LANGUAGE="VBScript" RUNAT="Server">

</SCRIPT>
```

```
<SCRIPT LANGUAGE="VBScript" RUNAT="Server">
Sub Application_OnStart

</SCRIPT>
```

1 Start the text editor you want to use to create the Global.asa file.

2 Type **<SCRIPT LANGUAGE="VBScript" RUNAT="Server">**. Then press Enter twice and type **</SCRIPT>**.

3 To create a subroutine that is processed when the application starts, click between the <SCRIPT> and </SCRIPT> tags and type **Sub Application_OnStart**. Then press Enter.

Extra

Users cannot access the Global.asa file, so do not include content to be displayed in a Web browser in the file. The Global.asa file should contain only code that performs tasks such as creating variables and opening or closing database connections.

You do not have to specify the path of the Global.asa file in your application to use the subroutines you create in the file. When the application starts or ends, the Web server automatically searches for the Global.asa file and processes the appropriate subroutine.

If the Web server may be accessed by users you do not trust, you should ensure that the correct security permissions are set for the Global.asa file. The Global.asa file can contain information that could constitute a security risk if the information was made public. You can consult your Web server and operating system documentation for information about how to set permissions for a file.

You are not required to use a Global.asa file in your application. If you have created a Global.asa file you no longer need, you should rename or remove the file. This will slightly increase the speed at which users can access the application.

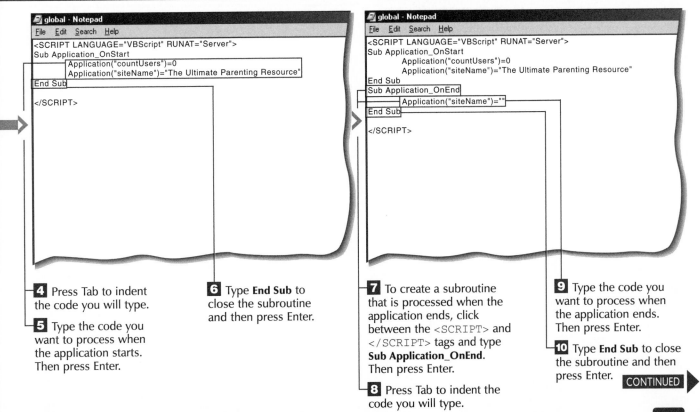

4 Press Tab to indent the code you will type.

5 Type the code you want to process when the application starts. Then press Enter.

6 Type **End Sub** to close the subroutine and then press Enter.

7 To create a subroutine that is processed when the application ends, click between the `<SCRIPT>` and `</SCRIPT>` tags and type **Sub Application_OnEnd**. Then press Enter.

8 Press Tab to indent the code you will type.

9 Type the code you want to process when the application ends. Then press Enter.

10 Type **End Sub** to close the subroutine and then press Enter. CONTINUED ▶

163

CREATE THE GLOBAL.ASA FILE
(CONTINUED)

I n addition to executing code when an application starts and ends, the Global.asa file can be used to process code when a session starts and ends. For information about sessions, see page 148.

A session starts when a new user requests a page from the application. When a session starts, the Web server automatically looks in the Global.asa file for a `Session_OnStart` subroutine. The Web server processes the `Session_OnStart` subroutine before processing the page the user requested. You may want to include code in the

`Session_OnStart` subroutine that opens a connection to a database or ensures users are logged on to the application properly.

The code in the `Session_OnEnd` subroutine is executed when a session ends. A session ends when the session times out or is abandoned. The `Session_OnEnd` subroutine is notoriously unreliable on many Web servers. If you must use the `Session_OnEnd` subroutine to process code when a session ends, you should test the code thoroughly and only include code that is not essential to the proper operation of your application.

CREATE SESSION_ONSTART AND SESSION_ONEND

```
global - Notepad
File  Edit  Search  Help
<SCRIPT LANGUAGE="VBScript" RUNAT="Server">
Sub Application_OnStart
        Application("countUsers")=0
        Application("siteName")="The Ultimate Parenting Resource"
End Sub
Sub Application_OnEnd
        Application("siteName")=""
End Sub
Sub Session_OnStart

</SCRIPT>
```

```
global - Notepad
File  Edit  Search  Help
<SCRIPT LANGUAGE="VBScript" RUNAT="Server">
Sub Application_OnStart
        Application("countUsers")=0
        Application("siteName")="The Ultimate Parenting Resource"
End Sub
Sub Application_OnEnd
        Application("siteName")=""
End Sub
Sub Session_OnStart
        Session("sessionMessage")="You are 1 visitor out of "
        Application("countUsers")=Application("countUsers") + 1
End Sub

</SCRIPT>
```

■1 To create a subroutine that is processed when a session starts, click between the `<SCRIPT>` and `</SCRIPT>` tags and type **Sub Session_OnStart**. Then press Enter.

■2 Press Tab to indent the code you will type.

■3 Type the code you want to process when a session starts. Then press Enter.

■4 Type **End Sub** to close the subroutine and then press Enter.

Extra

You can create your own subroutine in the Global.asa file and then call the subroutine from within one of the four pre-defined subroutines. All of the subroutine code in the Global.asa file must be processed in one of the four pre-defined subroutines. Creating your own subroutines can make the Global.asa file more versatile and easier to read and troubleshoot. You cannot call a subroutine you create in the Global.asa file elsewhere in your application.

Example:
```
Sub Session_OnStart
    Call VerifyUserName
    Call SendWelcomeMessage
End Sub
```

The Web server will ignore any code you create in the Global.asa file that does not apply to the application or a session. The Web server will also ignore any HTML code you include in the Global.asa file.

If you make changes to the Global.asa file, the Web server will automatically reread the file. It is good programming practice to make changes to the file when the application is not being accessed. Changing the Global.asa file when users are accessing the application may interrupt the activities of the users.

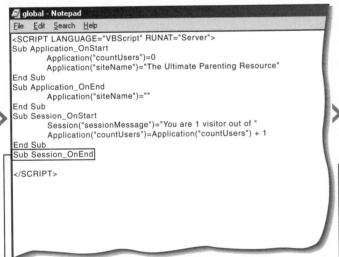

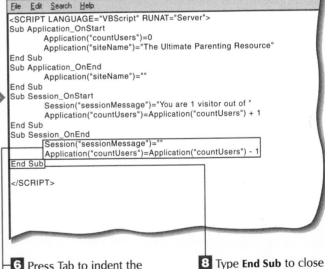

5 To create a subroutine that is processed when a session ends, click between the `<SCRIPT>` and `</SCRIPT>` tags and type **Sub Session_OnEnd**. Then press Enter.

6 Press Tab to indent the code you will type.

7 Type the code you want to process when a session ends. Then press Enter.

8 Type **End Sub** to close the subroutine and then press Enter.

DECLARE AN OBJECT IN THE GLOBAL.ASA FILE

The `<OBJECT>` tag allows you to declare an object in the Global.asa file. Using the `<OBJECT>` tag is an efficient way of declaring an object that will be used several times throughout multiple ASP pages. For information about the Global.asa file, see page 162.

If the Global.asa file contains a script, the object must be declared outside the `<SCRIPT>` and `</SCRIPT>` tags.

The RUNAT attribute of the `<OBJECT>` tag allows you to specify that the object will be created on the Web server. The SCOPE attribute determines

if the object will be used in a session or an application. The ID attribute allows you to give the object a name. You will use the name to access the object from ASP pages. The PROGID attribute allows you to specify the type of object you want to declare.

When you declare an object in the Global.asa file, the object is created only when an ASP page accesses the object. The object is not created when the Global.asa file is processed. This saves the Web server from creating objects that may not be used, which conserves server resources.

DECLARE AN OBJECT IN THE GLOBAL.ASA FILE

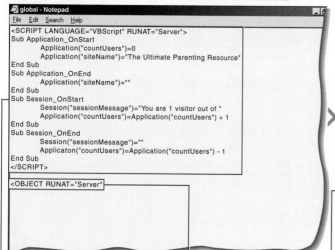

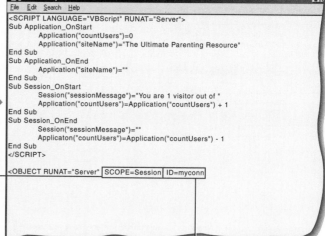

1 Display the code for the Gobal.asa file in which you want to declare an object.

■ If the Gobal.asa file does not already exist, start the text editor you want to use to create the file.

2 Click where you want to declare the object and type **<OBJECT RUNAT="Server"**.

■ Objects must be declared outside the `<SCRIPT>` and `</SCRIPT>` tags.

3 Type **SCOPE=** followed by the scope of the object.

■ The scope of an object can be either Session or Application.

4 Type **ID=** followed by the name you want to use for the object.

■ You will use the name to access the object in your ASP pages.

Extra

Once you have declared an object in the Global.asa file, you can use the name you specified for the `ID` attribute to access the object in an ASP page. For example, if you declare the `ADODB.Connection` object in the Global.asa and assign the object the 'myconn' `ID`, you can use the object to connect to a database in an ASP page.

Example:
```
myconn.ConnectionTimeout=60
myconn.Open "DSN=mydatabase"
```

If you only need to access an object once, you should use the `Server.CreateObject` statement to create the object in an ASP page, instead of using the `<OBJECT>` tag in the Global.asa file. When you use the `Server.CreateObject` statement, the object is created when the ASP page is processed, whether the object is accessed or not.

If you want to declare an ActiveX object you have created and you have a *ClassID* for the object, you can use the `CLASSID` attribute instead of the `PROGID` attribute to specify the type of object you want to create.

Example:
```
<OBJECT RUNAT="Server" SCOPE=Session ID=objMyObject
CLASSID="c8ca28fd-3911-44da-91a7-45897bf4fb4b">
</OBJECT>
```

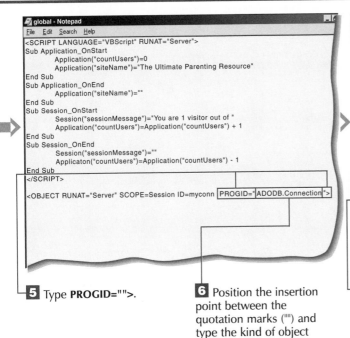

5 Type **PROGID="">.**

6 Position the insertion point between the quotation marks ("") and type the kind of object you want to declare.

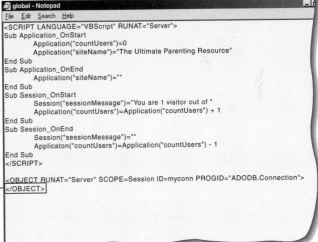

7 Click where you want to close the `<OBJECT>` tag and type **</OBJECT>**.

8 Save the Global.asa file. The file must be named Gobal.asa and stored in the root directory of the application.

■ You should restart the Web server before using the object in your ASP pages.

DECLARE A TYPE LIBRARY IN THE GLOBAL.ASA FILE

A type library stores information about a component, such as the *constants* used by the component. For example, the type library for the ActiveX Data Objects component stores constants you can use to work more efficiently with databases. Declaring a type library for a component in the Global.asa file allows you to access these constants throughout your application. For information about the Global.asa file, see page 162.

Once you have declared a type library for a component, you can use the constants defined in the type library in your ASP pages. Using constants instead of alphanumeric values in ASP code can

make the code easier to read and understand. For example, when retrieving records from a database, you can specify the cursor type using the constant `adOpenDynamic` instead of the value 2. For information about cursor types, see page 202.

The `<METADATA>` tag is used to declare the type library for a component and should be placed at the top of the Global.asa file. The `TYPE` attribute of the tag specifies you want to declare a type library and the `FILE` attribute specifies the path of the type library. The path must be a physical path, not a *virtual* path.

You must be using Active Server Pages 3.0 to declare a type library.

DECLARE A TYPE LIBRARY IN THE GLOBAL.ASA FILE

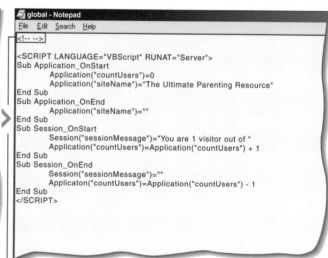

1 Display the code for the Global.asa file in which you want to declare a type library.

■ If the Global.asa file does not already exist, start the text editor you want to use to create the file.

2 Click where you want to declare a type library and type the HTML comment tags (`<!--` and `-->`). Then press Enter.

■ A type library should be declared at the top of the Global.asa file.

Extra

Other components that offer a type library include the Ad Rotator component and the IIS Log component. You can consult the documentation that came with the Web server for more information about the type libraries for these components.

If you only need to use the information in the type library for a component in one ASP page, you can declare the type library in that page instead of in the Global.asa file. The <METADATA> tag should be placed at the top of the page.

Example:

```
<!-- METADATA TYPE="TypeLib"
FILE="C:\Program Files\Common
Files\System\ado\msado15.dll" -->
<HTML>
<HEAD> </HEAD>
<BODY>
```

Some components, such as ActiveX Data Objects, also have a file that defines the constants used by the component. You can include the file in an ASP page as a *Server Side Include* to be able to use the constants in the page. For information about Server Side Includes, see page 174. Declaring a type library in the Global.asa file is more efficient than using Server Side Includes.

Example:

```
<!-- #include file="adovbs.inc" -->
```

---

global - Notepad
File Edit Search Help

```
<!-- METADATA TYPE="TypeLib" FILE="" -->

<SCRIPT LANGUAGE="VBScript" RUNAT="Server">
Sub Application_OnStart
        Application("countUsers")=0
        Application("siteName")="The Ultimate Parenting Resource"
End Sub
Sub Application_OnEnd
        Application("siteName")=""
End Sub
Sub Session_OnStart
        Session("sessionMessage")="You are 1 visitor out of "
        Application("countUsers")=Application("countUsers") + 1
End Sub
Sub Session_OnEnd
        Session("sessionMessage")=""
        Applicaton("countUsers")=Application("countUsers") - 1
End Sub
</SCRIPT>
```

global - Notepad
File Edit Search Help

```
<!-- METADATA TYPE="TypeLib" FILE="C:\Program Files\Common
Files\System\ado\msado15.dll" -->

<SCRIPT LANGUAGE="VBScript" RUNAT="Server">
Sub Application_OnStart
        Application("countUsers")=0
        Application("siteName")="The Ultimate Parenting Resource"
End Sub
Sub Application_OnEnd
        Application("siteName")=""
End Sub
Sub Session_OnStart
        Session("sessionMessage")="You are 1 visitor out of "
        Application("countUsers")=Application("countUsers") + 1
End Sub
Sub Session_OnEnd
        Session("sessionMessage")=""
        Applicaton("countUsers")=Application("countUsers") - 1
End Sub
</SCRIPT>
```

3 Position the insertion point after the <!-- comment tag and type a space followed by **METADATA TYPE="TypeLib" FILE=""**.

4 Position the insertion point between the quotation marks ("") and type the path of the type library.

Note: The path must be a physical path.

5 Save the Global.asa file. The file must be named Global.asa and stored in the root directory of the application.

CALL AN ASP PAGE

The `Server.Execute` statement allows you to access an ASP page from within another ASP page. This allows you to break ASP code into manageable sections and use the sections to build your pages.

Using the `Server.Execute` statement is similar to calling a subroutine or a function and is an alternative to using *Server-Side Includes* to perform specific tasks in an ASP page.

When the Web server processes an ASP page and finds a `Server.Execute` statement, the server processes the ASP file specified in the statement. When the Web server finishes

processing the file, the server returns to the original ASP page and continues to process the page.

Any information, such as session or application variables, available to the calling ASP page will also be available to the called ASP page.

After data has been sent to a Web browser by the calling ASP page, the called ASP page must not attempt to generate any HTTP header information. If the called page generates header information, an error will occur.

In order for you to call an ASP page, the Web server must be running Active Server Pages 3.0.

CREATE AN ASP PAGE YOU WANT TO CALL

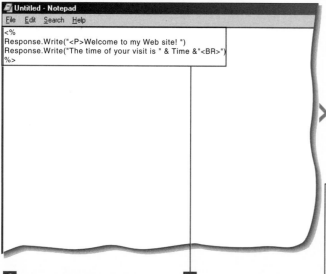

1 Start the text editor you will use to create the ASP page you want to include in other ASP pages.

2 Type the code you want to be able to execute in other ASP pages.

3 Save the file on the Web server in a text only format with the .asp extension.

Extra

Calling an ASP page from within other ASP pages allows you to quickly update code in your pages. For example, to display the same footer information at the bottom of several ASP pages, you could use a `Server.Execute` statement to call a footer.asp file from within each page. To update the footer information in every page, you simply change the footer.asp file.

If an ASP page is stored in the same directory as the page that calls it, you only need to include the name of the ASP page in the `Server.Execute` statement. If the pages are stored in different directories, you must include the name of the directory that stores the ASP page you want to call in the `Server.Execute` statement.

Example:

```
<%
Server.Execute("/asppages/banner.asp")
%>
```

You can append a query string to the name of an ASP page specified in a `Server.Execute` statement. The query string will be processed as if it was entered into the address bar of a Web browser, provided by a form using the `GET` method or submitted as part of a hyperlink.

Example:

```
<%
Server.Execute("message.asp?name=Sue")
%>
```

CALL AN ASP PAGE

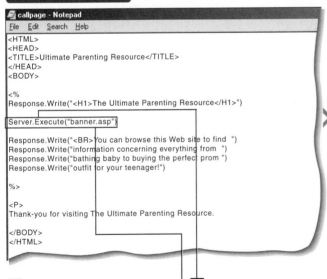

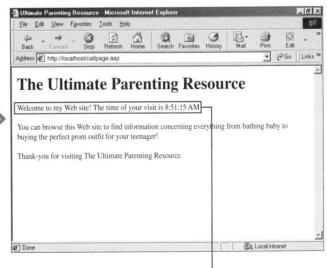

1 In a text editor, display the code for the ASP page in which you want to call another ASP page.

2 Click where you want to call an ASP page and type **Server.Execute("")**. Then press Enter.

3 Position the insertion point between the quotation marks ("") and type the name of the ASP page you want to call.

4 Display the ASP page that calls another ASP page in a Web browser.

■ The Web browser displays the result of calling an ASP page.

TRANSFER CONTROL TO ANOTHER ASP PAGE

The Server.Transfer statement is used to transfer control from one ASP page to another. For example, when an error occurs during the processing of an ASP page, you can use a Server.Transfer statement to transfer control to another ASP page that handles errors and displays help information for the user. Using the Server.Transfer statement allows you to efficiently manage the ASP code in your pages.

When the Web server processes an ASP page that contains a Server.Transfer statement, the server stops processing the page and executes the code in the ASP file specified in the statement. The Web server does not return to the original ASP page.

Any information available to the original ASP page will also be available to the ASP page control is transferred to. Information available to the controlling ASP page includes application variables, session variables and any data stored in a Request statement, such as Request.Form or Request.QueryString. The ASP page control is transferred to can access this information even if the page is not part of the same application as the original ASP page.

In order for you to transfer control to another ASP page, the Web server must be running Active Server Pages 3.0.

CREATE AN ASP PAGE YOU WANT TO TRANSFER CONTROL TO

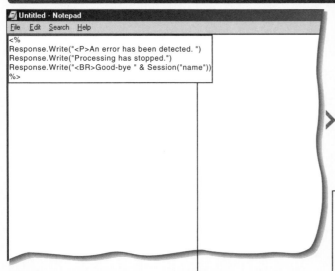

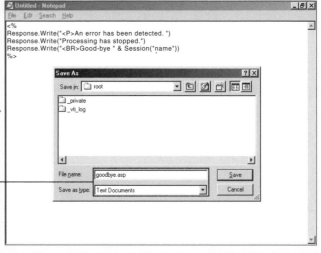

1 Start the text editor you will use to create the ASP page you want to transfer control to.

2 Type the code you want to be able to execute when you transfer control to the page.

3 Save the file on the Web server in a text only format with the .asp extension.

The `Server.Transfer` statement is often used to transfer control to another ASP page depending on the outcome of testing a condition. This gives you greater flexibility when you are creating complex Web sites.

Example:

```
<%
userName=Request.QueryString("name")

If userName="Webmaster" Then
    Server.Transfer("websiteadmin.asp")
Else
    Response.Write("You are not authorized to ")
    Response.Write("administer the Web site.")
    Server.Transfer("goodbye.asp")
End If
%>
```

If the ASP page you want to transfer control to is stored in the same directory as the original ASP page, the `Server.Transfer` statement only needs to include the name of the page control will be transferred to. If the pages are stored in different directories, the `Server.Transfer` statement must also include the name of the directory that stores the ASP page you want to transfer control to.

Example:

```
<%
Server.Transfer("/asppages/goodbye.asp")
%>
```

TRANSFER CONTROL TO ANOTHER ASP PAGE

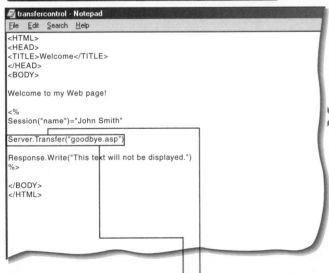

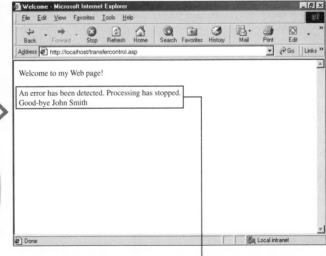

1 In a text editor, display the code for the ASP page in which you want to transfer control to another ASP page.

2 Click where you want to transfer control and type **Server.Transfer("")**. Then press Enter.

3 Position the insertion point between the quotation marks ("") and type the name of the ASP page you want to transfer control to.

4 Display the ASP page that transfers control to another ASP page in a Web browser.

■ The Web browser displays the result of transferring control to another ASP page.

USING SERVER-SIDE INCLUDES

Server-Side Includes (SSI) allow you to use one file in several different Web pages. This can save you time when you need to include the same code in multiple pages. If you change the code in the file, all of the Web pages that include the file will be updated.

You must first create the file you want to include. The file can contain HTML code, such as a table, header or footer. The file can also contain ASP code, enclosed within the ASP delimiters (<% and %>), such as a subroutine or function. You can save the file with the .inc extension on the Web server.

To include the file in a Web page, you add a #include file statement to the page. The #include file statement contains the name of the file you want to include and must be enclosed within HTML comment tags (<!-- and -->). If the included file contains ASP code, the Web page must have the .asp extension.

The Web server processes the #include file statement in a Web page before executing any scripts and replaces the statement with the contents of the specified file. The Web server then finishes processing the Web page and sends the page to a Web browser.

CREATE A FILE YOU WANT TO INCLUDE

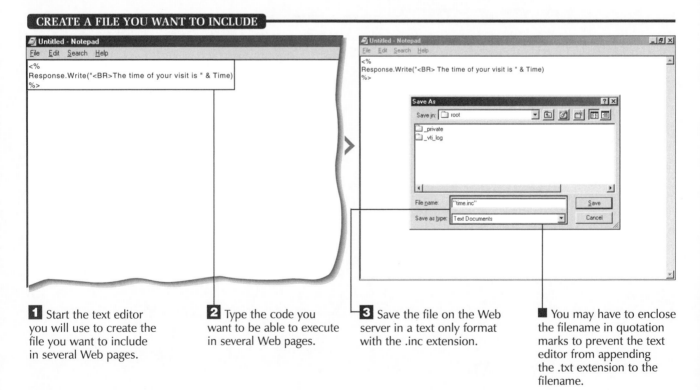

1 Start the text editor you will use to create the file you want to include in several Web pages.

2 Type the code you want to be able to execute in several Web pages.

3 Save the file on the Web server in a text only format with the .inc extension.

■ You may have to enclose the filename in quotation marks to prevent the text editor from appending the .txt extension to the filename.

Extra

The `#include file` statement allows you to include a file that is stored in the same directory as the Web page including the file or in a sub-directory of that directory. In this example, the Web page is stored in a directory called test and the time.inc file is stored in a sub-directory called test\pages.

Example:

```
<!-- #include file="pages\time.inc" -->
```

The `#include virtual` statement allows you to include a file that is not stored in the same directory structure as the Web page. In this example, the file named banner.inc is stored in a *virtual* directory named includes.

Example:

```
<!-- #include virtual="includes/banner.inc" -->
```

Using Server-Side Includes allows you to break code into manageable sections and then include the code in Web pages as needed. Each Server-Side Include file should contain code specific to only one task. If you create a file that contains code for many tasks, the Web pages may not use all the code and the Web server's resources will be wasted.

USE A SERVER-SIDE INCLUDE FILE

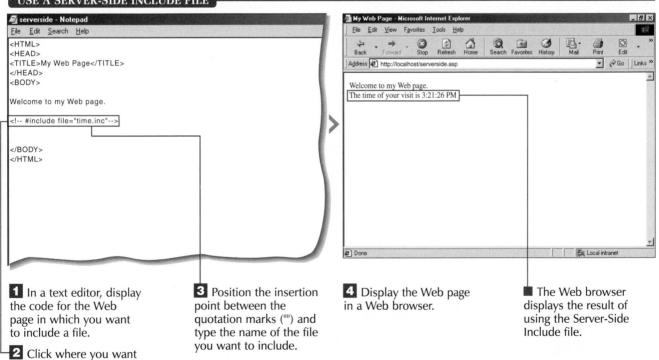

1 In a text editor, display the code for the Web page in which you want to include a file.

2 Click where you want to include a file and type **<!-- #include file="" -->**. Then press Enter.

3 Position the insertion point between the quotation marks ("") and type the name of the file you want to include.

4 Display the Web page in a Web browser.

■ The Web browser displays the result of using the Server-Side Include file.

CREATE A WINDOWS SCRIPT COMPONENT

A script component, or scriptlet, is a small script that is created and saved in a file separate from the ASP pages on the Web server. ASP pages can access and process the code in the script component.

Creating a scriptlet allows you to use the same code in several different ASP pages. For example, you may have many pages that need to access a database on the Web server. Instead of inserting the code required to establish a connection to the database into all the ASP pages, the code required to establish the connection can be placed in a single scriptlet that all the ASP pages can access. Using a script component also makes it easier to update the information in your ASP pages, because only the script component needs to be updated.

As well as the actual scripting code, a script component requires additional information to be specified before the script component can be used. You must specify the program identification, or PROGID, which is a unique name you use to identify the script component in your ASP pages. You can also specify a description for your scriptlet to help you identify the purpose of the scriptlet.

SPECIFY REGISTRATION INFORMATION

```
Untitled - Notepad
File  Edit  Search  Help
<SCRIPTLET>

</SCRIPTLET>
```

```
Untitled - Notepad
File  Edit  Search  Help
<SCRIPTLET>
<REGISTRATION PROGID=""

</REGISTRATION>

</SCRIPTLET>
```

1 Start the text editor you want to use to create the scriptlet.

2 Type **<SCRIPTLET>**. Then press Enter twice and type **</SCRIPTLET>**.

3 To create the registration information, click between the <SCRIPTLET> and </SCRIPTLET> tags and type **<REGISTRATION PROGID="">**. Then press Enter twice.

4 Type **</REGISTRATION>** and then press Enter.

Extra

You can specify a version number for your script component in the <REGISTRATION> tag. Specifying a version number can help you keep track of the changes you make to the script component.

Example:
```
<REGISTRATION PROGID="MakeMessage.wsc"
    VERSION="3"
    DESCRIPTION="Scriptlet to display a message">
</REGISTRATION>
```

You can include a CLASSID number in the <REGISTRATION> tag to provide extra identification for a scriptlet on the Web server. If you have Microsoft Visual Studio installed on your computer, you can use the *uuidgen* utility to generate a CLASSID number for your scriptlet. Use the Windows Command Prompt to run the uuidgen utility and then copy the CLASSID number into your scriptlet.

Example:
```
<REGISTRATION PROGID="MakeMessage.wsc"
    VERSION="3"
    CLASSID="{ec5a4f77-6b50-4d57-beac-3b53ea69a0dc}"
    DESCRIPTION="Scriptlet to display a message">
</REGISTRATION>
```

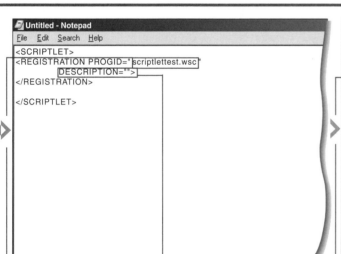

5 Position the insertion point between the quotation marks ("") and type the name of the scriptlet you want to create.

6 To create a description for the scriptlet, click between the <REGISTRATION> and </REGISTRATION> tags and press Tab to indent the code you will type.

7 Type **DESCRIPTION="">**.

8 Position the insertion point between the quotation marks ("") and type a description of the scriptlet.

CONTINUED ▶

CREATE A WINDOWS SCRIPT COMPONENT (CONTINUED)

After specifying the registration information for a scriptlet, the implementation information must be specified. The implementation information is specified between the <IMPLEMENTS> and </IMPLEMENTS> tags.

The implementation information is used to specify how an ASP page will communicate with the script component and consists of property information and method information.

Property information allows you to make variables you create in the scriptlet available to the ASP pages that will access the scriptlet. You use the

<PROPERTY/> tag to name a variable and make the variable accessible to ASP pages.

Specifying method information in the script component allows you to make functions and procedures in your script component available to ASP pages. As with variables, you must specify the name of the function or procedure. The <METHOD/> tag makes functions and procedures accessible to ASP pages.

Using the <PROPERTY/> and <METHOD/> tags to make variables, functions and procedures accessible to ASP pages is referred to as *exposing* the information.

SPECIFY IMPLEMENTATION INFORMATION

Untitled - Notepad
File   Edit   Search   Help

```
<SCRIPTLET>
<REGISTRATION PROGID="scriptlettest.wsc"
        DESCRIPTION="Scriptlet to display a test message">
</REGISTRATION>
<IMPLEMENTS ID=Automation TYPE=Automation>

</IMPLEMENTS>

</SCRIPTLET>
```

Untitled - Notepad
File   Edit   Search   Help

```
<SCRIPTLET>
<REGISTRATION PROGID="scriptlettest.wsc"
        DESCRIPTION="Scriptlet to display a test message">
</REGISTRATION>
<IMPLEMENTS ID=Automation TYPE=Automation>
        <PROPERTY NAME="message"/>

</IMPLEMENTS>

</SCRIPTLET>
```

1 Click where you want to place the implementation information and type **<IMPLEMENTS ID=Automation TYPE=Automation>**. Then press Enter twice.

2 Type **</IMPLEMENTS>** and then press Enter.

3 To specify property information, click between the <IMPLEMENTS> and </IMPLEMENTS> tags, press Tab and then type **<PROPERTY NAME=""/>**. Then press Enter.

4 Position the insertion point between the quotation marks ("") and type the name of a variable you will use in the scriptlet.

You may want to use different variable, function or procedure names in the scriptlet than the variable, function or procedure names you use in your ASP pages. This allows you to use names in your scriptlet that may not make sense in an ASP page. You must specify both names in the implementation information. In the `<PROPERTY/>` or `<METHOD/>` tag, use the `NAME` attribute to specify the variable, function or procedure name you will use in your ASP pages. Use the `INTERNALNAME` attribute to specify the variable, function or procedure name you will use in the scriptlet.

Example:

```
<IMPLEMENTS ID=Automation TYPE=Automation>
    <PROPERTY NAME="message" INTERNALNAME="textVariable"/>
    <METHOD NAME="calculate" INTERNALNAME="generateFinalNumbers"/>
</IMPLEMENTS>
```

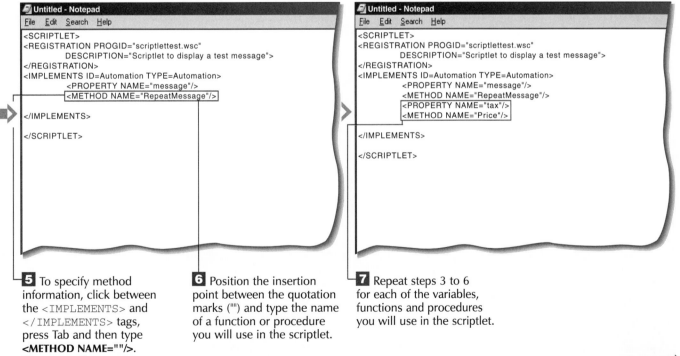

5 To specify method information, click between the `<IMPLEMENTS>` and `</IMPLEMENTS>` tags, press Tab and then type **<METHOD NAME=""/>**. Then press Enter.

6 Position the insertion point between the quotation marks ("") and type the name of a function or procedure you will use in the scriptlet.

7 Repeat steps 3 to 6 for each of the variables, functions and procedures you will use in the scriptlet.

CONTINUED

CREATE A WINDOWS
SCRIPT COMPONENT (CONTINUED)

T he final step in creating a scriptlet is writing the script code that will be executed to generate the values for the variables, functions and procedures you specified in the implementation information.

The code you want to execute in the script component must be enclosed within the <SCRIPT> and </SCRIPT> tags. The LANGUAGE attribute for the <SCRIPT> tag allows you to specify which scripting language the scriptlet will use.

Any variable name or function and procedure names used in the script that you want to expose must be

specified in a <PROPERTY/> or <METHOD/> tag in the implementation information. Otherwise, the ASP pages that access the scriptlet will not be able to access the variables, functions or procedures.

Specifying variables or functions and procedures as properties or methods also ensures that the ASP pages that access the scriptlet will not be affected by any of the additional code in the scriptlet. This allows you to add and remove code in your scriptlet without having to worry about the changes having an adverse effect on the ASP pages that access the scriptlet.

CREATE THE SCRIPT

```
<SCRIPTLET>
<REGISTRATION PROGID="scriptlettest.wsc"
        DESCRIPTION="Scriptlet to display a test message">
</REGISTRATION>
<IMPLEMENTS ID=Automation TYPE=Automation>
        <PROPERTY NAME="message"/>
        <METHOD NAME="RepeatMessage"/>
        <PROPERTY NAME="tax"/>
        <METHOD NAME="Price"/>

</IMPLEMENTS>
<SCRIPT LANGUAGE="">

</SCRIPT>
</SCRIPTLET>
```

```
<SCRIPTLET>
<REGISTRATION PROGID="scriptlettest.wsc"
        DESCRIPTION="Scriptlet to display a test message">
</REGISTRATION>
<IMPLEMENTS ID=Automation TYPE=Automation>
        <PROPERTY NAME="message"/>
        <METHOD NAME="RepeatMessage"/>
        <PROPERTY NAME="tax"/>
        <METHOD NAME="Price"/>

</IMPLEMENTS>
<SCRIPT LANGUAGE="VBScript">

</SCRIPT>
</SCRIPTLET>
```

■1 Click where you want to begin the script for the scriptlet and type **<SCRIPT LANGUAGE="">**. Then press Enter twice and type **</SCRIPT>**.

■2 Position the insertion point between the quotation marks ("") and type the name of the scripting language you will use to create the script.

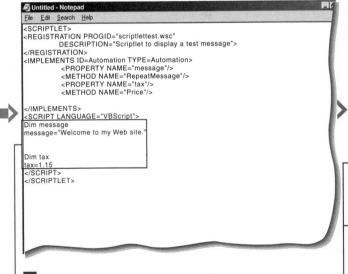

Extra

Script components are not limited to code written with VBScript. You can create scriptlets using many different scripting languages, including JavaScript. The ability to use different scripting languages gives you the freedom to choose the language that best suits the tasks you want the scriptlet to perform. Keep in mind, however, that using many different scripting languages in a single script component can negatively impact the performance of the Web server.

Use the `<SCRIPT>` and `</SCRIPT>` tags to separate code written in different languages in a scriptlet.

Example:

```
<SCRIPT LANGUAGE="VBScript">
message="Hello World"
</SCRIPT>

<SCRIPT LANGUAGE="JavaScript">
var errorMessage="System halted"
</SCRIPT>
```

3 Click between the `<SCRIPT>` and `</SCRIPT>` tags and type the code that declares the variables you will use in the scriptlet and assigns values to the variables.

4 Type the functions or procedures you want to execute in the scriptlet.

CONTINUED

CREATE A WINDOWS SCRIPT COMPONENT (CONTINUED)

O nce you have created a scriptlet, you must save the scriptlet and then register it with the operating system running on the Web server.

Script components must be saved in a text only format with the .wsc extension. If you are creating scriptlets with a text editor, you can place quotation marks around the filename of the scriptlet to ensure the .txt or other extension is not appended to the filename.

Before you can use a scriptlet you have saved, you must register the scriptlet. Registering a

script component places information about the scriptlet in the registry of the Web server's operating system. The operating system's registry is used to keep track of hardware configuration and any programs that have been installed.

In order to register the script component on the Web server, you must be logged onto the server as an administrator.

If a user attempts to access a script component from an ASP page before you register the script component, an error will occur.

SAVE AND REGISTER THE SCRIPTLET

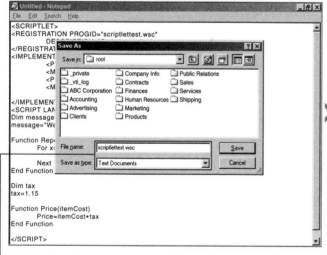

1 Save the scriptlet on the Web server in a text only format with the .wsc extension.

2 On the Web server, start Windows Explorer and locate the scriptlet.

Extra

You can also register a script component from the command prompt using a utility called *regsvr32*. In the Windows Command Prompt on the Web server, type **regsvr32** followed by the name and path of the script component you want to register.

When you no longer require a scriptlet, you can unregister the scriptlet. You can perform steps 2 to 4 below, selecting Unregister in step 4. You can also use the regsvr32 utility to unregister a scriptlet. In the Windows Command Prompt on the Web server, type **regsvr32 /u** followed by the name and path of the scriptlet you want to unregister.

A script component must not contain any <HTML> or <BODY> tags. If the scriptlet contains these types of tags, you will not be able to register the scriptlet.

The Windows Script Component Wizard allows you to quickly create and register scriptlets. The wizard will automatically generate the implementation and registration information based on information you provide. The Windows Script Component Wizard is available for download at the msdn.microsoft.com/scripting Web site.

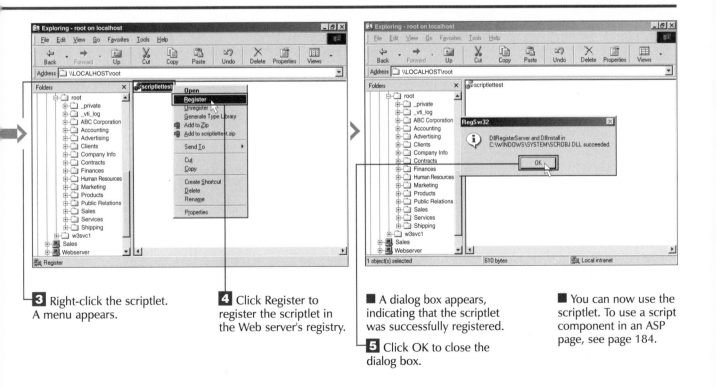

3 Right-click the scriptlet. A menu appears.

4 Click Register to register the scriptlet in the Web server's registry.

■ A dialog box appears, indicating that the scriptlet was successfully registered.

5 Click OK to close the dialog box.

■ You can now use the scriptlet. To use a script component in an ASP page, see page 184.

USING A WINDOWS SCRIPT COMPONENT

After a Windows script component has been created, saved and registered on the Web server, the script component is accessible to ASP pages processed on the server.

To use a scriptlet in an ASP page, you use a `Server.CreateObject` statement to create an instance of the scriptlet in the page. Creating an instance of a script component is similar to creating an instance of an *object* for use in an ASP page.

When creating an instance of a script component, a variable name must be assigned to the instance.

Once a variable name has been assigned to the instance of the scriptlet, the ASP page can access the methods and properties of the scriptlet.

If the methods in a script component require an argument list, you must take care to ensure that the correct number and type of arguments are used when accessing the methods. Using an incorrect number of arguments or using incorrect argument types, such as using text instead of a number, may cause the Web server to stop processing the ASP page that is using the scriptlet.

USING A WINDOWS SCRIPT COMPONENT

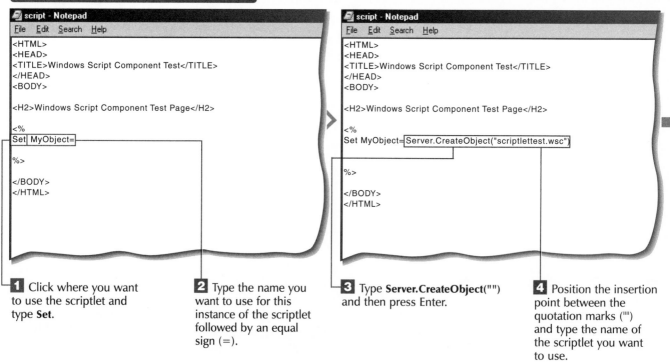

1 Click where you want to use the scriptlet and type **Set**.

2 Type the name you want to use for this instance of the scriptlet followed by an equal sign (=).

3 Type **Server.CreateObject("")** and then press Enter.

4 Position the insertion point between the quotation marks ("") and type the name of the scriptlet you want to use.

Extra

Scriptlets are very versatile and powerful tools that can be used to create sophisticated Web sites. You can create and use Windows script components to accomplish many types of tasks in your ASP pages. For more information and technical support about Windows script components, visit the Microsoft Windows Script Technologies Web site at msdn.microsoft.com/scripting.

If needed, Active Server Pages code and HTML code can be included in Web pages using *Server-Side Includes*. While not as powerful as script components, Server-Side Includes may be preferred for incorporating small sections of code.

If the script component you want to use is stored on a different Web server than the Web server that stores the ASP page, you can include the name of the server storing the scriptlet in the `Server.CreateObject` statement. In this example, the ASP page will access the script component named scriptlettest.asp on the Web server named server2.

Example:

```
Set newExample=CreateObject("scriptlettest.asp", "server2")
```

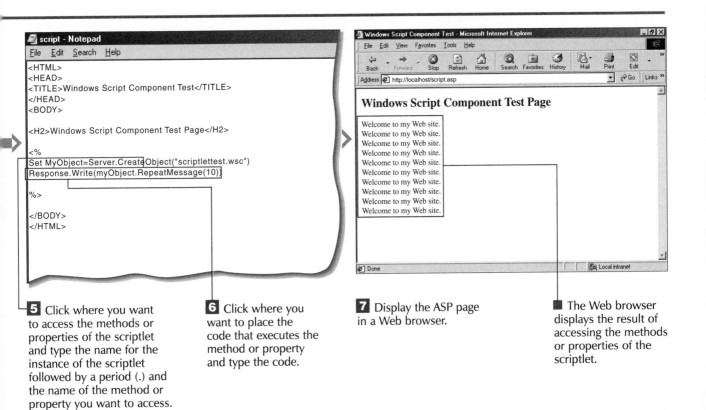

5 Click where you want to access the methods or properties of the scriptlet and type the name for the instance of the scriptlet followed by a period (.) and the name of the method or property you want to access.

6 Click where you want to place the code that executes the method or property and type the code.

7 Display the ASP page in a Web browser.

■ The Web browser displays the result of accessing the methods or properties of the scriptlet.

INTRODUCTION TO DATABASES

One of the most important features of Active Server Pages is the ability to connect to a database.

Databases store and manage large collections of information. ASP pages can be used to make this information available to the users who visit your Web site.

Instead of storing information in text files or static Web pages, an ASP page can be set up to retrieve, format and display data from a database. When a user accesses the ASP page, the information displayed by the page will be created from the current information in the database. An ASP page can also allow users to manipulate the data in a database.

Using databases to store information and ASP pages to access the information is an efficient method of displaying up-to-date information in a Web site.

DATABASE PROGRAMS

There are several different programs available that you can use to create a database. The two most popular database programs used when working with Active Server Pages are Microsoft Access and Microsoft SQL Server. Microsoft Access is useful for creating relatively small databases. For information about Microsoft Access, you can visit the www.microsoft.com/office/access Web site. SQL Server is useful for creating large databases, such as a database used to provide information to a busy e-commerce Web site. For information about Microsoft SQL Server, you can visit the www.microsoft.com/sql Web site.

DATABASE STRUCTURE

A database is made up of one or more tables. A table contains records that store the information entered into the table. For example, a record could store the information for one customer. Each record is divided into fields. A field is a specific piece of information in a record, such as the first name of a customer.

Great care should be taken when initially planning and designing the structure of a database. A well-planned database ensures that tasks, such as adding or deleting records, can be performed efficiently and accurately. Poor database design may cause problems if the database needs to be changed in the future.

CONNECT TO A DATABASE

Before an ASP page can access a database, you must create a connection to the database. You create a Data Source Name (DSN) for the database to tell your ASP pages what kind of database you want to connect to and where the database is located. You can then use the DSN with the `Connection` object in an ASP page to connect the page to the database.

Once connected, you can use the `Execute` method of the `Connection` object or the `Recordset` object to retrieve records from the database. The `Execute` method is useful for performing simple tasks on a small number of records. The `Recordset` object offers more flexibility than the `Execute` method and can be used to work with a large number of records.

STRUCTURED QUERY LANGUAGE

In order for an ASP page to work with the records in a
database, the page must be able to communicate with the
database. You use the Structured Query Language (SQL) in
an ASP page you want to communicate with a database.

SQL FEATURES

Standardized

SQL is the industry standard language for
managing and manipulating data in a database.
SQL can be used to work with many types of
databases, which makes it easy to upgrade
from one database program to another. For
example, a small Web site might start out using
a Microsoft Access database, but then grow
large enough to require a database created
using Microsoft SQL Server. You only have to
learn one language to have your ASP pages
communicate with both types of databases.

Easy to Use

SQL is a very simple language to work with and uses
many easy-to-understand commands. For example,
SQL uses the INSERT statement to add information
to a database. These plain-language commands make
it easy for you to read code created using SQL and
determine the purpose of the code.

Powerful

Although SQL is easy to use, it is a very powerful
language. As well as being suitable for retrieving data
from a database and performing simple tasks such
as adding and deleting records, SQL can be used to
perform complicated procedures, such as compiling
different types of data from multiple data sources.

SQL STATEMENTS

Although SQL is made up of many statements
and clauses, you will only need to be familiar with
a few to perform the examples in this chapter.

SELECT

The SELECT statement specifies
the records you want to retrieve
from a database. The SELECT
statement uses the FROM clause
to specify the name of the table
that stores the records you want
to retrieve. The WHERE clause
specifies exactly which records
you want to retrieve.

Example:

```
SELECT Total FROM invoiceNumbers
WHERE Total > '$100'
```

INSERT

The INSERT statement allows you to
add records to a database. The INSERT
statement uses the INTO clause to specify
the name of the table to which you want
to add a record and the names of the fields
that store the information in the table. The
VALUES clause specifies the field values
that make up the record you are adding.

Example:

```
INSERT INTO invoiceNumbers(INVOICE,TOTAL)
VALUES (12843, '$34.56')
```

DELETE

The DELETE statement is used to
remove records from a database.
The DELETE statement uses the
FROM clause to specify the name
of the table that stores the records
you want to delete. The WHERE
clause contains information that
uniquely identifies the records you
want to delete.

Example:

```
DELETE FROM invoiceNumbers
WHERE year < 1996
```

CREATE A DATA SOURCE NAME

After you have created a database, you must assign a Data Source Name (DSN) to the database.

A DSN stores information that tells Web applications how to access a specific database. You include the data source name in the ASP pages you want to connect to the database.

You only have to create a DSN once for a database. You do not have to create a new name when you change or update the structure of the database.

The data source name must be created on the Web server that stores the database and

the ASP pages that will access the database. If a Web presence provider is hosting your database and ASP pages, the Web presence provider will usually create the DSN for you.

To create a data source name, you specify the driver for the program you used to create the database, such as Microsoft Access or SQL Server. You then specify the DSN you want to use and the location of the database. The data source name does not have to be the same as the name of the database.

The steps below create a system DSN for a Microsoft Access database stored on a Web Server running Windows 2000.

CREATE A DATA SOURCE NAME

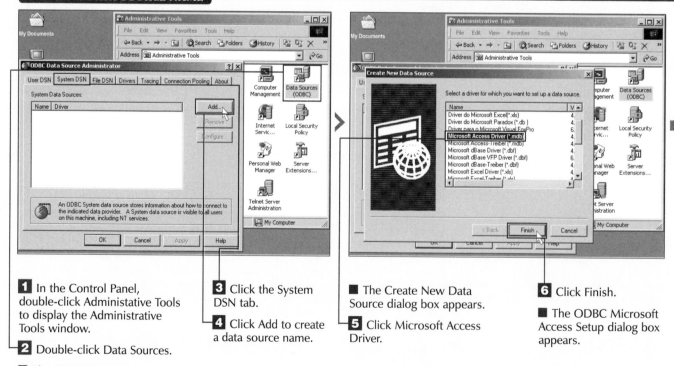

1 In the Control Panel, double-click Administrative Tools to display the Administrative Tools window.

2 Double-click Data Sources.

■ The ODBC Data Source Administrator dialog box appears.

3 Click the System DSN tab.

4 Click Add to create a data source name.

■ The Create New Data Source dialog box appears.

5 Click Microsoft Access Driver.

6 Click Finish.

■ The ODBC Microsoft Access Setup dialog box appears.

Extra

TYPES OF DATA SOURCE NAMES

There are three main types of data source names. The types of data source names differ in where the information about a database is stored and who can use the DSN. The administrator of the Web server usually specifies the type of DSN that must be used.

System DSN

The information in a system DSN is stored in the registry of the Web server. Any user that has access to the server will be able to use a system DSN to access the database.

User DSN

The information in a user DSN is stored in the registry of the Web server, but only a specific user account can use the DSN. User data source names are often used when developing intranet Web applications that require secure access to a database.

File DSN

The information in a file DSN is stored in a text file on the Web server. File data source names make it easy to transfer databases and data source names between different Web servers. Any user that has access to the Web server will be able to use a file DSN to access the database.

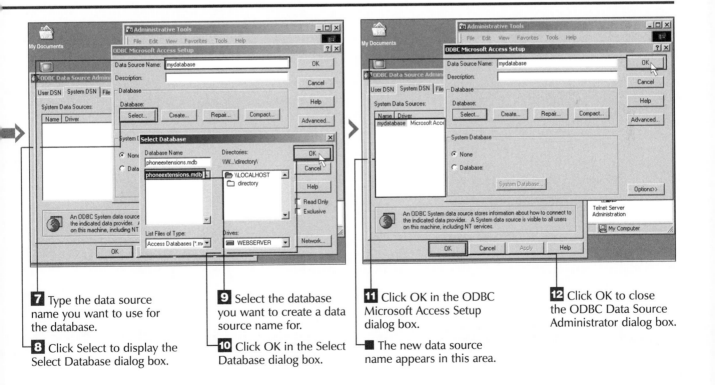

7 Type the data source name you want to use for the database.

8 Click Select to display the Select Database dialog box.

9 Select the database you want to create a data source name for.

10 Click OK in the Select Database dialog box.

11 Click OK in the ODBC Microsoft Access Setup dialog box.

■ The new data source name appears in this area.

12 Click OK to close the ODBC Data Source Administrator dialog box.

CONNECT TO A DATABASE

Once a data source name has been created for a database, you can set up a connection to the database in an ASP page. You can then use the ASP page to access the database.

In order to set up a connection to a database, an instance of the Connection object must be created and assigned a name. You can then use the properties and methods of the Connection object to connect to the database.

You should use the ConnectionTimeout property to specify a timeout setting for the connection. The timeout setting specifies the length of time, in seconds, the Web server

will attempt to open the connection before generating an error.

The Open method is used to specify the data source name of the database you want to open a connection to.

When an ASP page that opens a connection to a database finishes processing, the connection is automatically closed. However, it is good programming practice to use the Close method to explicitly close a database connection in an ASP page. You should then use the Nothing keyword to free up the portion of the Web server's memory that was used by the Connection object.

CONNECT TO A DATABASE

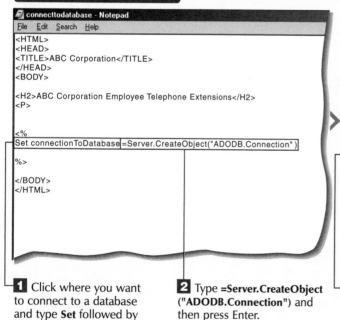

1 Click where you want to connect to a database and type **Set** followed by the name you want to use for this instance of the Connection object.

2 Type **=Server.CreateObject ("ADODB.Connection")** and then press Enter.

3 Type the name for this instance of the Connection object followed by a period (.).

4 Type **ConnectionTimeout=** followed by the number of seconds you want the Web server to attempt to establish a connection. Then press Enter.

Extra

If several of your ASP pages need to access the same database, you may want to place the code that opens the connection to the database in a *Server-Side Include* file. If you later need to make changes to the connection information, the Server-Side Include file will allow you to quickly update the information in all the ASP pages.

You may want to begin the name of an instance of the `Connection` object with `obj`. This can help you differentiate an instance of the object from other code elements, such as variables or functions.

Example:

```
Set objReceiptDatabase=Server.CreateObject("ADODB.Connection")
objReceiptDatabase.ConnectionTimeout=60
objReceiptDatabase.Open "DSN=invoiceNumbers"
```

You can access more than one database in an ASP page by creating multiple instances of the `Connection` object.

Example:

```
Set objClientDatabase=Server.CreateObject("ADODB.Connection")
objClientDatabase.ConnectionTimeout=20
objClientDatabase.Open "DSN=customerInformation"

Set objSalesDatabase=Server.CreateObject("ADODB.Connection")
objSalesDatabase.ConnectionTimeout=40
objSalesDatabase.Open "DSN=salesData"
```

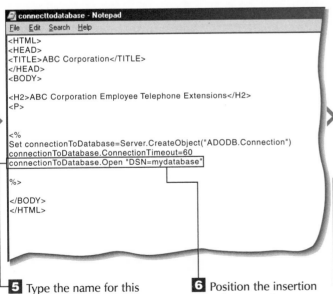

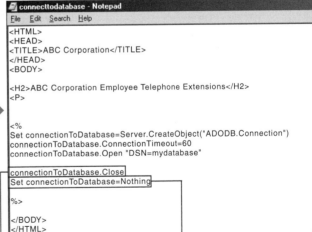

5 Type the name for this instance of the `Connection` object followed by a period (.). Type **Open** "" and then press Enter.

6 Position the insertion point between the quotation marks ("") and type **DSN=** followed by the data source name of the database you want to open a connection to.

7 Click where you want to place the code that closes the connection to the database and type the name for this instance of the `Connection` object followed by a period (.). Type **Close** and then press Enter.

8 To free up the Web server's memory, type **Set** followed by the name for this instance of the `Connection` object and an equal sign (=). Type **Nothing** and then press Enter.

RETRIEVE INFORMATION FROM A DATABASE Using the Execute Method

After setting up a connection to a database in an ASP page, you can use the ASP page to retrieve records from the database. A group of records retrieved from a database is referred to as a recordset.

To create a recordset, you use the Execute method of the Connection object to issue an SQL SELECT statement to the database. The SELECT statement specifies the records you want to retrieve for the recordset and the name of the table in the database that stores the records. An asterisk (*) can be used with the SELECT statement to retrieve all the records from a table.

To access each record in a recordset, you can use code that creates a loop, such as a Do While statement.

You use the EOF (End Of File) property to determine when the last record in the recordset has been accessed.

You must add the MoveNext method to the code that accesses each record in a recordset. The MoveNext method allows the code to move to the next record. For information about other methods that can be used to move through the records in a recordset, see the top of page 195.

To access each field in a record, you can use another loop, such as a For...Next statement. You can determine the total number of fields a record contains using the Count property.

USING THE EXECUTE METHOD

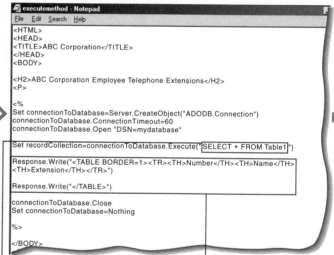

```
executemethod - Notepad
File  Edit  Search  Help
<HTML>
<HEAD>
<TITLE>ABC Corporation</TITLE>
</HEAD>
<BODY>

<H2>ABC Corporation Employee Telephone Extensions</H2>
<P>

<%
Set connectionToDatabase=Server.CreateObject("ADODB.Connection")
connectionToDatabase.ConnectionTimeout=60
connectionToDatabase.Open "DSN=mydatabase"

Set recordCollection =connectionToDatabase.Execute("")

connectionToDatabase.Close
Set connectionToDatabase=Nothing

%>

</BODY>
</HTML>
```

```
executemethod - Notepad
File  Edit  Search  Help
<HTML>
<HEAD>
<TITLE>ABC Corporation</TITLE>
</HEAD>
<BODY>

<H2>ABC Corporation Employee Telephone Extensions</H2>
<P>

<%
Set connectionToDatabase=Server.CreateObject("ADODB.Connection")
connectionToDatabase.ConnectionTimeout=60
connectionToDatabase.Open "DSN=mydatabase"

Set recordCollection=connectionToDatabase.Execute("SELECT * FROM Table1")

Response.Write("<TABLE BORDER=1><TR><TH>Number</TH><TH>Name</TH>
<TH>Extension</TH></TR>")

Response.Write("</TABLE>")

connectionToDatabase.Close
Set connectionToDatabase=Nothing

%>

</BODY>
```

1 Click where you want to retrieve information from a database and type **Set** followed by the name you want to use for the recordset.

2 Type an equal sign (=) and the name for this instance of the Connection object followed by a period (.). Type **Execute("")** and then press Enter.

3 Position the insertion point between the quotation marks ("") and type **SELECT * FROM** followed by the name of the table in the database you want to retrieve information from.

4 Click where you want to place the code that formats the information in the recordset and type the code.

Extra

Instead of using a loop to access each
field in a record, you can use the field
names from the table in the database.

TYPE THIS:

```
Response.Write("<TABLE BORDER=1><TR><TH>Number</TH><TH>Name</TH><TH>Extension</TH></TR>")

Do While Not recordCollection.EOF
    Response.Write("<TR>")
    Response.Write("<TD>" & recordCollection("ID_NUMBER") & "</TD>")
    Response.Write("<TD>" & recordCollection("NAME") & "</TD>")
    Response.Write("<TD>" & recordCollection("EXTENSION") & "</TD>")
    Response.Write("</TR>")
recordCollection.MoveNext
Loop
Response.Write("</TABLE>")
```

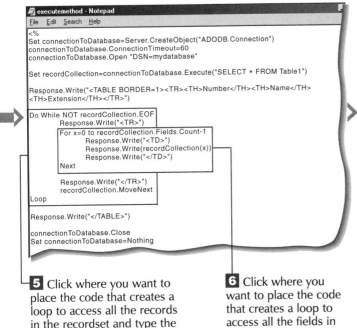

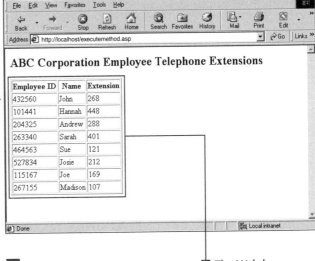

5 Click where you want to
place the code that creates a
loop to access all the records
in the recordset and type the
code.

*Note: To move to the next record in
the recordset each time the loop is
executed, include the* MoveNext
method in the code for the loop.

6 Click where you
want to place the code
that creates a loop to
access all the fields in
each record and type
the code.

7 Display the ASP page
in a Web browser.

■ The Web browser
displays the result of
retrieving information
from a database.

RETRIEVE INFORMATION FROM A DATABASE Using the Recordset Object

The Recordset object can be used to retrieve information from a database once a connection to the database has been established. The Recordset object is useful for working with a large number of records or frequently updating the database.

To use the Recordset object, an instance of the object must be created and assigned a name. You can then use the Open method of the object to issue an SQL SELECT statement to the database. The SELECT statement specifies the records you want to retrieve and the name of the table in the database that stores the

records. The Open method also specifies the name of the connection to the database.

A group of records retrieved from a database is referred to as a recordset. To access each record in a recordset, you can use code that creates a loop, such as a Do While statement. You use the EOF (End Of File) property to determine when the last record in the recordset has been accessed.

To access each field in a record, you can use the field names from the table in the database.

USING THE RECORDSET OBJECT

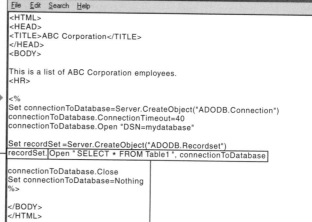

```
recordset - Notepad
File  Edit  Search  Help
<HTML>
<HEAD>
<TITLE>ABC Corporation</TITLE>
</HEAD>
<BODY>

This is a list of ABC Corporation employees.
<HR>

<%
Set connectionToDatabase=Server.CreateObject("ADODB.Connection")
connectionToDatabase.ConnectionTimeout=40
connectionToDatabase.Open "DSN=mydatabase"

Set recordSet =Server.CreateObject("ADODB.Recordset")

connectionToDatabase.Close
Set connectionToDatabase=Nothing
%>

</BODY>
</HTML>
```

```
recordset - Notepad
File  Edit  Search  Help
<HTML>
<HEAD>
<TITLE>ABC Corporation</TITLE>
</HEAD>
<BODY>

This is a list of ABC Corporation employees.
<HR>

<%
Set connectionToDatabase=Server.CreateObject("ADODB.Connection")
connectionToDatabase.ConnectionTimeout=40
connectionToDatabase.Open "DSN=mydatabase"

Set recordSet =Server.CreateObject("ADODB.Recordset")
recordSet.Open " SELECT * FROM Table1 ", connectionToDatabase

connectionToDatabase.Close
Set connectionToDatabase=Nothing
%>

</BODY>
</HTML>
```

■1 Type the code that connects the ASP page to the database. See page 190 to connect to a database.

■2 Click where you want to use the Recordset object to retrieve information from the database and type **Set** followed by the name you want to use for this instance of the Recordset object.

■3 Type **=Server.CreateObject ("ADODB.Recordset")** and then press Enter.

■4 Type the name for this instance of the Recordset object followed by a period (.).

■5 Type **Open** "" followed by a comma (,) and the name for this instance of the Connection object. Then press Enter.

■6 Position the insertion point between the quotation marks ("") and type **SELECT * FROM** followed by the name of the table in the database you want to retrieve information from.

Extra There are several methods of the `Recordset` object that you can use to navigate or move through the records in a recordset. You will have to change the *cursor type* for the recordset to use a method other than `MoveNext`. The cursor type determines how the records in a recordset can be accessed.

METHOD NAME	DESCRIPTION
MoveNext	Moves to the next record in a recordset
MovePrevious	Moves to the previous record in a recordset.
MoveFirst	Moves to the first record in a recordset.
MoveLast	Moves to the last record in a recordset.
Move(2)	Moves forward 2 records in a recordset.
Move(-3)	Moves backward 3 records in a recordset.

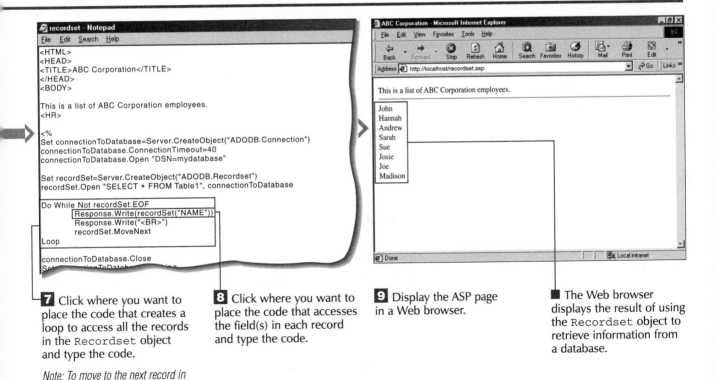

7 Click where you want to place the code that creates a loop to access all the records in the `Recordset` object and type the code.

Note: To move to the next record in the recordset each time the loop is executed, include the `MoveNext` method in the code for the loop.

8 Click where you want to place the code that accesses the field(s) in each record and type the code.

9 Display the ASP page in a Web browser.

■ The Web browser displays the result of using the `Recordset` object to retrieve information from a database.

EDIT A RECORD

Once a recordset has been created, you can edit a record in the recordset. Working with records in a recordset is more efficient than working with records directly in the database.

After you create and name an instance of the `Recordset` object, you use the `Open` method to issue an SQL `SELECT` statement to the database. The `SELECT` statement uses the `FROM` clause to specify the name of the database table that stores the record you want to retrieve and uses the `WHERE` clause to specify exactly which record you want to retrieve.

The `Open` method also specifies the name of the connection to the database, the *cursor type* and

the *lock type*. It is important to specify the correct cursor and lock types. For example, if the cursor type is read-only, your editing changes may generate an error. For information about cursor types, see page 202. For information about lock types, see page 203.

When you have specified all the changes you want to make to a record, the `Update` method is used to save the changes to the database. If the ASP page stops processing due to an error or the Web server is shut down before the `Update` method is processed, the database will not reflect your changes.

EDIT A RECORD

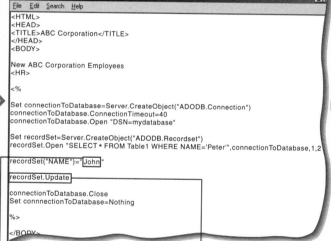

1 Perform steps 1 to 6 on page 194 to connect the ASP page to the database and create an instance of the `Recordset` object.

2 Click where you want to edit a record and type the name for this instance of the `Recordset` object followed by ("")="". Then press Enter.

3 Position the insertion point between the first set of quotation marks ("") and type the name of the field you want to change.

4 Position the insertion point between the second set of quotation marks and type a new value for the field.

5 Click where you want to update the record in the database and type the name for this instance of the `Recordset` object followed by a period(.). Type **Update** and then press Enter.

Extra

You can use the `OriginalValue` property to return a field to its original value. Using the `OriginalValue` property can help prevent invalid information from being added to the database. For example, when updating the NAME field in a database, you can check to make sure the new value for the field is not empty. If the new value is empty, you can use the `OriginalValue` property to recover the original value of the field.

Example:

```
If recordSet("NAME")="" Then
    recordSet("NAME")=recordSet("NAME").OriginalValue
End If
recordSet.Update
```

If multiple users have access to the database, it is good programming practice to use the `Close` method of the `Recordset` object to explicitly close the recordset before closing the connection to the database.

Example:

```
recordSet.Close
connectionToDatabase.Close
Set connnectionToDatabase=Nothing
```

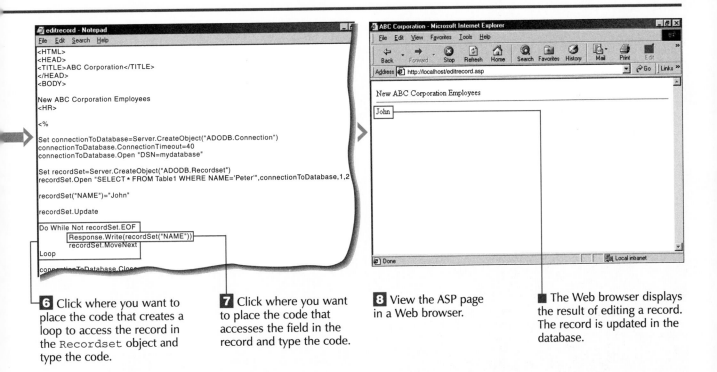

6 Click where you want to place the code that creates a loop to access the record in the `Recordset` object and type the code.

7 Click where you want to place the code that accesses the field in the record and type the code.

8 View the ASP page in a Web browser.

■ The Web browser displays the result of editing a record. The record is updated in the database.

ADD A RECORD

After a connection to a database has been opened, the SQL INSERT statement can be used to add a record to the database.

The SQL INSERT statement is used with the Execute method of the Connection object. The INSERT statement uses the INTO clause to specify the name of the database table you want to add a record to and the names of the fields that store information in the table. The VALUES clause specifies the field values that make up the record you are adding to the database. You may have to enclose the field values in single or double quotation marks, depending on your database program.

It is common programming practice to store an SQL INSERT statement in a variable. Using variables can help make your code easier to read and update.

Forms provide an easy-to-use interface for working with a database and are commonly used to add records. When you create the code for a form that will be used to add records to a database, you must specify the name of the ASP page that will connect to the database and add the record specified in the form.

ADD A RECORD

```
addrecord - Notepad
File  Edit  Search  Help
<HTML>
<HEAD>
<TITLE>ABC Corporation</TITLE>
</HEAD>
<BODY>

<%
frmID_NUMBER=Request.Form("ID_NUMBER")
frmNAME=Request.Form("NAME")
frmEXTENSION=Request.Form("EXT")

Set connectionToDatabase=Server.CreateObject("ADODB.Connection")
connectionToDatabase.ConnectionTimeout=40
connectionToDatabase.Open "DSN=mydatabase"

sqlStatement="INSERT INTO"

connectionToDatabase.Close
Set connectionToDatabase=Nothing
%>

Thank you. <BR>
The record has been added to the database.
<P>
<A HREF="directory.asp">Return to the Home page</A>
```

```
addrecord - Notepad
File  Edit  Search  Help
<HTML>
<HEAD>
<TITLE>ABC Corporation</TITLE>
</HEAD>
<BODY>

<%
frmID_NUMBER=Request.Form("ID_NUMBER")
frmNAME=Request.Form("NAME")
frmEXTENSION=Request.Form("EXT")

Set connectionToDatabase=Server.CreateObject("ADODB.Connection")
connectionToDatabase.ConnectionTimeout=40
connectionToDatabase.Open "DSN=mydatabase"

sqlStatement="INSERT INTO Table1( ID_NUMBER,NAME,EXTENSION ) VALUES ( "&
frmID_NUMBER & "," & frmNAME & "," & frmEXTENSION & " )"

connectionToDatabase.Close
Set connectionToDatabase=Nothing
%>

Thank you. <BR>
The record has been added to the database.
<P>
```

■1 Type the code that accesses information passed by the form users will use to add a record.

■2 Type the code that connects the ASP page to the database. See page 190 to connect to a database.

■3 Click where you want to create a variable name to store the SQL INSERT statement and type the name followed by ="".

■4 Position the insertion point between the quotation marks ("") and type **INSERT INTO**.

■5 Type the name of the table in the database you want to add a record to followed by ( ) **VALUES** ( ).

■6 Position the insertion point between the first set of parentheses ( ) and type the name of each field in the table, separated by a comma.

■7 Position the insertion point between the second set of parentheses and type the code that accesses information passed by the form.

Extra

SQL statements are often very long, which can make your code difficult to read. You can use a space followed by an underscore character (_) to split a long statement and display the statement over several lines. A line that ends with a space and an underscore character and the line that follows are processed as one statement.

Example:

```
sqlStatement= _
"INSERT INTO Table1(ID_NUMBER,NAME,EXTENSION)" & _
"VALUES" & _
"("& frmID_NUMBER & ",'" & frmNAME & "'," & frmEXTENSION & ")"
```

You can also use the `Recordset` object to add a record to a database. After you connect to the database, use the `AddNew` method to add a record and the `Update` method to save the new record to the database.

Example:

```
Set recordSet=Server.CreateObject("ADODB.Recordset")
recordSet.Open "SELECT * FROM Table1",connectionToDatabase,1,2
recordSet.AddNew
recordSet("NAME")="Andrew"
recordSet("ID_NUMBER")="439476"
recordSet("EXTENSION")="526"
recordSet.Update
```

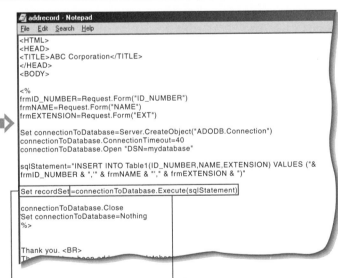

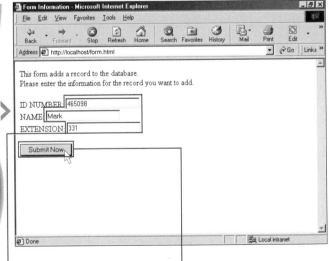

8 Click where you want to retrieve information from a database and type **Set** followed by the name you want to use for the recordset.

9 Type an equal sign (=) and the name for this instance of the `Connection` object followed by a period (.). Type **Execute( )** and then press Enter.

10 Position the insertion point between the parentheses ( ) and type the variable name that stores the SQL `INSERT` statement.

11 Display the form you created to add records to the database in a Web browser.

12 Enter the required information into the form.

13 Click the button that submits the information in the form to the ASP page that will add the record to the database.

■ The contents of the ASP page that adds the record will appear and the record will be added to the database.

DELETE A RECORD

The SQL DELETE statement can be issued from an ASP page to delete a record from a database. The SQL DELETE statement is used with the Execute method of the Connection object.

The DELETE statement uses the FROM clause to specify the name of the database table that stores the record you want to delete. The WHERE clause contains information that uniquely identifies the record. You should be careful when identifying the record you want to delete, as information accidentally deleted from a database often cannot be recovered.

You can have a variable store the SQL DELETE statement. Using variables to store statements is common programming practice and can make your code easier to read.

Many ASP developers create a form to provide an easy-to-use interface for deleting records from a database. In the code for the form, remember to specify the name of the ASP page that will connect to the database and delete the record specified in the form.

DELETE A RECORD

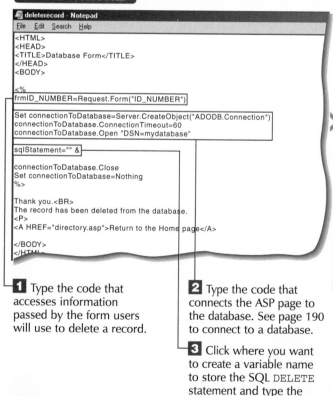

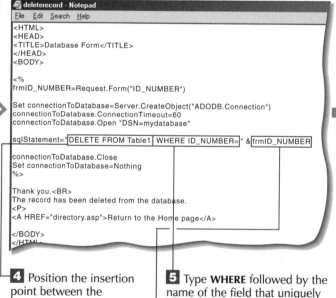

1 Type the code that accesses information passed by the form users will use to delete a record.

2 Type the code that connects the ASP page to the database. See page 190 to connect to a database.

3 Click where you want to create a variable name to store the SQL DELETE statement and type the name followed by **="" &**.

4 Position the insertion point between the quotation marks ("") and type **DELETE FROM** followed by the name of the table that stores the record you want to delete.

5 Type **WHERE** followed by the name of the field that uniquely identifies the record you want to delete and an equal sign (=).

6 Position the insertion point after the ampersand (&) and type the code that accesses information passed by the form.

Extra

If you want to remove all the records from a table at one time, you can use the SQL DELETE statement without including the WHERE clause. This will erase all of the data in the table, but the table will still exist in the database.

Example:

```
sqlStatement="DELETE FROM tblInvoices"
Set Recordset=connectionToDatabase.Execute(sqlStatement)
```

If you want to remove a table from a database, you can use the SQL DROP TABLE command. This will remove the table and all the data stored in the table from the database.

Example:

```
sqlStatement="DROP TABLE tblSales"
Set Recordset=connectionToDatabase.Execute(sqlStatement)
```

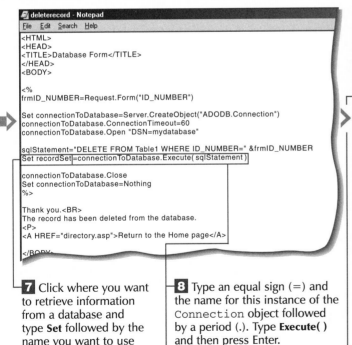

7 Click where you want to retrieve information from a database and type **Set** followed by the name you want to use for the recordset.

8 Type an equal sign (=) and the name for this instance of the Connection object followed by a period (.). Type **Execute( )** and then press Enter.

9 Position the insertion point between the parentheses ( ) and type the variable name that stores the SQL DELETE statement.

10 Display the form you created to delete records from the database in a Web browser.

11 Enter the required information into the form.

12 Click the button that submits the information in the form to the ASP page that will delete the record from the database.

■ The contents of the ASP page that deletes the record will appear and the record will be deleted from the database.

201

SET THE CURSOR TYPE

W hen retrieving records from a database using the Open method of the Recordset object, the cursor type can be set to specify how you want the records to be used. You can allow users to only read records or perform a task such as adding records. The cursor type also determines how users can move through records. For information about moving through records, see the top of page 195.

Each of the four cursor types is represented by a value. The value 0 allows read-only access to records and is the default cursor type. Users can only move forward from the current record using this cursor type.

The value 1 allows read and write access to records. Users can add, delete and edit records but not view changes made by others while the recordset is open. Users can move forward and backward through records using this cursor type.

The value 2 allows read and write access to records as well as forward and backward movement through records. This cursor type also allows users to view changes made by others while the recordset is open.

The value 3 allows read-only access but users can move forward and backward through records with this cursor type.

SET THE CURSOR TYPE

```
cursortype - Notepad
File  Edit  Search  Help
<HTML>
<HEAD>
<TITLE>Database</TITLE>
</HEAD>
<BODY>

<%

Set connectionToDatabase=Server.CreateObject("ADODB.Connection")
connectionToDatabase.ConnectionTimeout=40
connectionToDatabase.Open "DSN=mydatabase"

Set recordSet=Server.CreateObject("ADODB.Recordset")
recordSet.Open "SELECT * FROM Table1", connectionToDatabase

connectionToDatabase.Close
Set connectionToDatabase=Nothing

%>

</BODY>
</HTML>
```

```
cursortype - Notepad
File  Edit  Search  Help
<HTML>
<HEAD>
<TITLE>Database</TITLE>
</HEAD>
<BODY>

<%

Set connectionToDatabase=Server.CreateObject("ADODB.Connection")
connectionToDatabase.ConnectionTimeout=40
connectionToDatabase.Open "DSN=mydatabase"

Set recordSet=Server.CreateObject("ADODB.Recordset")
recordSet.Open "SELECT * FROM Table1", connectionToDatabase, 1

connectionToDatabase.Close
Set connectionToDatabase=Nothing

%>

</BODY>
</HTML>
```

1 Perform steps 1 to 6 on page 194 to connect the ASP page to the database and create an instance of the Recordset object.

2 Position the insertion point after the name for this instance of the Connection object and type a comma (,) followed by the cursor type value you want to use.

■ You can now specify a lock type for the recordset. See page 203 to specify a lock type.

SET THE LOCK TYPE

When a database is stored on a Web server, several users may be accessing the database at the same time. If several users attempt to change the same record at once, only one user's changes will be accepted by the database. The other users' changes may be ignored. To prevent this problem, you can set the lock type for the recordset. You must use the Open method of the Recordset object to create a recordset you want to set the lock type for.

Each of the four lock types is represented by a value. The lock type you should set

depends on the number of users accessing the database and the tasks they are performing.

The value 1 allows read-only access and is the default lock type. The value 2 locks the record a user is editing. The value 3 locks the record a user is updating. The value 4 locks multiple records when a user performs a batch update of records.

Setting the lock type affects the performance of a database. While a record is locked by one user, other users will have to wait until the record is unlocked to access the record.

SET THE LOCK TYPE

```
locktype - Notepad
File  Edit  Search  Help
<HTML>
<HEAD>
<TITLE>Database</TITLE>
</HEAD>
<BODY>

<%

Set connectionToDatabase=Server.CreateObject("ADODB.Connection")
connectionToDatabase.ConnectionTimeout=40
connectionToDatabase.Open "DSN=mydatabase"

Set recordSet=Server.CreateObject("ADODB.Recordset")
recordSet.Open "SELECT * FROM Table1", connectionToDatabase, 1

connectionToDatabase.Close
Set connectionToDatabase=Nothing

%>

</BODY>
</HTML>
```

```
locktype - Notepad
File  Edit  Search  Help
<HTML>
<HEAD>
<TITLE>Database</TITLE>
</HEAD>
<BODY>

<%

Set connectionToDatabase=Server.CreateObject("ADODB.Connection")
connectionToDatabase.ConnectionTimeout=40
connectionToDatabase.Open "DSN=mydatabase"

Set recordSet=Server.CreateObject("ADODB.Recordset")
recordSet.Open "SELECT * FROM Table1", connectionToDatabase, 1, 2

connectionToDatabase.Close
Set connectionToDatabase=Nothing

%>

</BODY>
</HTML>
```

1 Perform steps 1 and 2 on page 202 to connect the ASP page to the database, create an instance of the Recordset object and specify a cursor type.

2 Position the insertion point after the cursor type value and type a comma (,) followed by the lock type value you want to use.

■ You can now create the code for the task you want to perform on the records in the database.

USING THE COUNTERS COMPONENT

There are many aspects of a Web site that you may want to track using a counter, such as the number of people accessing a file or the number of times a form has been processed. The Counters component allows you to create a Counters object that you can use to create, store and manipulate all the counters for your ASP pages.

Once a counter is created, any of your ASP pages stored on the Web server can access the counter.

You can use the Increment method on an ASP page to increase the value of a counter by 1 each time the method is processed. If you use the

Increment method with a counter that has not yet been created, the counter will be automatically created with a starting value of 1.

The Get method retrieves the current value of a counter. This allows you to use or display the value of the counter in an ASP page. If you use the Get method with a counter that has not yet been created, the counter will be automatically created with a starting value of 0.

If you want to count Web page hits, you can use the Page Counter component. For information about the Page Counter component, see page 206.

USING THE COUNTERS COMPONENT

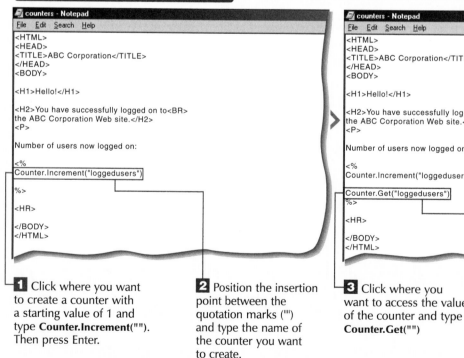

■1 Click where you want to create a counter with a starting value of 1 and type **Counter.Increment("")**. Then press Enter.

■2 Position the insertion point between the quotation marks ("") and type the name of the counter you want to create.

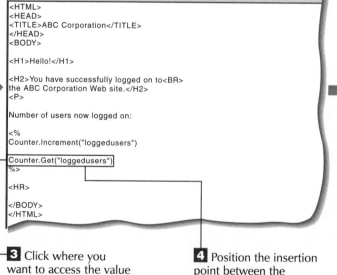

■3 Click where you want to access the value of the counter and type **Counter.Get("")**

■4 Position the insertion point between the quotation marks ("") and type the name of the counter whose value you want to access.

Extra

Most Web servers automatically create the `Counters` object for you. If the `Counters` object is not available to your ASP pages, create the *Global.asa* file containing the following code and place the file in the root directory of the Web server.

TYPE THIS:

```
<OBJECT RUNAT="Server" SCOPE="Application"
ID="Counter" PROGID="MSWC.Counters">
</OBJECT>
```

The information used by the `Counters` object is stored in a file called Counters.txt, which is usually found in the \system32\inetsrv\Data folder in the Windows operating system folder. You can open the file to see the name and current value of each counter being used on the Web server, but you should not modify any information in the file.

The `Set` method is used to change the value of an existing counter. When the value of a counter is changed, the new value will be used by any page on the Web server that accesses the counter. You can also use the `Set` method to create a counter with a specific starting value.

TYPE THIS:

```
Counter.Set "users", 98
```

Removing a counter that is no longer needed frees up resources on the Web server, allowing the server to operate more efficiently. If a counter that has been removed is later accessed using either the `Set` or `Get` methods, the counter will be recreated on the server.

TYPE THIS:

```
Counter.Remove("users")
```

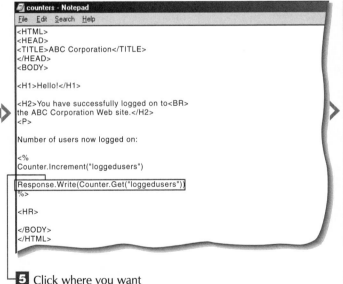

5 Click where you want to place the code that executes the `Counter.Get` statement and type the code.

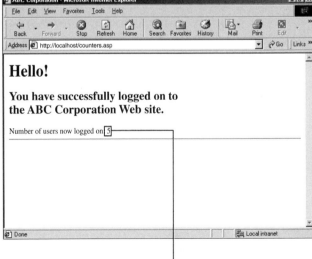

6 Display the ASP page in a Web browser.

■ The Web browser displays the result of using the Counters component. The value of the counter will increase by 1 each time the counter is incremented.

USING THE PAGE COUNTER COMPONENT

There are many components available that can be used to enhance and add functionality to a Web site. The Page Counter component is used to track the number of times ASP pages are viewed, or *hit*.

To use the Page Counter component, you create an instance of the component in an ASP page and then use various methods to access and manipulate the data in the component.

The PageHit method is used to increase the number of hits for an ASP page by one each time the page is opened or refreshed. The PageHit method should

be used on every ASP page you want to keep track of the number of hits for.

The Hits method is used to access and display the number of hits a page has received. The Hits method is read-only, which means you cannot manually modify the value it returns.

Unlike other methods of tracking ASP page visits, the Page Counter component is able to keep track of the number of page hits even when the Web server is restarted. The component periodically records the number of hits in a text file stored on the Web server. The text file is not erased when the server is restarted.

USING THE PAGE COUNTER COMPONENT

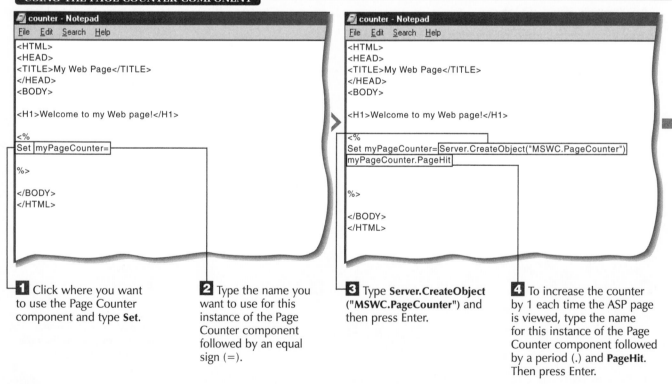

1 Click where you want to use the Page Counter component and type **Set**.

2 Type the name you want to use for this instance of the Page Counter component followed by an equal sign (=).

3 Type **Server.CreateObject ("MSWC.PageCounter")** and then press Enter.

4 To increase the counter by 1 each time the ASP page is viewed, type the name for this instance of the Page Counter component followed by a period (.) and **PageHit**. Then press Enter.

Extra

You can view the text file on the Web server where the Page Counter component records the number of hits for your ASP pages. By default, the file is called HitCnt.cnt and is stored in the WINNT\system32\inetsrv\Data folder.

Example of the HitCnt.cnt File

5	/sales/contacts.asp
14	/sales/default.asp
67	/resources/default.asp
93	/login/join.asp

You can adjust the hit count of ASP pages in a Web site by editing the HitCnt.cnt file on the Web server. When editing the HitCnt.cnt file, you must be careful not to alter the structure of the file inadvertently, such as adding or deleting a line of text.

You can change the name and location of the HitCnt.cnt file by altering the Web server's registry. The Page Counter component information is stored in the HKEY_CLASSES_ROOT\MSWC.PageCounter key.

You can change the frequency with which the Page Counter component records page count information in the HitCnt.cnt file on the Web server. In the registry of the server, display the Page Counter component information. The File_Location value indicates the number of hits that must be received before the HitCnt.cnt file will be updated.

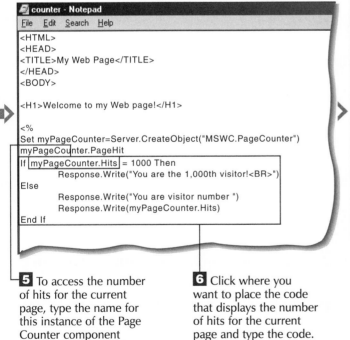

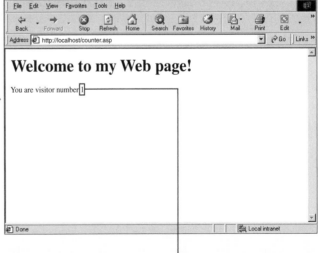

5 To access the number of hits for the current page, type the name for this instance of the Page Counter component followed by a period (.) and **Hits**.

6 Click where you want to place the code that displays the number of hits for the current page and type the code.

7 Display the ASP page in a Web browser.

■ The Web browser displays the result of using the Page Counter component. The counter will increase each time the page is opened or refreshed.

USING THE CONTENT ROTATOR COMPONENT Create the Content Schedule File

The Content Rotator component makes it easy to include content that changes each time an ASP page is viewed. You can use the component to rotate through HTML content such as a collection of quotations, hyperlinks or pictures. You can even use the component to rotate through different backgrounds for an ASP page.

Before you can use the Content Rotator component, you must create a text file referred to as the Content Schedule file. This file contains the sections of content you want to rotate through on the ASP page. The Content Schedule

file can only contain HTML code. The file cannot contain Active Server Pages code.

A line containing two percentage signs (%%) must separate each section of HTML content in the Content Schedule file.

You can include a text description of each section of HTML content you create. The description will not be visible to a user displaying the ASP page in a Web browser, but other people working with the Content Schedule file may find the description useful.

CREATE THE CONTENT SCHEDULE FILE

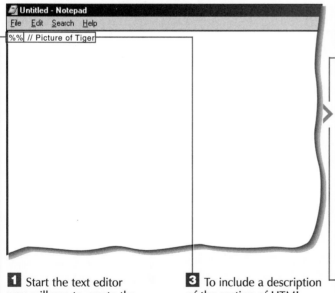

1 Start the text editor you will use to create the Content Schedule file.

2 To begin a section of HTML content you want to include in an ASP page, type **%%**.

3 To include a description of the section of HTML content, type **//** followed by the description. Then press Enter.

4 Type the HTML code you want to use to create the section of content. Then press Enter.

■ The content can consist of text, HTML formatting, images and hyperlinks.

Extra

You can use a weight number to specify how often you want a section of HTML content to be displayed compared to the other sections. For example, a section of content with a weight of 10 will be displayed twice as many times as a section of content with a weight of 5 and 10 times more than a section of content with a weight of 1. The weight number is assigned by placing a pound character (#) and the weight number after the percentage signs for the HTML content. By default, each section of content has a weight of 1.

Example:

```
%% #5 // Red quote
<FONT COLOR="red">
Absence makes the heart grow fonder.
</FONT>

%% #3 // Blue quote
<FONT COLOR="blue">
An apple a day keeps the doctor away.
</FONT>
```

You can include content in the Content Schedule file that you do not want to display in an ASP page. This is useful if you want to include HTML code in the file for use at a later time. To prevent content from appearing in an ASP page, give the content a weight number of 0.

You can include more than one line of description text for each section of HTML content. You must begin each line of description text with the %% // characters.

Example:

```
%% // Link to www.maran.com
%% // A great source for computer books
Try the <A HREF="http://www.maran.com">
maranGraphics</A> Web site!
```

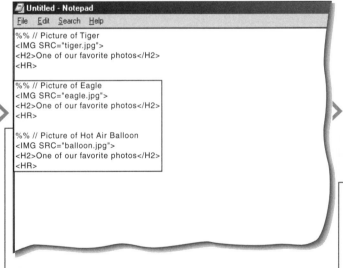

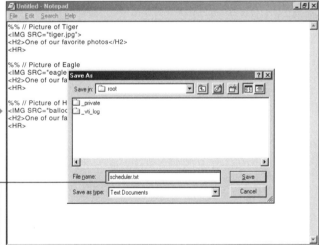

5 Repeat steps 2 to 4 for each section of HTML content you want to include.

6 Save the file on the Web server with the .txt extension.

■ You can now use the Content Rotator component to include the HTML content in an ASP page.

CONTINUED ▶

USING THE CONTENT ROTATOR COMPONENT Using the ContentRotator Object

Once the Content Schedule file has been created, the `ContentRotator` object can be used in an ASP page. This allows the ASP page to access and display a section of HTML content stored in the Content Schedule file. A different section of content will be displayed each time the ASP page is opened or refreshed.

The `ContentRotator` object randomly selects a section of HTML content from the Content Schedule file for display in a Web browser. There is no way to control which section of code will

be selected. The frequency with which each section of content is selected depends on the weight number assigned to each section. If a section is assigned a high weight number compared to other sections of content, the section may be displayed several times in a row.

To use the `ContentRotator` object, you must assign a name to this instance of the object. You then use a `Response.Write` statement with the `ChooseContent` method to display a section of HTML content on the screen.

USING THE CONTENTROTATOR OBJECT

rotator - Notepad
File Edit Search Help

```
<HTML>
<HEAD>
<TITLE>Photographer of the Month</TITLE>
</HEAD>
<BODY>

<%
Set rotating =Server.CreateObject("MSWC.ContentRotator")

%>

<H2>Photographer of the Month</H2>
Our Photographer of the Month, Jim Gray, has been taking pictures
ever since he purchased his first camera as a teenager.
<P>Since then, his work has been featured in hundreds of newspapers and doz
magazines.</P>
<P>Although he carries his camera everywhere and enjoys photographing anyth
sees, his favorites subjects are people.</P>
<P>&quot;People interest me a great deal,&quot; says Gray. &quot;I like to cap
emotions in my photographs and hopefully my pictures will tell a story.&quot;
```

rotator - Notepad
File Edit Search Help

```
<HTML>
<HEAD>
<TITLE>Photographer of the Month</TITLE>
</HEAD>
<BODY>

<%
Set rotating=Server.CreateObject("MSWC.ContentRotator")
    Response.Write(rotating.)
%>

<H2>Photographer of the Month</H2>
Our Photographer of the Month, Jim Gray, has been taking pictures
ever since he purchased his first camera as a teenager.
<P>Since then, his work has been featured in hundreds of newspapers and doz
magazines.</P>
<P>Although he carries his camera everywhere and enjoys photographing anyth
sees, his favorites subjects are people.</P>
<P>&quot;People interest me a great deal,&quot; says Gray. &quot;I like to cap
emotions in my photographs and hopefully my pictures will tell a story.&quot;
```

1 Click where you want to display changing HTML content and type **Set** followed by the name you want to use for this instance of the `ContentRotator` object.

2 Type **=Server.CreateObject ("MSWC.ContentRotator")** and then press Enter.

3 Press Tab to indent the code you will type.

4 Type **Response.Write()** and then press Enter.

5 Position the insertion point between the parentheses ( ) and type the name for the instance of the `ContentRotator` object followed by a period(.).

Extra

If the Content Schedule file is stored in the same directory as the ASP page that will display the content, the `ChooseContent` method only needs to specify the name of the file. If the file and the ASP page are stored in different directories, the `ChooseContent` method must also include the name of the directory that stores the Content Schedule file.

Example:

```
Response.Write(rotating.ChooseContent("/newfiles/scheduler.txt"))
```

You can use the `GetAllContent` method of the Content Rotator component to display all the sections of HTML content in the Content Schedule file at once. Each section of content is separated by a horizontal rule. You do not need to use the `Response.Write` statement when using the `GetAllContent` method.

TYPE THIS:

```
<%
Set rotating=Server.CreateObject("MSWC.ContentRotator")
    rotating.GetAllContent("quotes.txt")
%>
```

RESULT:

Absence makes the heart grow fonder.

An apple a day keeps the doctor away.

Don't cry over spilled milk.

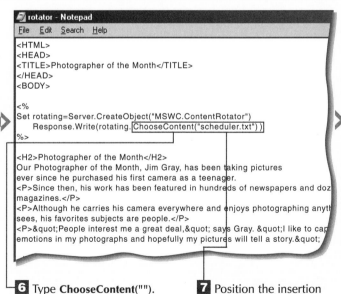

6 Type **ChooseContent("")**.

7 Position the insertion point between the quotation marks ("") and type the name of the Content Schedule file.

8 Display the ASP page in a Web browser.

■ The Web browser displays the result of using the Content Rotator component. A different section of HTML content will appear each time the page is opened or refreshed.

USING THE AD ROTATOR COMPONENT

Many Web sites display advertisements in order to generate revenue. An advertisement is usually an image. When a user clicks the image, the advertiser's Web page is displayed in the user's Web browser.

The Ad Rotator component makes it easy to incorporate advertisements into an ASP page. A different advertisement appears each time the ASP page is opened or refreshed.

Before you can use the Ad Rotator component, you must create a Redirection file. When an advertisement is clicked by a user, the name

of the advertisement and the URL associated with the advertisement are passed to the Redirection file in the form of a query string. The Redirection file then sends the user to the advertiser's Web page.

After creating the Redirection file, the Rotator Schedule file can be created. The Rotator Schedule file consists of two sections. The first section contains information about how the images for each advertisement should be displayed. You can specify the width, height and border thickness you want to use for all the images.

CREATE THE REDIRECTION FILE

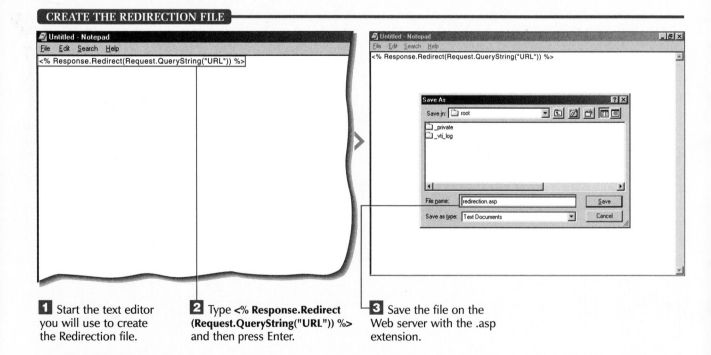

1 Start the text editor you will use to create the Redirection file.

2 Type **<% Response.Redirect (Request.QueryString("URL")) %>** and then press Enter.

3 Save the file on the Web server with the .asp extension.

Extra

You may want to include additional code in the Redirection file, such as code that keeps track of how many times an advertisement is clicked. You can then save this information to a database. This is useful for determining how successful an advertisement is and can help you set advertising rates for your ASP pages. If you choose to include additional code in the Redirection file, make sure the code is not long, as it may negatively affect the performance of the Web site.

When users access your ASP pages and click on the advertisements, information such as the user's IP number, the date and time and the URL of the advertiser's Web page is stored in the Web server's log file. There are many third-party applications that can be used to review and analyze the information in the log file to help you improve your ASP pages and the advertisements. One of the most popular log analysis tools is WebTrends, which is available at the www.webtrends.com/products/Log/default.htm Web site.

CREATE THE ROTATOR SCHEDULE FILE

■1 Start the text editor you will use to create the Rotator Schedule file.

2 Type **REDIRECT** followed by the name of the Redirection file on the Web server. Then press Enter.

3 Type **WIDTH** followed by the width you want each advertisement to display, in pixels. Then press Enter.

4 Type **HEIGHT** followed by the height you want each advertisement to display, in pixels. Then press Enter.

5 Type **BORDER** followed by the thickness of the border you want each advertisement to display, in pixels. Then press Enter.

CONTINUED ▶

USING THE AD ROTATOR COMPONENT

An asterisk (*) separates the first section of the Rotator Schedule file from the second section of the file. The first section consists of information that applies to every advertisement displayed on an ASP page. The second section provides specific information about each advertisement.

You must provide the name of an advertisement you want to display on an ASP page. To have the advertisement display another page when clicked, you must include the URL of the page you want to be displayed.

Some users have Web browsers that cannot display images, while others turn off the display of images to browse the Web more quickly. You can provide text that will be displayed if an advertisement does not appear on an ASP page. This will give users who do not see images information about the missing advertisement.

Each advertisement is assigned a weight number to specify how often the advertisement should appear on an ASP page compared to other advertisements. For example, an advertisement with a weight of 3 will be displayed 30 percent of the time, whereas an advertisement with a weight of 6 will be displayed 60 percent of the time. The weight number can be any whole number between 0 and 10000.

CREATE THE ROTATOR SCHEDULE FILE (CONTINUED)

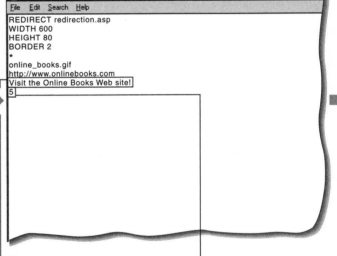

6 Type an asterisk (*) and then press Enter.

7 Type the name of an advertisement you want to display on an ASP page and then press Enter.

8 Type the URL of the page you want to display when a user clicks the advertisement and then press Enter.

9 Type the text you want to display if a user's Web browser does not support images and then press Enter.

10 Type a number that represents how often you want the advertisement to be displayed compared to other advertisements. Then press Enter.

Extra

If the Rotator Schedule file is stored in the same directory as the advertisements, you only need to specify the name of the advertisement in the Rotator Schedule file, such as advert1.gif. If the advertisements are stored in different directories, you must also include the name of the directory, such as \Ads\advert1.gif, or the entire path for the advertisement, such as http://www.abccorp.com/Ads/advert1.gif.

You must ensure that the combined weight number of all the advertisements listed in the Rotator Schedule file does not exceed 10000. If the combined weight is higher than this number, an error message will appear the first time the Rotator Schedule file is accessed by an ASP page.

The Ad Rotator component can also be used to display simple images. To display an image that is not a hyperlink, enter a dash (-) below the name of the image in the Rotator Schedule file instead of a URL.

Example:

```
\Ads\advert1.gif
-
Coming Soon
20
```

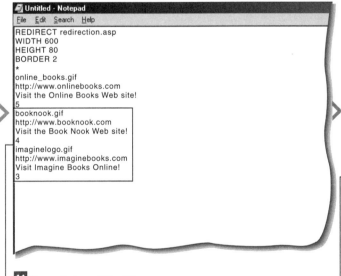

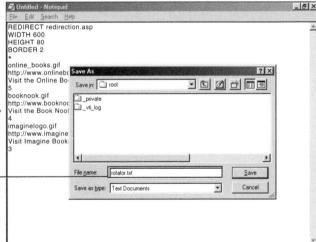

11 Repeat steps 7 to 10 for each advertisement you want to include in an ASP page.

12 Save the file on the Web server with the .txt extension.

■ You can now use the AdRotator object to include the advertisements in an ASP page.

CONTINUED ▶

USING THE AD ROTATOR COMPONENT

O nce the Redirection and Rotator Schedule files have been created, you can use the Ad Rotator component to create an `AdRotator` object, which will insert advertisements into an ASP page. This allows the ASP page to access and display an advertisement listed in the Rotator Schedule file. A different advertisement will be displayed each time the ASP page is opened or refreshed.

The `AdRotator` object randomly selects an advertisement from the Rotator Schedule file for display in a Web browser. The frequency with which each advertisement is selected depends on the weight number assigned to each advertisement. If an advertisement is assigned a high weight

number compared to other advertisements, the advertisement may be displayed several times in a row.

To use the `AdRotator` object, you must assign a name to this instance of the object. You then use a `Response.Write` statement with the `GetAdvertisement` method to display an advertisement on the screen.

When the `GetAdvertisement` method is used, the `AdRotator` object generates HTML code to display the advertisement. The HTML code consists of the `<IMG>` tag and the `<A HREF>` tag. The width, height and border settings specified in the Rotator Schedule file are included in the `<IMG>` tag.

USING THE ADROTATOR OBJECT

```
ads - Notepad
File  Edit  Search  Help
<HTML>
<HEAD>
<TITLE>The Online Book Club</TITLE>
</HEAD>
<BODY>

<%
Set advertisement =Server.CreateObject("MSWC.AdRotator")

%>

<HR>
<H2>Book of the Month</H2>
Our Book of the Month, The Journey Home, is written by renowned author, <B>Jim
<BR>Ever since he published his first book 25 years ago, Gray's work has won him
literary awards.
<P>His writing is humorous, uplifting and insightful.</P>
<P>&quot;I really try to portray the characters in my novels as realistically as possi
says Gray. &quot;When people are finished reading one of my books, I want them to
though they really got to know the characters.&quot;</P>

</BODY>
</HTML>
```

```
ads - Notepad
File  Edit  Search  Help
<HTML>
<HEAD>
<TITLE>The Online Book Club</TITLE>
</HEAD>
<BODY>

<%
Set advertisement=Server.CreateObject("MSWC.AdRotator")
Response.Write(advertisement.)

%>

<HR>
<H2>Book of the Month</H2>
Our Book of the Month, The Journey Home, is written by renowned author, <B>Jim
<BR>Ever since he published his first book 25 years ago, Gray's work has won him
literary awards.
<P>His writing is humorous, uplifting and insightful.</P>
<P>&quot;I really try to portray the characters in my novels as realistically as possi
says Gray. &quot;When people are finished reading one of my books, I want them to
though they really got to know the characters.&quot;</P>

</BODY>
</HTML>
```

1 Click where you want to display an advertisement and type **Set** followed by the name you want to use for this instance of the `AdRotator` object.

2 Type **=Server.CreateObject ("MSWC.AdRotator")** and then press Enter.

3 Type **Response.Write()** and then press Enter.

4 Position the insertion point between the parentheses ( ) and type the name for this instance of the `AdRotator` object followed by a period (.).

Extra

You can use the `Clickable` property to turn off the feature of the `AdRotator` object that makes advertisements hyperlinks. This allows you to test the appearance of the advertisements on an ASP page without affecting any counters you have set up.

TYPE THIS:

```
Set advertisement=Server.CreateObject("MSWC.AdRotator")
advertisement.Clickable=FALSE
Response.Write(advertisement.GetAdvertisement("page_ads.txt"))
```

If an ASP page uses frames, you can use the `TargetFrame` property of the `AdRotator` object to place advertisements in specific frames.

TYPE THIS:

```
Set advertisement=Server.CreateObject("MSWC.AdRotator")
advertisement.TargetFrame=MainFrame
Response.Write(advertisement.GetAdvertisement("page_ads.txt"))
```

You can use multiple advertisements from one Rotator Schedule file with a single instance of the `AdRotator` object. This allows you to place advertisements at both the top and bottom of an ASP page.

TYPE THIS:

```
Set advertisement=Server.CreateObject("MSWC.AdRotator")
Response.Write(advertisement.GetAdvertisement("page_ads.txt"))
Response.Write("<P>")
Response.Write(advertisement.GetAdvertisement("page_ads.txt"))
```

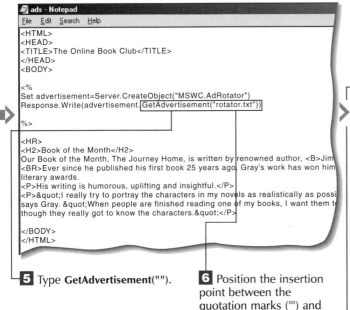

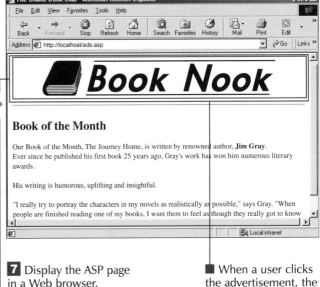

5 Type **GetAdvertisement("")**.

6 Position the insertion point between the quotation marks ("") and type the name of the Rotator Schedule file.

7 Display the ASP page in a Web browser.

■ The Web browser displays the result of using the Ad Rotator component. A different advertisement will appear each time the page is opened or refreshed.

■ When a user clicks the advertisement, the advertiser's Web page will appear on the screen.

USING THE MYINFO COMPONENT

The MyInfo component allows you to create a `MyInfo` object that can be used to define and store information about your Web site, such as the administrator's name and telephone number or the company's name and address. Once the `MyInfo` object is created, any of your ASP pages stored on the Web server can access the information in the object.

The information in the `MyInfo` object is stored in a file named Myinfo.xml on the Web server. The file is created when information is first assigned to the `MyInfo` object.

Using the `MyInfo` object to define and store information is useful for organizations that have more than one person administering their Web sites. For example, in a large corporation where each department has its own Web server, the `MyInfo` object allows the administrator of each server to store their own personal information. The same ASP page, which accesses and displays the personal information for the server's administrator, can be saved on each Web server. This allows the corporation's ASP developer to create a single ASP page to display administrator information, instead of having to create a specific ASP page for each Web server.

ASSIGN INFORMATION TO THE MYINFO OBJECT

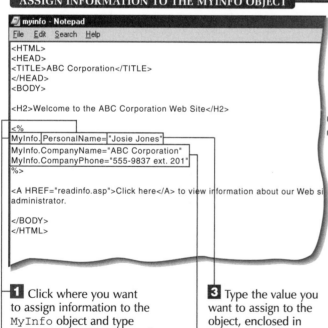

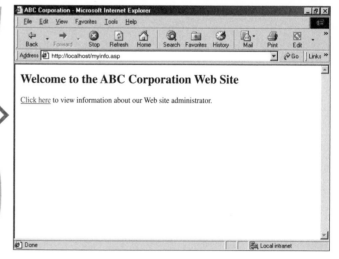

■1 Click where you want to assign information to the `MyInfo` object and type **MyInfo** followed by a period (.).

■2 Type the name of the property you want to use to assign information to the object, followed by an equal sign (=).

■3 Type the value you want to assign to the object, enclosed in quotation marks ("").

■ You can repeat steps 1 to 3 for each value you want to assign to the object.

■4 Display the ASP page in a Web browser.

■ The Web browser displays the contents of the ASP page. The information you assigned to the `MyInfo` object is now saved in the Myinfo.xml file on the Web server.

■ You can now use the information in the `MyInfo` object in other ASP pages in your Web site.

Extra

Most Web servers automatically create the `MyInfo` object for you. If the `MyInfo` object is not available to your ASP pages, create the *Global.asa* file containing the following code and place the file in the root directory of the Web server.

Although there are predefined properties for the `MyInfo` object, it is possible to create custom properties you can use to store information in the Myinfo.xml file. To create a custom property, simply assign a value to a property name that describes the information you want to store.

TYPE THIS:

```
<OBJECT RUNAT="Server" SCOPE="Application"
ID="MyInfo" PROGID="MSWC.MyInfo">
</OBJECT>
```

Example:

```
<%
MyInfo.Gender = "Male"
Response.Write(MyInfo.Gender)
%>
```

COMMONLY USED PROPERTIES

Personal
MyInfo.PersonalName
MyInfo.PersonalAddress
MyInfo.PersonalPhone
MyInfo.PersonalMail
MyInfo.PersonalWords

Company
MyInfo.CompanyName
MyInfo.CompanyAddress
MyInfo.CompanyPhone
MyInfo.CompanyDepartment
MyInfo.CompanyWords

Home
MyInfo.HomeOccupation
MyInfo.HomePeople
MyInfo.HomeWords

School
MyInfo.SchoolName
MyInfo.SchoolAddress
MyInfo.SchoolPhone
MyInfo.SchoolDepartment
MyInfo.SchoolWords

Organization
MyInfo.OrganizationName
MyInfo.OrganizationAddress
MyInfo.OrganizationPhone
MyInfo.OrganizationWords

Community
MyInfo.CommunityName
MyInfo.CommunityLocation
MyInfo.CommunityPopulation
MyInfo.CommunityWords

URLs
MyInfo.URL(n)
MyInfo.URLWords(n)

Miscellaneous
MyInfo.PageType
MyInfo.Style
MyInfo.Background
MyInfo.Title
MyInfo.Guestbook
MyInfo.Messages

CONTINUED

USING THE MYINFO COMPONENT

You can use an ASP page to access and display information stored in the MyInfo object. You can also delete information you no longer need from the MyInfo object.

The Myinfo.xml file is created when the first value is assigned to the MyInfo object and is usually found in the \system32\inetsrv\Data folder in the Windows operating system folder on the Web server. You can open the Myinfo.xml file in a text editor to see the current value of each property that has been assigned information.

You cannot rename the Myinfo.xml file on the Web server. Only one Myinfo.xml file can be used on a Web server, so it is not possible to have multiple Myinfo.xml files for different sites or virtual directories on a server.

You cannot remove information from the MyInfo object using an ASP page. To remove information from the MyInfo object, you must open the Myinfo.xml file in a text editor and delete the information you no longer want the object to store. The Web server should be stopped before you edit the Myinfo.xml file.

ACCESS INFORMATION IN THE MYINFO OBJECT

```
readinfo - Notepad
File   Edit   Search   Help
<HTML>
<HEAD>
<TITLE>ABC Corporation</TITLE>
</HEAD>
<BODY>

<H2>Welcome to the ABC Corporation Web Site</H2>

<H3>Web Site Administrator Page</H3>

<%
Response.Write("Administrator Name: ")
Response.Write( MyInfo. PersonalName  & "<BR>")

Response.Write("Administrator's Telephone Number: ")
Response.Write(MyInfo.CompanyPhone & "<BR>")
%>

<HR>
Thank you for visiting the ABC Corporation Web site.

</BODY>
</HTML>
```

ABC Corporation - Microsoft Internet Explorer

Address http://localhost/readinfo.asp

Welcome to the ABC Corporation Web Site

Web Site Administrator Page

Administrator Name: Josie Jones
Administrator's Telephone Number: 555-9837 ext. 201

Thank you for visiting the ABC Corporation Web site.

■1 Click where you want to access information in the MyInfo object and type **MyInfo** followed by a period (.).

■2 Type the name of the property that stores the value you want to access and then press Enter.

■3 Click where you want to place the code that executes the MyInfo statement and type the code.

■ You can repeat steps 1 to 3 for each value you want to access.

■4 Display the ASP page in a Web browser.

■ The Web browser displays the result of accessing information in the MyInfo object.

Extra

The Myinfo.xml file may not be created or updated immediately after you assign information to the `MyInfo` object. You will be able to immediately access the information in the object using an ASP page, but if you want to open the Myinfo.xml file on the Web server to display the information, you may first have to restart the server. You may also have to restart the server before any changes you make in the Myinfo.xml file will take effect.

When accessing information in the `MyInfo` object, the ASP page will display an empty string if the property you specify does not exist in the object. The ASP page will not generate an error message.

The Myinfo.xml file is created using code written to XML standards. Similar to HTML, XML stores values in tags, which indicate the name of the value. You can find more information about the XML language and its standards at the www.w3.org/TR/REC-xml.html Web site.

DELETE INFORMATION FROM THE MYINFO OBJECT

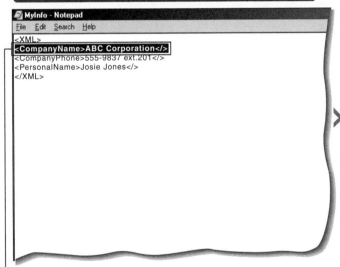

1 Stop the Web server and open the Myinfo.xml file in a text editor.

2 Select the line containing the value you want to remove.

3 Press Delete to remove the value from the `MyInfo` object.

■ You can repeat steps 2 and 3 for each value you want to remove.

4 Save the Myinfo.xml file and then restart the Web server.

USING THE BROWSER CAPABILITIES COMPONENT

One of the difficulties faced by people building ASP pages is the vast range of Web browsers that may be used to view a page, because each type of browser can display pages differently. Fortunately, the Browser Capabilities component can be used to determine the features of a Web browser accessing an ASP page. Once the features of a Web browser have been determined, the content of the ASP page can be tailored to that specific browser.

The Browser Capabilities component allows you create a BrowserType object. When a Web browser requests a page from a Web server, the browser sends the server a header that describes

the browser. The BrowserType object compares the information in the header to the information in the *browscap.ini* file to identify the browser. When the browser is identified, you can access the properties of the BrowserType object in your ASP page to determine the capabilities of the browser and then adjust the content of the page accordingly.

It is important to note that while the Browser Capabilities component can be used to determine if a browser is capable of a certain feature, such as cookies, it does not determine whether the user has that feature enabled.

USING THE BROWSER CAPABILITIES COMPONENT

capabilities - Notepad
File Edit Search Help
```
<HTML>
<HEAD>
<TITLE>ABC Corporation</TITLE>
</HEAD>
<BODY>

<%
Set browser=Server.CreateObject("MSWC.BrowserType")

%>

</BODY>
</HTML>
```

capabilities - Notepad
File Edit Search Help
```
<HTML>
<HEAD>
<TITLE>ABC Corporation</TITLE>
</HEAD>
<BODY>

<%
Set browser=Server.CreateObject("MSWC.BrowserType")

browser.Frames
%>

</BODY>
</HTML>
```

1 Click where you want to use the Browser Capabilities component and type **Set** followed by the name you want to use for this instance of the BrowserType object.

2 Type **=Server.CreateObject ("MSWC.BrowserType")** and then press Enter.

3 Click where you want to access a property of the BrowserType object and type the name for the instance of the BrowserType object followed by a period (.).

4 Type the name of the property you want to access and then press Enter.

Extra

There are several properties of the BrowserType object that you can access to find specific information about a user's Web browser.

BROWSERTYPE OBJECT PROPERTIES	DESCRIPTION
ActiveXControls	Determines if the browser supports ActiveX controls.
Backgroundsounds	Determines if the browser supports background sounds.
Beta	Determines if the browser is beta software.
Browser	Returns the name of the browser.
Cookies	Determines if the browser supports cookies.
Frames	Determines if the browser supports frames.
Javaapplets	Determines if the browser supports Java applets.
Javascript	Determines if the browser supports JavaScript.
Platform	Returns the name of the user's operating system.
Tables	Determines if the browser supports tables.
Vbscript	Determines if the browser supports VBScript.
Version	Returns the version number of the browser.

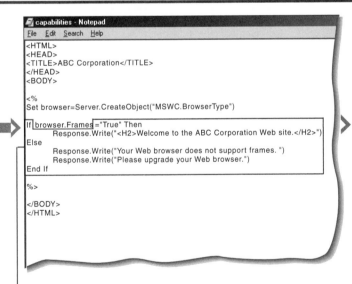

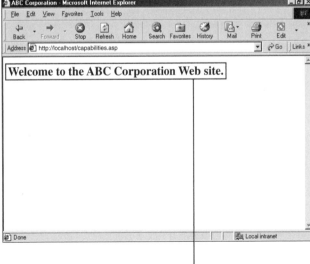

5 Click where you want to place the code that executes the property of the BrowserType object you specified and type the code.

6 Display the ASP page in a Web browser.

■ The Web browser displays the result of using the Browser Capabilities component.

CONTINUED ▶

USING THE BROWSER CAPABILITIES COMPONENT Edit The Browscap.ini File

The Browser Capabilities component uses the browscap.ini file to identify a Web browser that accesses an ASP page. The browscap.ini file stores information about the capabilities of many types of Web browsers.

The browscap.ini file is usually found in the \system32\inetsrv\Data folder in the Windows operating system folder on the Web server. You can open the browscap.ini file in a text editor to view and edit the information in the file.

The browscap.ini file is broken into sections. Typically, a major version of a browser, such as Internet Explorer 5 or Netscape Navigator 4,

is contained in a section of the file. Each section has smaller sub-sections that provide details about the minor versions of the browser, such as Internet Explorer 5.01 or Netscape Navigator 4.3.

A minor version of a Web browser will often have the parent property, which specifies which major version the minor version is based on. When adding information for a minor version of a browser to the browscap.ini file, you can use the parent property to avoid including every property for the browser. You simply specify the information that is different from the parent version. If a browser does not have a parent property, you must specify all the properties for the browser.

EDIT THE BROWSCAP.INI FILE

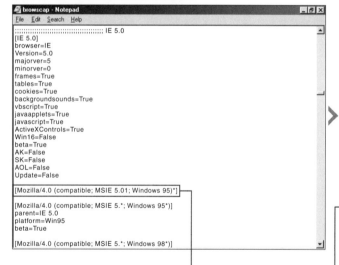

1 Open the browscap.ini file in a text editor.

2 Click where you want to include information about a new Web browser version in the browscap.ini file and type the title for the new section.

Note: The title of the section must match the text that is sent by the Web browser in the header.

3 Type the information you want to specify for the browser.

■ Each property and value must be typed on its own line in the file.

Extra

The header sent by the Web browser when requesting a page is usually stored in the server log on the Web server. You may want to check the header entries in the server log periodically to ensure that the browscap.ini file is still recognizing the most popular Web browsers used to access your ASP pages.

Instead of constantly updating your version of the browscap.ini file, you can download the most up-to-date version of the file from the Web. Visit the www.cyscape.com/browscap Web site to obtain the latest version of the browscap.ini file.

There are third-party programs you can use to find even more information about a Web browser accessing your ASP page. For example, the BrowserHawk program allows you to determine which capabilities a user has disabled for a Web browser. For information about BrowserHawk, visit the www.cyscape.com Web site.

The last section of the browscap.ini file usually stores the default information. If the header sent by a Web browser does not match any of the entries in the browscap.ini file, the information in the default section will be used. If no default value has been specified for a property, the property will return a value of unknown to the ASP page.

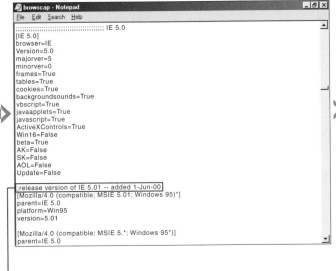

4 To add a comment to the file, type a semi-colon (;) and then type the comment you want to add.

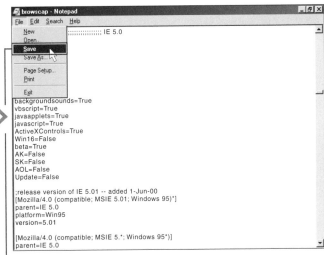

5 Save the browscap.ini file and then close the file.

■ The information you added to the browscap.ini file can now be used when you use the Browser Capabilities component in your ASP pages.

USING THE CONTENT LINKING COMPONENT Create the Content Linking List File

Many Web sites contain pages that are accessed sequentially, similar to pages in a book. Instruction manuals, news articles and long stories are common examples of information that can be spread over many sequential Web or ASP pages.

One of the problems associated with creating a collection of sequential Web or ASP pages is that if a page is added or removed, the navigation links in the other pages and the table of contents must also be updated. To avoid these time-consuming tasks, the Content Linking

component can be used to create an easy-to-update list of pages in a collection.

The first step in using the Content Linking component is to create the Content Linking List file. The Content Linking List file contains the file name of each Web or ASP page to be accessed, in order, and a description of each page. The Content Linking component uses this list to access the pages from another ASP page. Any navigation links or tables of contents created using the Content Linking component will be automatically updated when you modify the information in the Content Linking List file.

CREATE THE CONTENT LINKING LIST FILE

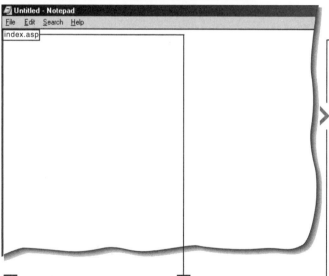

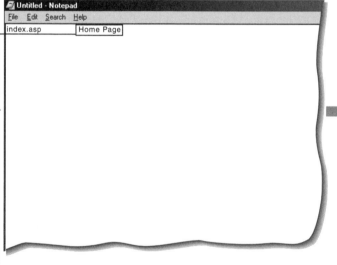

1 Start the text editor you will use to create the Content Linking List file.

2 Type the name of the first page you want to include in the collection.

3 To include a description of the page, press Tab and type the description. Then press Enter.

Extra

You can enter comments into the Content Linking List file if you wish. Comments can provide additional information to help you identify individual pages in a large collection of Web and ASP pages. Be careful not to start a new line when entering a long comment line. Each entry in the Content Linking List file must be contained in one line. After typing the file name and description, press Tab and then type the comments for the page.

Example:

```
page1.html    Page one of my story      My childhood
page2.html    Page two of my story      Needs more work
page3.html    Page three of my story    Stories about school
page4.html    Page four of my story     My first job
```

You cannot use an absolute URL to identify a Web or ASP page you want to include in the Content Linking List file. For example, the URL `http://www.abccorp.com/page1.html` will not be accepted by the Content Linking component.

If the Web or ASP page you want to include in the Content Linking List file is not located in the same directory as the ASP page that will use the Content Linking component, you must specify the name of the directory that stores the page.

Example:

`/myWebpages/page1.html`

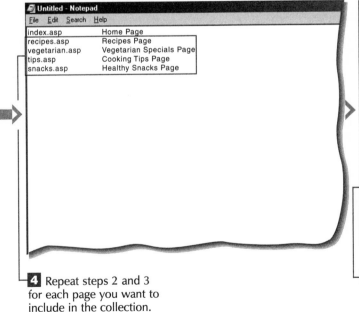

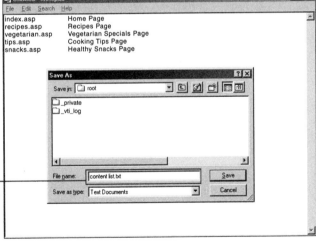

4 Repeat steps 2 and 3 for each page you want to include in the collection.

5 Save the file on the Web server with the .txt extension.

■ You can now use the Content Linking component to access the collection of pages in the Content Linking List file.

CONTINUED ▶

USING THE CONTENT LINKING COMPONENT Create a Table of Contents

O nce the Content Linking List file has been created, the Content Linking component can be used to access the information about the Web or ASP pages in the list. For example, you can use the information about the pages to create a table of contents for the Web site.

The Content Linking component allows you to create a NextLink object. You use the GetNthURL and GetNthDescription methods of the NextLink object to retrieve the names and descriptions of pages in the Content Linking List file.

To create a table of contents that lists each page from the Content Linking List file, you must create a loop that cycles through the list and accesses the names and descriptions of each page.

Entries in the Content Linking List file are numbered sequentially, beginning with the number 1. When using the GetNthURL and GetNthDescription methods, you must specify the name of the Content Linking List file and the number of the entry you want to access or the variable that represents the position of each entry in the list.

CREATE A TABLE OF CONTENTS

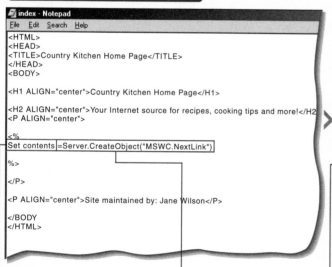

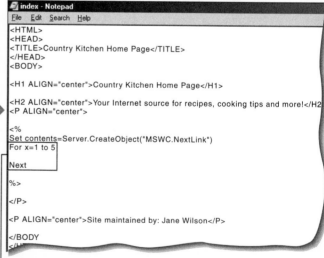

1 Click where you want to use the Content Linking component and type **Set** followed by the name you want to use for this instance of the NextLink object.

2 Type **=Server.CreateObject ("MSWC.NextLink")** and then press Enter.

3 Click where you want to create a table of contents and type the code that creates a loop to cycle through the pages in the Content Linking List file.

Extra

When working with an unknown number of entries in the Content Linking List file, you can use the `GetListCount` method to determine the exact number of entries in the list.

Example:

```
For x=1 to contents.GetListCount("content list.txt")
    Response.Write(contents.GetNthURL("content list.txt",x))
    Response.Write(contents.GetNthDescription("content list.txt",x))
Next
```

You can use HTML table formatting to neatly display the table of contents in an ASP page. Include the `<TABLE>`, `<TD>` and `<TR>` tags to format the information.

Example:

```
<TABLE BORDER="1">
<%
Set contents=Server.CreateObject("MSWC.NextLink")
For x=1 to 5
    Response.Write("<TR><TD>")
    Response.Write(contents.GetNthURL("content list.txt",x))
    Response.Write("</TD><TD>")
    Response.Write(contents.GetNthDescription("content list.txt",x))
    Response.Write("</TD></TR>")
Next
%>
</TABLE>
```

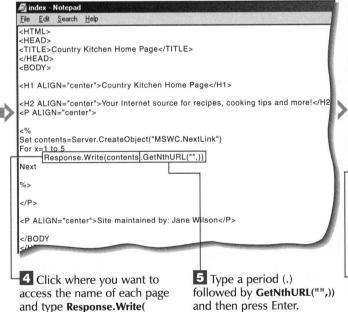

4 Click where you want to access the name of each page and type **Response.Write(** followed by the name for this instance of the `NextLink` object.

5 Type a period (.) followed by **GetNthURL("",))** and then press Enter.

6 Position the insertion point between the quotation marks ("") and type the name of the Content Linking List file.

7 Position the insertion point after the comma (,) and type the variable that represents the position of each page in the list.

CONTINUED ▶

229

USING THE CONTENT LINKING COMPONENT Create a Table of Contents (Continued)

The Content Linking component is most useful when it is used to create a collection of hyperlinks to the Web or ASP pages in the Content Linking List file. The collection of hyperlinks creates a linkable table of contents for the Web site.

Creating a table of contents that displays links to each page listed in the Content Linking List file involves carefully combining the HTML <A> tag with the information retrieved from the list using the Content Linking component. Typically, the

information retrieved with the GetNthURL method is used as the target of the link. The information retrieved with the GetNthDescription method is used as the text of the link.

When using Active Server Pages code to produce HTML code, quotation marks (") cannot be used as other characters can. To produce quotation marks with ASP code, such as in a Response.Write statement, you must use the string function Chr(34).

CREATE A TABLE OF CONTENTS (CONTINUED)

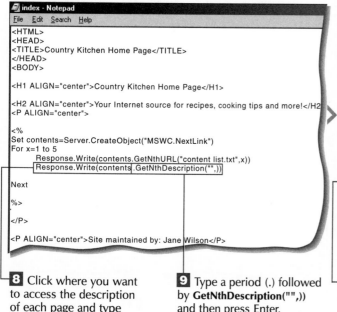

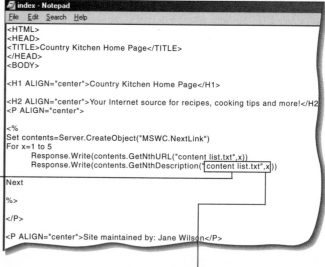

8 Click where you want to access the description of each page and type **Response.Write(** followed by the name for this instance of the NextLink object.

9 Type a period (.) followed by **GetNthDescription("",))** and then press Enter.

10 Position the insertion point between the quotation marks (**""**) and type the name of the Content Linking List file.

11 Position the insertion point after the comma (,) and type the variable that represents the position of each page in the list.

Apply It

When using Active Server Pages code to create an HTML link, you may want to use the short form of the `Response.Write` statement to access the information in the Content Linking List file. Placing the code between the `<%=` and `%>` delimiters may make the code easier to understand and work with.

TYPE THIS:

```
<%
Set contents=Server.CreateObject("MSWC.NextLink")
For x=1 to 5
%>

<A HREF="<%=contents.GetNthURL("content list.txt",x)%>">
<%=contents.GetNthDescription("content list.txt",x)%>
</A>
<BR>

<% Next %>
```

RESULT:

Home Page
Recipes Page
Vegetarian Specials Page
Cooking Tips Page
Healthy Snacks Page

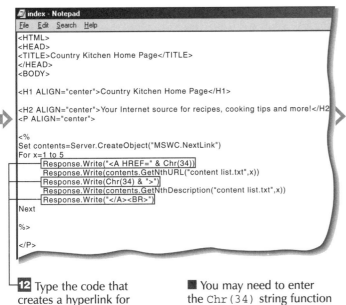

```
index - Notepad
File  Edit  Search  Help
<HTML>
<HEAD>
<TITLE>Country Kitchen Home Page</TITLE>
</HEAD>
<BODY>

<H1 ALIGN="center">Country Kitchen Home Page</H1>

<H2 ALIGN="center">Your Internet source for recipes, cooking tips and more!</H2>
<P ALIGN="center">

<%
Set contents=Server.CreateObject("MSWC.NextLink")
For x=1 to 5
      Response.Write("<A HREF=" & Chr(34))
      Response.Write(contents.GetNthURL("content list.txt",x))
      Response.Write(Chr(34) & ">")
      Response.Write(contents.GetNthDescription("content list.txt",x))
      Response.Write("</A><BR>")
Next

%>

</P>
```

Country Kitchen Home Page - Microsoft Internet Explorer

Address http://localhost/index.asp

Country Kitchen Home Page

Your Internet source for recipes, cooking tips and more!

Home Page
Recipes Page
Vegetarian Specials Page
Cooking Tips Page
Healthy Snacks Page

Site maintained by: Jane Wilson

■2 Type the code that creates a hyperlink for each page.

■ You may need to enter the `Chr(34)` string function to create quotation marks within a `Response.Write` statement.

■3 Display the ASP page in a Web browser.

■ The Web browser displays the result of using the Content Linking component to create a linkable table of contents.

CONTINUED ▶

USING THE CONTENT LINKING COMPONENT   Create Navigation Links

Another powerful feature of the Content Linking component is the ability to create navigation links on an ASP page listed in the Content Linking List file. Navigation links allow readers to easily move backwards and forwards through the ASP pages in the Web site.

Creating navigation links without using the Content Linking component can be difficult and time-consuming because you must always keep the order of the pages in mind. If the order of the pages changes, you must recreate all the navigation links to reflect the change. However, the Content

Linking component allows you to use the Content Linking List file to keep track of the order of the pages and update the navigation links automatically when the order of the pages changes.

To create a link to the previous page in a sequence of pages, you use the GetPreviousURL method, which retrieves the URL of the page preceding the current ASP page in the Content Linking List file. Similarly, the GetNextURL method allows you to retrieve the location of the next page in the Content Linking List file.

CREATE NAVIGATION LINKS

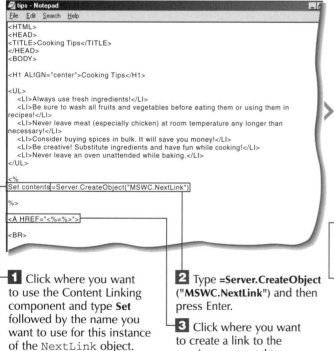

1 Click where you want to use the Content Linking component and type **Set** followed by the name you want to use for this instance of the NextLink object.

2 Type **=Server.CreateObject ("MSWC.NextLink")** and then press Enter.

3 Click where you want to create a link to the previous page and type **<A HREF="<%=%>">** and then press Enter.

4 Position the insertion point between the <%= and %> delimiters and type the name for this instance of the NextLink object. Type a period (.) followed by **GetPreviousURL("")**.

5 Position the insertion point between the quotation marks ("") and type the name of the Content Linking List file.

Extra

You can use images for the navigation links in your Web site. Images for navigation links are available at many Web sites, including www.bycarel.com/buttons and www.station4.com/buttonfactory. To use an image for a navigation link, you must include the `<IMG SRC>` tag in the code.

Example:

```
<A HREF="<%=contents.GetNextURL("content list.txt")%>">
<IMG SRC="nextbutton.gif"></A>
```

You can use the `GetPreviousDescription` or `GetNextDescription` methods to display the description of a page from the Content Linking List file as the text for a navigation link.

Example:

```
<A HREF="<%=contents.GetNextURL("content list.txt")%>">
<%=contents.GetNextDescription("content list.txt")%></A>
```

The `GetListIndex` method and `GetListCount` method can be used to inform users of where they are in your Web site. The `GetListIndex` method returns the entry number of the current page. The `GetListCount` method returns the total number of entries in the Content Linking List file.

Example:

```
You are reading page
<%=contents.GetListIndex("content list.txt")%>
of
<%=contents.GetListCount("content list.txt")%>
pages.
```

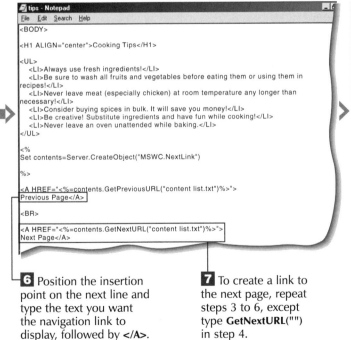

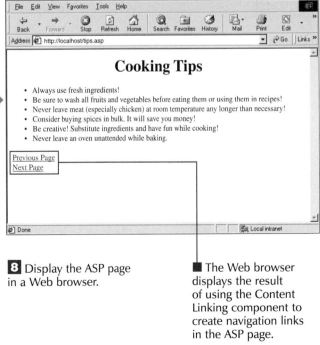

6 Position the insertion point on the next line and type the text you want the navigation link to display, followed by **</A>**. Then press Enter.

7 To create a link to the next page, repeat steps 3 to 6, except type **GetNextURL("")** in step 4.

8 Display the ASP page in a Web browser.

■ The Web browser displays the result of using the Content Linking component to create navigation links in the ASP page.

USING THE PERMISSION CHECKER COMPONENT

You can use the security measures provided by the Web server software and operating system to restrict access to a file on the server. You can then use the Permission Checker component in an ASP page to determine whether a user accessing the page has permission to access the file.

File permissions are based on the login name of the user who is accessing the Web server.

File restrictions are typically only feasible on Web servers that are accessed by users on an intranet. Users accessing a Web server on an intranet have

a unique login name and belong to a specific group or groups. Different access permissions may be assigned to different groups.

The Permission Checker component allows you to create a `PermissionChecker` object. You use the `HasAccess` method of the `PermissionChecker` object to determine whether a user has permission to access a file on the Web server.

The Permission Checker component can be used only on Web servers running Microsoft Internet Information Server (IIS) 5.0.

USING THE PERMISSION CHECKER COMPONENT

```
permission - Notepad
File  Edit  Search  Help
<HTML>
<HEAD>
<TITLE>ABC Corporation</TITLE>
</HEAD>
<BODY>

<H2>You have successfully logged on to<BR>
the ABC Corporation Web site.</H2>
<P>

<%
Set objPchecker=Server.CreateObject("MSWC.PermissionChecker")
%>

</BODY>
</HTML>
```

```
permission - Notepad
File  Edit  Search  Help
<HTML>
<HEAD>
<TITLE>ABC Corporation</TITLE>
</HEAD>
<BODY>

<H2>You have successfully logged on to<BR>
the ABC Corporation Web site.</H2>
<P>

<%
Set objPchecker=Server.CreateObject("MSWC.PermissionChecker")
objPchecker.HasAccess(" \News\index.txt ")
%>

</BODY>
</HTML>
```

1 Click where you want to use the Permission Checker component and type **Set** followed by the name you want to use for this instance of the `PermissionChecker` object.

2 Type **=Server.CreateObject ("MSWC.PermissionChecker")** and then press Enter.

3 Click where you want to check a user's permission to access a file and type the name for this instance of the `PermissionChecker` object followed by a period (.).

4 Type **HasAccess("")** and then press Enter.

5 Position the insertion point between the quotation marks ("") and type the path of the file for which you want to check a user's permission.

Extra

You can assign the `HasAccess` method to a variable to make your code easier to read and update.

Example:

```
<%
Set objPchecker=Server.CreateObject("MSWC.PermissionChecker")
grantAccess=objPchecker.HasAccess("\News\index.txt")

If grantAccess="True" Then
    Response.Write("You have access to the file.")
Else
    Response.Write("Sorry, access forbidden.")
End If
%>
```

The Permission Checker component can be used to determine if a user has permission to access a file located within the folder structure of the Web server or in a folder located outside the folder structure of the server. Care should be taken when allowing users access to files located outside the folder structure of the Web server.

To check user permissions for a file located in the folder structure of the Web server, type:

```
grantAccess=objPchecker.HasAccess("/home/Web pages/public/index.html")
```

To check user permissions for a file located outside the folder structure of the Web server, type:

```
grantAccess=objPchecker.HasAccess("C:\work\files\data.txt")
```

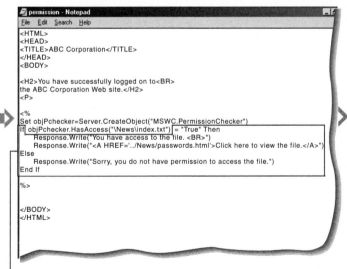

6 Click where you want to place the code that executes the `PermissionChecker` object and type the code.

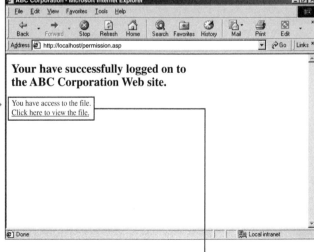

7 Display the ASP page in a Web browser.

■ The Web browser displays the result of using the Permission Checker component.

235

USING THE TOOLS COMPONENT
Check If A File Exists

The Tools component allows you to create the Tools object. The FileExists method of the Tools object allows you to determine whether a file you want to work with on the Web server exists. If the file exists, the FileExists method returns the value -1. The value 0 is returned if the file does not exist.

If the file you want to check the existence of is not located in the same directory as the ASP page that executes the FileExists method, you must specify the name of the directory that stores the file.

It is good programming practice to verify whether a file you want your ASP page to access exists before trying to use the file. Checking the existence of a file allows the ASP page to take a course of action other than simply generating an error in the event the file does not exist. For example, an ASP page can execute the FileExists method for a database before attempting to open a connection to the database. If the database exists, the ASP page can proceed to connect to the database. If the database does not exist, the ASP page can perform an action such as displaying a message that provides users with further instructions or sending users to another ASP page.

CHECK IF A FILE EXISTS

```
checkforfile - Notepad
File  Edit  Search  Help
<HTML>
<HEAD>
<TITLE>Databases</TITLE>
</HEAD>
<BODY>

Checking if the database exists on the Web server.<P>

<%
Set utilities=Server.CreateObject("MSWC.Tools")

%>

</BODY>
</HTML>
```

```
checkforfile - Notepad
File  Edit  Search  Help
<HTML>
<HEAD>
<TITLE>Databases</TITLE>
</HEAD>
<BODY>

Checking if the database exists on the Web server.<P>

<%
Set utilities=Server.CreateObject("MSWC.Tools")
utilities.FileExists("inventory.mdb")

%>

</BODY>
</HTML>
```

1 Click where you want to use the Tools component and type **Set** followed by the name you want to use for this instance of the Tools object.

2 Type **=Server.CreateObject ("MSWC.Tools")** and then press Enter.

3 Click where you want to check if a file exists and type the name for this instance of the Tools object followed by a period (.).

4 Type **FileExists("")** and then press Enter.

5 Position the insertion point between the quotation marks ("") and type the name of the file you want to check the existence of.

Apply It

If the file you want to work with on the Web server is an ASP file, you can use the `Server.Execute` statement to have the Web server process the file after determining it exists. When the Web server finishes processing the file, the server returns to the original ASP page and continues to process the page. For example, an ASP page could check for a file that displays current news bulletins. If the file exists, the server will process the file to display the current news bulletins and then continue processing the original ASP page. If the file has been deleted from the server because the news is no longer current, the rest of the original ASP page will still be processed.

TYPE THIS:

```
Checking for current news bulletins.<P>
<%
Set utilities=Server.CreateObject("MSWC.Tools")

If utilities.FileExists("news.asp")=-1 Then
    Server.Execute("news.asp")
Else
    Response.Write("There are no news bulletins today.")
End If
%>
<P> Please remember to check for news bulletins
on a regular basis.
```

RESULT:

Checking for current news bulletins.

There are no news bulletins today.

Please remember to check for news bulletins on a regular basis.

6 Click where you want to place the code that executes the `FileExists` method of the `Tools` object and type the code.

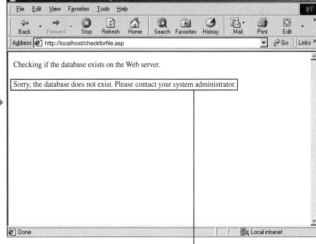

7 Display the ASP page in a Web browser.

■ The Web browser displays the result of checking if a file exists.

CONTINUED ▶

USING THE TOOLS COMPONENT
Generate a Random Number

Random numbers can be used as unique file names or to create values that instruct an ASP page to pause for varying lengths of time. Although it may seem relatively simple, one of the most difficult tasks in computer programming is generating a truly random number.

Any formula used to generate random numbers could easily produce the same set of random numbers each time the computer is restarted.

If a program is used to generate random numbers based on the date and time, any of the random numbers generated could be repeated by simply adjusting the computer's clock.

The Tools component allows you to create a Tools object. The Random method of the Tools object is used to generate a truly random number between -32768 and 32767. Using the Random method saves you from having to create your own code to generate a truly random number.

GENERATE A RANDOM NUMBER

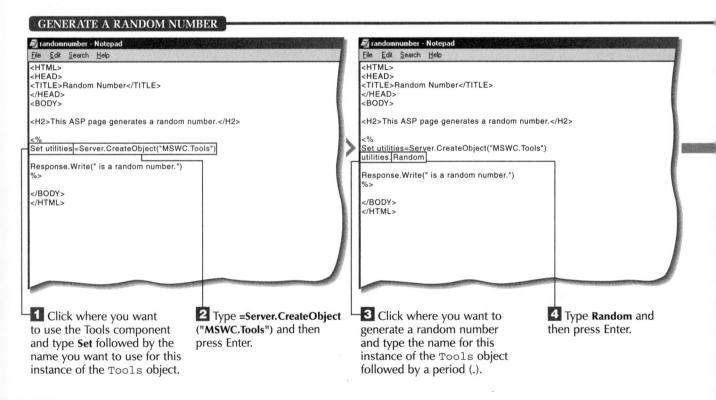

1 Click where you want to use the Tools component and type **Set** followed by the name you want to use for this instance of the Tools object.

2 Type **=Server.CreateObject ("MSWC.Tools")** and then press Enter.

3 Click where you want to generate a random number and type the name for this instance of the Tools object followed by a period (.).

4 Type **Random** and then press Enter.

Extra

Using a variable to store code, such as the `Random` method, is common programming practice and can make your code easier to read.

Example:

```
randomNum=utilities.Random
```

To generate a random number outside the range of -32768 and 32767, you can multiply random numbers using the VBScript multiplication operator (*).

Example:

```
largeRandomNum=utilities.Random *
utilities.Random
```

If you require a positive random number, you can use the VBScript Abs function to convert a negative number returned by the `Random` method to a positive number. If the number returned by the `Random` method is already positive, the `Abs` function will have no effect on the number.

Example:

```
positiveRandomNum=Abs(utilities.Random)
```

The VBScript `Mod` operator can be used to generate a random number between the negative and positive of a specific number.

To generate a random number between -10 and 10, type

```
randomNumber=utilities.Random Mod 10
```

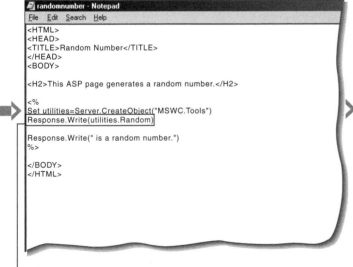

5 Click where you want to place the code that executes the `Random` method of the `Tools` object and type the code.

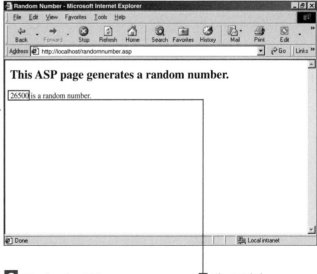

6 Display the ASP page in a Web browser.

■ The Web browser displays the result of generating a random number.

CONTINUED ▶

USING THE TOOLS COMPONENT
Process a Form

T he ProcessForm method of the Tools object can be used to process information submitted by a form or a query string and then save the result in a file on the Web server.

To use the ProcessForm method, you must first create a template file. The template file contains the information you want to save to a file, which can include text and ASP code, such as code that processes information from a form or a query string.

Any Active Server Pages code enclosed in the <% and %> delimiters will be placed in the file without being processed in the template file. This is useful

if the file will be used to create an ASP page. ASP code you want to be processed in the template file must be enclosed in the <%% and %%> delimiters. The template file is saved with the .asp extension.

After you create the template file, you use the Tools component to create an instance of the Tools object in an ASP page. You then use the ProcessForm method to specify the name of the file you want to create on the Web server and the name of the template file. The file is automatically created in the directory that stores the template file and the ASP page that executes the ProcessForm method.

CREATE A TEMPLATE FILE

```
template - Notepad
File  Edit  Search  Help
The form was submitted by:

<%%
Response.Write(Request.Form("firstName") & " ")
Response.Write(Request.Form("lastName") & " ")
Response.Write(Request.Form("clientID"))
%%>
```

PROCESS A FORM

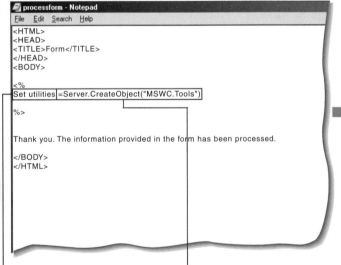

```
processform - Notepad
File  Edit  Search  Help
<HTML>
<HEAD>
<TITLE>Form</TITLE>
</HEAD>
<BODY>

<%
Set utilities =Server.CreateObject("MSWC.Tools")

%>

Thank you. The information provided in the form has been processed.

</BODY>
</HTML>
```

1 Start the text editor you will use to create the template file.

2 Type the text you want to save to a file on the Web server.

3 Type **<%%**. Press Enter twice and then type **%%>**.

4 Click between the <%% and %%> delimiters and type the ASP code you want to use to process information from a form or a query string.

5 Save the file on the Web server with the .asp extension.

1 Display the code for the ASP page you want to process a form in a text editor.

2 Click where you want to use the Tools component and type **Set** followed by the name you want to use for this instance of the Tools object.

3 Type **=Server.CreateObject ("MSWC.Tools")** and then press Enter.

Extra

When you create a form you want to process, you must specify the name of the ASP page that executes the `ProcessForm` method in the code for the form. In order for a query string to be processed, the query string must be appended to the name of the ASP page that executes the `ProcessForm` method.

If you use the same ASP page and template file to process information from a form or query string more than once, the information in the file will be overwritten with the new information. Information cannot be appended to the existing file. To avoid overwriting an existing file, you can use the `Random` method of the `Tools` object to generate a unique name for each file you create.

Example:

```
<%
Set utilities=Server.CreateObject("MSWC.Tools")
randomNumber=Abs(utilities.Random)
outputFileName= randomNumber & ".txt"
utilities.ProcessForm outputFileName,"template.asp"
%>
```

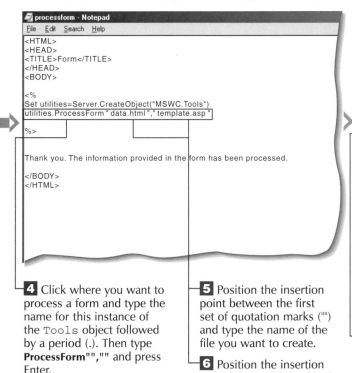

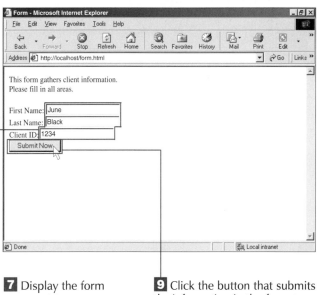

4 Click where you want to process a form and type the name for this instance of the `Tools` object followed by a period (.). Then type **ProcessForm**"","" and press Enter.

5 Position the insertion point between the first set of quotation marks ("") and type the name of the file you want to create.

6 Position the insertion point between the second set of quotation marks and type the name of the template file.

7 Display the form you want to process in a Web browser.

8 Enter the required information into the form.

9 Click the button that submits the information in the form to the ASP page that executes the `ProcessForm` method.

■ The contents of the ASP page that executes the `ProcessForm` method will appear and the file will be created on the Web server.

USING THE IIS LOG COMPONENT
Read a Log File

The IIS Log component is used to create an instance of the IISLog object. The methods and properties of the IISLog object allow you to read log files on the Web server. A log file contains records that store information about the files on the server, such as Web pages, ASP pages and images, that have been accessed by users. In order to use the IIS Log component, the Web server must be running Internet Information Server (IIS) 5.0 and you must be logged on to the server as an administrator.

You use the OpenLogFile method to specify the location of the log file you want to open. Log files are usually found in the \system32\LogFiles\W3SVC1

folder in the Windows operating system folder on the Web server.

To read each record in the log file, you include the ReadLogRecord method in code that creates a loop, such as a Do While statement. You can then use a property of the IISLog object to extract the information you want to read from each log record. For example, the URIStem property returns the name of the file that was accessed. For information about other properties you can use, see the top of page 245.

You use the AtEndOfLog method to stop the loop when the last record in the log file has been read.

READ A LOG FILE

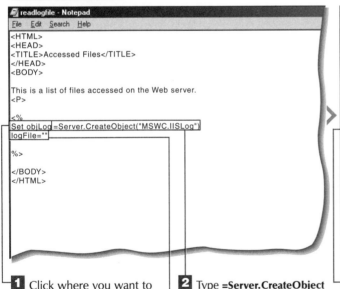

1 Click where you want to use the IIS Log component and type **Set** followed by the name you want to use for this instance of the IISLog object.

2 Type **=Server.CreateObject ("MSWC.IISLog")** and then press Enter.

3 Click where you want to create a variable name to store the location of the log file you want to open and type the name followed by ="".

4 Position the insertion point between the quotation marks ("") and type the location of the log file.

5 Click where you want to open the log file and type the name for this instance of the IISLog object followed by a period (.). Then type **OpenLogFile**.

6 Type the name of the variable that stores the location of the log file followed by the parameters you will use to open the log file, separated by commas. Then press Enter.

Extra

The `OpenLogFile` method has several parameters that you can use to control how a log file is opened. If you do not want to specify a value for a text parameter, you can use double quotation marks ("") in place of the parameter.

```
OpenLogFile FileName, IOMode, ServiceName, ServiceInstance, FileFormat
```

FileName
Specifies the location of a log file you want to open.

IOMode
Specifies if you want to open a log file for reading or writing. The value 1 opens a log file for reading and is the default value. The value 2 opens a log file for writing.

ServiceName
Specifies the service that generates the records you want to read, usually "W3SVC1". This is an optional text parameter.

ServiceInstance
Specifies the Web server that generates the records you want to read. This is an optional parameter that is used when multiple Web servers are available.

FileFormat
Specifies the format of a log file opened for writing. This is an optional text parameter. For information about log file formats, see page 24.

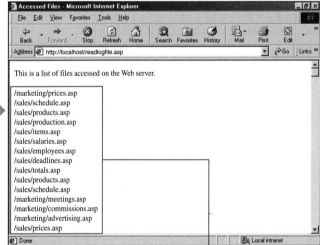

7 Click where you want to place the code that creates a loop to read all the records in the log file and type the code.

Note: To access the name of the file in each log record, include the URIStem property in the code for the loop.

8 Display the ASP page in a Web browser.

■ The Web browser displays the result of reading a log file.

CONTINUED ▶

USING THE IIS LOG COMPONENT
Filter Records by Date and Time

The way the log file stores records is determined by the configuration of the Web server. For example, depending on the server, all the records could be stored in one large log file or a new log file could be created each day to store records.

When working with a large log file, you may want to filter records to read only the records that fall between specific dates and times. For example, you can see how busy the Web server was during a weekend by filtering records to read only records created on Saturday and Sunday.

You could also filter records to read only the records that were created today between 9:00 and 10:00.

To filter records, you must create an instance of the IISLog object and use the OpenLogFile method to specify the location of the log file you want to open. You can then use the ReadFilter method to specify a start date and time and an end date and time for the filter. The ReadFilter method and the property you are using to extract information from records are placed in a loop that reads each record in the log file.

FILTER RECORDS BY DATE AND TIME

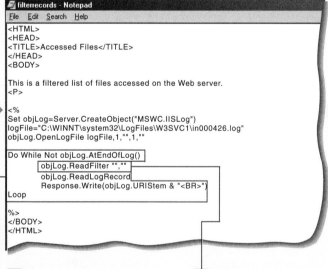

filterrecords - Notepad
File Edit Search Help

```
<HTML>
<HEAD>
<TITLE>Accessed Files</TITLE>
</HEAD>
<BODY>

This is a filtered list of files accessed on the Web server.
<P>

<%
Set objLog=Server.CreateObject("MSWC.IISLog")
logFile="C:\WINNT\system32\LogFiles\W3SVC1\in000426.log"
objLog.OpenLogFile logFile,1,"",1,""

%>
</BODY>
</HTML>
```

filterrecords - Notepad
File Edit Search Help

```
<HTML>
<HEAD>
<TITLE>Accessed Files</TITLE>
</HEAD>
<BODY>

This is a filtered list of files accessed on the Web server.
<P>

<%
Set objLog=Server.CreateObject("MSWC.IISLog")
logFile="C:\WINNT\system32\LogFiles\W3SVC1\in000426.log"
objLog.OpenLogFile logFile,1,"",1,""

Do While Not objLog.AtEndOfLog()
        objLog.ReadFilter "",""
        objLog.ReadLogRecord
        Response.Write(objLog.URIStem & "<BR>")
Loop

%>
</BODY>
</HTML>
```

1 Perform steps 1 to 6 on page 242 to create an instance of the IISLog object and use the OpenLogFile method to specify the location of the log file you want to open.

2 Click where you want to place the code that creates a loop to read all the records in the log file and type the code.

Note: The property you want to use to extract information from each record must be included in the loop.

3 Click where you want to place the code that filters the records and type the name for this instance of the IISLog object followed by a period (.). Then type **ReadFilter"","".**

Extra The `IISLog` object provides several properties that can be used to return information from the records in a log file. You can find information such as when files were accessed and which Web browsers were used to access files. The information stored in the records of a log file depends on the format of the log file.

COMMON PROPERTIES	DESCRIPTION
`BytesReceived`	Returns the number of bytes received.
`BytesSent`	Returns the number of bytes sent.
`ClientIP`	Returns the IP number of a user.
`Cookie`	Returns the name of a user's cookie.
`DateTime`	Returns the date and time a file was accessed.
`ProtocolStatus`	Returns the status of a network protocol.
`Referer`	Returns the name of the file a user came from.
`ServiceName`	Returns the service used to create a record.
`TimeTaken`	Returns the time taken to process a request.
`URIQuery`	Returns any parameters sent with a request.
`URIStem`	Returns the name of an accessed file.
`UserAgent`	Returns the Web browser used to access a file.

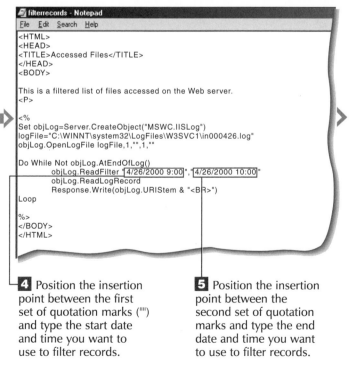

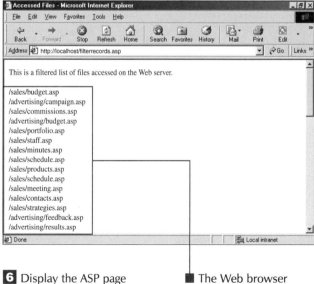

4 Position the insertion point between the first set of quotation marks ("") and type the start date and time you want to use to filter records.

5 Position the insertion point between the second set of quotation marks and type the end date and time you want to use to filter records.

6 Display the ASP page in a Web browser.

■ The Web browser displays the result of filtering records in the log file by date and time.

USING THE FILE ACCESS COMPONENT
Create or Open a File

I t is often necessary to access text files stored on the Web server from within ASP pages. Text files allow you to read, manipulate and store data, such as configuration settings, application information and Web pages.

You must use the FileSystemObject statement to prepare the Web server to interact with files. You then create a TextStream object in order to work with a specific file. You can create or open a file using the TextStream object.

You use the CreateTextFile statement to create a new file on the Web server. After creating a file, you can write data to the file.

If the file you want to work with already exists on the Web server, you use the OpenTextFile statement to open the file. When opening a file, you must specify whether you want to read the file, overwrite information in the file or append new data to the end of the file. After the file name in the OpenTextFile statement, you must include a 1 to read data, a 2 to overwrite existing data or an 8 to append data to the end of the file.

CREATE A FILE

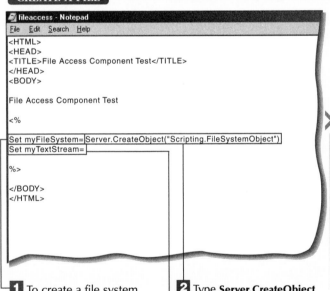

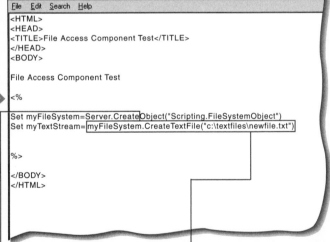

1 To create a file system object, type **Set** followed by the name you want to use for this instance of the file system object and an equal sign (=).

2 Type **Server.CreateObject ("Scripting.FileSystemObject")** and then press Enter.

3 To create a file, type **Set** followed by the name you want to use for this instance of the text stream object and an equal sign (=).

4 Type the name for this instance of the file system object followed by a period (.). Then type **CreateTextFile("")** and press Enter.

5 Position the insertion point between the quotation marks ("") and type the path and name of the file you want to use.

Extra

By default, if you attempt to create a file with the same name as an existing file, you will overwrite the existing file. If you do not want to overwrite an existing file, you can set the `Overwrite` parameter to `false` in the `CreateTextFile` statement.

Example:
```
Set newTextStream=myFileSystem.CreateTextFile("c:\textfiles\newfile.txt", false)
```

By default, a file you create is in the ASCII format. If you will share the file with other types of systems, such as a Macintosh or UNIX system, you may want to use the Unicode format for the file. To do so, you must add the `Unicode` parameter to the `CreateTextFile` statement.

Example:
```
Set unicodeTextStream=myFileSystem.CreateTextFile("c:\textfiles\unicodefile.txt",,true)
```

When opening a file, you can specify the format in which you want to open the file. By default, each file is opened in the ASCII format. To open a file created in the Unicode format, you include a `-1` at the end of the `OpenTextFile` statement. If you are unsure of the format, you include a `-2` to specify that you want to use the system's default format.

Example:
```
Set myTextStream=myFileSystem.OpenTextFile("c:\textfiles\newfile.txt", 8, -2)
```

OPEN A FILE

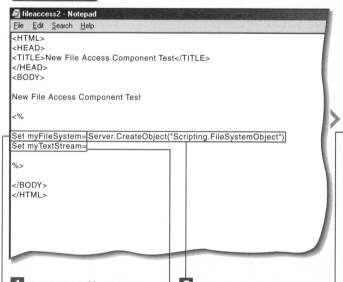

1 To create a file system object, type **Set** followed by the name you want to use for this instance of the file system object and an equal sign (=).

2 Type **Server.CreateObject ("Scripting.FileSystemObject")** and then press Enter.

3 To open a file, type **Set** followed by the name you want to use for this instance of the text stream object and an equal sign (=).

4 Type the name for this instance of the file system object followed by a period (.). Then type **OpenTextFile()** and press Enter.

5 Position the insertion point between the parentheses () and type the path and name of the file you want to open enclosed in quotation marks (""). Then type a comma (,) followed by the number (1, 2 or 8) for the task you want to perform.

CONTINUED ▶

USING THE FILE ACCESS COMPONENT
Write Data to a File

After you create a file system object and create a text file or open a text file for writing or appending, you can write data to the file.

You use the `Write` method to send data to an open file. When you use the `Write` method, the data you write does not include any line breaks. If you use the `Write` method several times in a row to write data to a file, all the text you enter will appear in one long line in the file.

If you want to split data into separate lines in a file, you can use the `WriteLine` method. The

`WriteLine` method inserts a line break at the end of each line of text you create.

You can also enter blank lines in a file. You must use the `WriteBlankLines` method and indicate the number of blank lines you want to create.

When you finish writing data to a file, you must close the file. Other users will not be able to access the file until it is closed.

After writing data to a file, you can use an ASP page to read the data. For information about reading data from a file, see page 250.

WRITE DATA TO A FILE

```
fileaccess - Notepad
File  Edit  Search  Help
<HTML>
<HEAD>
<TITLE>File Access Component Test</TITLE>
</HEAD>
<BODY>

File Access Component Test

<%

Set myFileSystem=Server.CreateObject("Scripting.FileSystemObject")
Set myTextStream=myFileSystem.CreateTextFile("c:\textfiles\newfile.txt")

myTextStream.Write "This is the first line of text. This line of text does not contain a line
break. "

%>

</BODY>
</HTML>
```

```
fileaccess - Notepad
File  Edit  Search  Help
<HTML>
<HEAD>
<TITLE>File Access Component Test</TITLE>
</HEAD>
<BODY>

File Access Component Test

<%

Set myFileSystem=Server.CreateObject("Scripting.FileSystemObject")
Set myTextStream=myFileSystem.CreateTextFile("c:\textfiles\newfile.txt")

myTextStream.Write "This is the first line of text. This line of text does not contain a line
break. "

myTextStream.WriteLine "This is the second line of text. This line ends with a line break."

%>

</BODY>
</HTML>
```

WRITE DATA

1 Type the name for this instance of the text stream object followed by a period (.) and then type **Write**.

2 Type the data you want to write to the file, enclosed in quotation marks, and then press Enter.

■ The text you enter will not include a line break.

WRITE ONE LINE OF DATA

1 Type the name for this instance of the text stream object followed by a period (.) and then type **WriteLine**.

2 Type the data you want to write to the file, enclosed in quotation marks, and then press Enter.

■ The text you enter will include a line break at the end of the text.

Extra

Before writing to files stored on a Web server, you must ensure the correct permissions are set for the Web server. You may also need to adjust file and folder permissions on the server. Refer to the Web server and operating system documentation for information about setting server, folder and file permissions.

When writing to a file using the `TextStream` object, you must write data sequentially. You cannot move back through data or jump ahead to insert data in the middle of the file. You must write data one line at a time.

If you do not include the `Close` method when writing to a file, the file will be closed automatically when the ASP page finishes processing.

You can use ASCII codes to format and manipulate the data you write to a file. For example, you can add a horizontal tab to the data you write to a file by entering `chr(9)` in the `Write` or `WriteLine` method.

TYPE THIS:

```
myTextStream.WriteLine "Name" &  chr(9) & "Phone"
myTextStream.WriteLine "Wanda" & chr(9) & "555-6374"
myTextStream.WriteLine "Paul" & chr(9) & "555-9830"
```

RESULT:

Name	Phone
Wanda	555-6374
Paul	555-9830

CLOSE A FILE

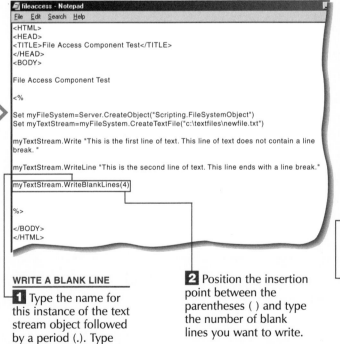

```
fileaccess - Notepad
File  Edit  Search  Help
<HTML>
<HEAD>
<TITLE>File Access Component Test</TITLE>
</HEAD>
<BODY>

File Access Component Test

<%

Set myFileSystem=Server.CreateObject("Scripting.FileSystemObject")
Set myTextStream=myFileSystem.CreateTextFile("c:\textfiles\newfile.txt")

myTextStream.Write "This is the first line of text. This line of text does not contain a line
break. "

myTextStream.WriteLine "This is the second line of text. This line ends with a line break."

myTextStream.WriteBlankLines(4)

%>

</BODY>
</HTML>
```

```
fileaccess - Notepad
File  Edit  Search  Help
<HTML>
<HEAD>
<TITLE>File Access Component Test</TITLE>
</HEAD>
<BODY>

File Access Component Test

<%

Set myFileSystem=Server.CreateObject("Scripting.FileSystemObject")
Set myTextStream=myFileSystem.CreateTextFile("c:\textfiles\newfile.txt")

myTextStream.Write "This is the first line of text. This line of text does not contain a line
break. "

myTextStream.WriteLine "This is the second line of text. This line ends with a line break."

myTextStream.WriteBlankLines(4)

myTextStream.WriteLine "End of blank lines."

myTextStream.Close

%>
```

WRITE A BLANK LINE

1 Type the name for this instance of the text stream object followed by a period (.). Type **WriteBlankLines( )** and then press Enter.

2 Position the insertion point between the parentheses ( ) and type the number of blank lines you want to write.

1 Type the name for this instance of the text stream object followed by a period (.). Type **Close** and then press Enter.

■ The text file will be closed.

CONTINUED ▶

USING THE FILE ACCESS COMPONENT
Read Data From a File

After you create a file system object and open a file for reading, you can access the contents of the file. This allows you to display the data in a Web browser or compare the data in the file to other data.

The Read method allows you to read a specific number of characters, beginning at the current position in the file.

The ReadLine method allows you to read a line of data, from the current position in the file to the next line break.

The ReadAll method is used to read all the data from a file at once. This statement is most

effective for files that contain a small amount of data. If you have read characters or lines from the file, the ReadAll method will read from the current position to the end of the file.

If you plan to display the data from a file in a Web browser, you can use the <PRE> tag to display the data exactly as it appears in the file. Place the <PRE> tag before the opening ASP delimiter and the </PRE> after the closing ASP delimiter. If you do not use the <PRE> tag, all the data in the file will appear in a Web browser with no line breaks or blank lines.

READ DATA FROM A FILE

```
fileaccess2 - Notepad
File  Edit  Search  Help
<HTML>
<HEAD>
<TITLE>New File Access Component Test</TITLE>
</HEAD>
<BODY>

New File Access Component Test

<PRE>
<%

Set myFileSystem=Server.CreateObject("Scripting.FileSystemObject")
Set myTextStream=myFileSystem.OpenTextFile("c:\textfiles\newfile.txt", 1)

Response.Write(myTextStream.Read(42))
Response.Write ("<HR>")

%>
</PRE>

</BODY>
</HTML>
```

```
fileaccess2 - Notepad
File  Edit  Search  Help
<HTML>
<HEAD>
<TITLE>New File Access Component Test</TITLE>
</HEAD>
<BODY>

New File Access Component Test

<PRE>
<%

Set myFileSystem=Server.CreateObject("Scripting.FileSystemObject")
Set myTextStream=myFileSystem.OpenTextFile("c:\textfiles\newfile.txt", 1)

Response.Write(myTextStream.Read(42))
Response.Write("<HR>")

Response.Write(myTextStream.ReadLine)
Response.Write("<HR>")

%>
</PRE>
```

READ CHARACTERS

1 Type the name for this instance of the text stream object followed by a period (.). Type **Read()** and then press Enter.

2 Position the insertion point between the parentheses ( ) and type the number of characters you want to read.

3 Click where you want to place the code that executes the statement to read characters from the file and type the code.

READ A LINE OF DATA

1 Type the name for this instance of the text stream object followed by a period (.). Type **ReadLine** and then press Enter.

2 Click where you want to place the code that executes the statement to read the line from the file and type the code.

Extra

You can display the number for the column or line of the current position in the text. This can help you determine where you are in the text.

Example:

```
Response.Write(myTextStream.Line)
Response.Write(myTextStream.Column)
```

Data in a file is read one line at a time. Although you cannot move back in the file, you can use the Skip method to skip ahead without reading characters. You must indicate the number of characters you want to skip. You can also use the SkipLine method to skip ahead an entire line.

Example:

```
myTextStream.Skip(10)
myTextStream.SkipLine
```

You can determine whether the current position in the text is at the end of a line using the AtEndOfLine method. You can also use the AtEndOfStream method to determine whether the current position is at the end of the file. When the position is at the end of a line or the file, the value of the method is true.

Example:

```
If myTextStream.AtEndOfLine=true Then
    Response.Write("End of Line<BR>")
Else
    Response.Write("Current column position: ")
    Response.Write(myTextStream.Column)
End If
```

VIEW DATA IN WEB BROWSER

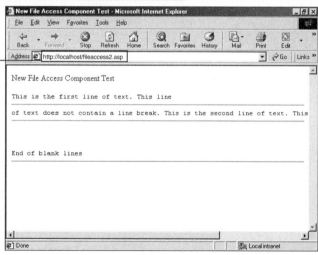

```
fileaccess2 - Notepad
File  Edit  Search  Help

<HTML>
<HEAD>
<TITLE>New File Access Component Test</TITLE>
</HEAD>
<BODY>

New File Access Component Test

<PRE>
<%

Set myFileSystem=Server.CreateObject("Scripting.FileSystemObject")
Set myTextStream=myFileSystem.OpenTextFile("c:\textfiles\newfile.txt", 1)

Response.Write(myTextStream.Read(42))
Response.Write("<HR>")

Response.Write(myTextStream.ReadLine)
Response.Write("<HR>")

Response.Write(myTextStream.ReadAll)
Response.Write("<HR>")
```

READ ALL DATA IN A FILE

1 Type the name for this instance of the text stream object followed by a period (.). Type **ReadAll** and then press Enter.

2 Click where you want to place the code that executes the statement to read all the data from the file and type the code.

1 Display the ASP page in a Web browser.

■ The Web browser displays the result of reading data from the file on the Web server.

CONTINUED ▶

USING THE FILE ACCESS COMPONENT
Work With Files and Folders

Besides reading and writing data to files, there are many methods available that you can use to work with files and folders on the Web server. For example, you can specify in an ASP page that you want to delete a file you no longer require from the Web server. You can also copy a file or folder to a new location or determine whether a file exists on the server.

Many of the methods associated with the FileSystemObject object are used to find information about a file or folder, such as the extension of a file, the drive where a file is located or which folder a file is stored in.

In order to work with files and folders on the Web server, you must ensure the correct permissions are set for the server, files and folders. You can refer to the Web server and operating system documentation for more information.

As with all procedures that allow users to interact with files on the Web server, you should ensure that proper security measures are in place on the Web server to prevent unauthorized access to files.

WORK WITH FILES AND FOLDERS

```
deletefile - Notepad
File   Edit   Search   Help
<HTML>
<HEAD>
<TITLE>Delete a File</TITLE>
</HEAD>
<BODY>

File Access Component Test

<%
Set myFileSystem= Server.CreateObject("Scripting.FileSystemObject")

%>


</BODY>
</HTML>
```

```
deletefile - Notepad
File   Edit   Search   Help
<HTML>
<HEAD>
<TITLE>Delete a File</TITLE>
</HEAD>
<BODY>

File Access Component Test

<%
Set myFileSystem=Server.CreateObject("Scripting.FileSystemObject")
myFileSystem.DeleteFile("c:\textfiles\newfile1.txt")

%>


</BODY>
</HTML>
```

DELETE A FILE

1 To create a file system object, type **Set** followed by the name you want to use for this instance of the file system object and an equal sign (=).

2 Type **Server.CreateObject ("Scripting.FileSystemObject")** and then press Enter.

3 To delete a file, type the name for this instance of the file system object followed by a period (.). Then type **DeleteFile("")** and press Enter.

4 Position the insertion point between the quotation marks ("") and type the path and name of the file you want to delete.

■ When this ASP page is displayed in a Web browser, the file will be deleted from the Web server.

FILESYSTEMOBJECT METHODS

BuildPath

Adds a folder or file name to a path.

`myFileSystem.BuildPath("c:\textfiles", "newfolder")`

CopyFolder

Copies a folder and all its files from one location to another on the Web server.

`myFileSystem.CopyFolder "c:\textfiles", "c:\inetpub\wwwroot\"`

CopyFile

Copies a file from one location to another on the Web server.

`myFileSystem.CopyFile "c:\textfiles\newfile.txt", "c:\"`

CreateFolder

Creates a new folder on the Web server.

`myFileSystem.CreateFolder("c:\textfiles")`

DeleteFolder

Deletes a folder and all its contents from the Web server.

`myFileSystem.DeleteFolder("c:\textfiles")`

DeleteFile

Deletes a file from the Web server.

`myFileSystem.DeleteFile("c:\textfiles\newfile.txt")`

DriveExists

Determines whether a drive exists on the Web server.

`myFileSystem.DriveExists("c:")`

FolderExists

Determines whether a folder exists on the Web server.

`myFileSystem.FolderExists("c:\textfiles")`

FileExists

Determines whether a file exists on the Web server.

`myFileSystem.FileExists("c:\textfiles\newfile.txt")`

GetAbsolutePathName

Returns the full path of a folder or file.

`myFileSystem.GetAbsolutePathName("c:\textfiles\newfile.txt")`

GetBaseName

Returns the base name of a folder or a file without the extension.

`myFileSystem.GetBaseName("c:\textfiles\newfile.txt")`

GetDrive

Returns a drive object. You can use properties such as `AvailableSpace` and `IsReady` with this object.

`Set obj= myFileSystem.GetDrive("c:")`
`obj.AvailableSpace`

GetDriveName

Returns the name of a drive storing a file.

`myFileSystem.GetDriveName("c:textfiles\newfile.txt")`

GetExtensionName

Returns the extension of a file.

`myFileSystem.GetExtensionName("c:\textfiles\newfile.txt")`

GetFile

Returns a file object. You can use properties such as `DateCreated` with this object.

`Set obj=myFileSystem.GetFile("c:\textfiles\newfile.txt")`
`obj.DateCreated`

GetFileName

Returns the last part of a file address, such as newfile.txt.

`myFileSystem.GetFileName("c:\textfiles\newfile.txt")`

GetFolder

Returns a folder object. You can use properties such as `DateLastAccessed` with this object.

`Set obj=myFileSystem.GetFolder("c:\textfiles")`
`obj.DateLastAccessed`

GetParentFolderName

Returns the name of the parent folder.

`myFileSystem.GetParentFolderName("c:\textfiles\newfolder\newfile.txt")`

GetSpecialFolder

Returns the path of a special Windows folder. 0 finds the folder that stores the operating system. 1 finds the folder that stores libraries and device drivers. 2 finds the Temp folder.

`myFileSystem.GetSpecialFolder(0)`

GetTempName

Generates a random name for a temporary file or folder.

`myFileSystem.GetTempName`

MoveFolder

Moves a folder and all its contents from one location to another on the Web server.

`myFileSystem.MoveFolder "c:\textfiles\newfolder", "c:\"`

MoveFile

Moves a file from one location to another on the Web server.

`myFileSystem.MoveFile "c:\textfiles\newfile.txt", "c:\newfolder\"`

CREATE AN ACTIVEX COMPONENT USING VISUAL BASIC

C reating a custom ActiveX component allows you to design a powerful component that can be used to perform a task specific to your ASP pages. Microsoft Visual Basic is a popular programming language used to create custom ActiveX components.

When you start Visual Basic, you must specify that you want to build an ActiveX DLL file. You can then enter the Visual Basic code that creates the function you want the ActiveX component to execute. When you access the ActiveX component in an ASP page, you will use the name of the function to call the component.

The next step in creating a component is naming a class. Visual Basic automatically creates and configures a class for you when creating an ActiveX DLL file. A descriptive class name that reflects the action performed by the class can help clarify the code used to call the component in an ASP page.

You must also specify a name for the project. A project is used to group related files together. The project name should indicate the purpose of the ActiveX component.

CREATE AN ACTIVEX COMPONENT USING VISUAL BASIC

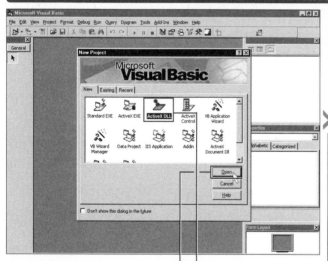

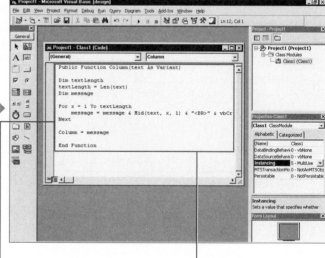

1 Start Visual Basic.

■ The Visual Basic window and New Project dialog box appear.

2 To create an ActiveX component, click ActiveX DLL.

3 Click Open.

■ The Code window appears.

4 Type the code to create a function that performs a specific task.

■ In this example, we create a function that displays text in a column.

Extra

There are different versions of Microsoft Visual Basic available. In the example below, Visual Basic 6.0 is used, but the same task can be accomplished using other versions of the programming language. If you are using a different version of Visual Basic, you should consult the documentation for the version to find information about creating ActiveX DLL files.

An ActiveX component can contain several related functions. For example, you could create one function to display text in a column from top to bottom, another function to display text in a column from bottom to top and another to display text from right to left. You do not have to create separate ActiveX components for each of these related functions. When you access the component from an ASP page, you specify which function you want to execute.

If the Code window does not appear, you can display the window by clicking the View Code button (□) in the Project window.

If the Properties window is not displayed in the Visual Basic window, click the Properties Window button (□).

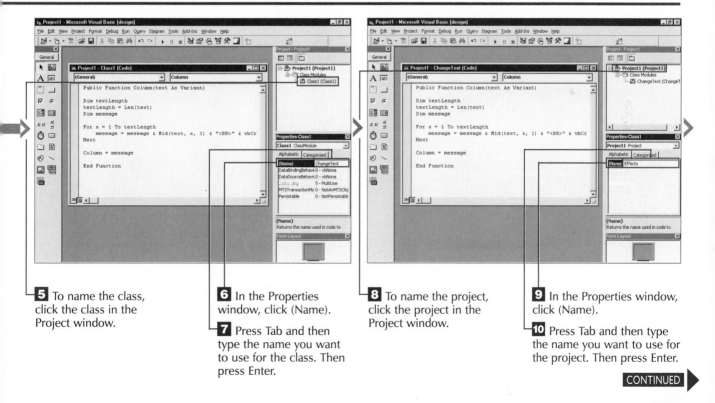

5 To name the class, click the class in the Project window.

6 In the Properties window, click (Name).

7 Press Tab and then type the name you want to use for the class. Then press Enter.

8 To name the project, click the project in the Project window.

9 In the Properties window, click (Name).

10 Press Tab and then type the name you want to use for the project. Then press Enter.

CONTINUED ▶

CREATE AN ACTIVEX COMPONENT USING VISUAL BASIC (CONTINUED)

After the function for the ActiveX component has been created and the class and project have been named, the ActiveX component should be saved.

When saving a component, the class is saved first as a separate file. You can then use the same class with other components, which can help reduce the time required to create new components.

Once the class file is saved, Visual Basic allows you to save the project you created.

After saving the class and project, you can create the DLL file for the ActiveX component. To create the DLL file, Visual Basic compiles the code you created for the component, combines it with any required Visual Basic files and then saves all the information as one file. The name that was used to save the project is the same name you will use for the DLL file. This makes the code used to call the component in an ASP page easier to understand.

After creating the ActiveX DLL file, you must transfer the DLL file to the Web server.

CREATE AN ACTIVEX COMPONENT USING VISUAL BASIC (CONTINUED)

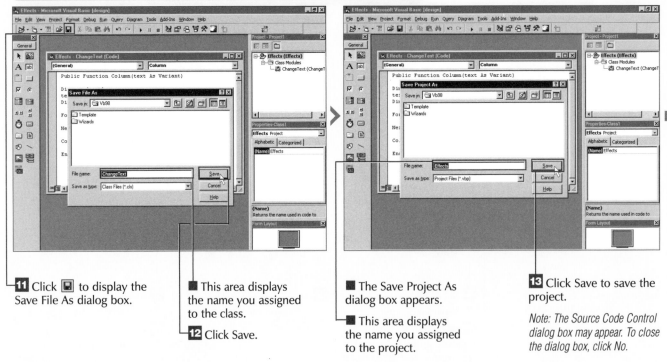

■11 Click 🖫 to display the Save File As dialog box.

■ This area displays the name you assigned to the class.

■12 Click Save.

■ The Save Project As dialog box appears.

■ This area displays the name you assigned to the project.

■13 Click Save to save the project.

Note: The Source Code Control dialog box may appear. To close the dialog box, click No.

Extra

Once you have transferred the ActiveX DLL file to the Web server, the DLL file must be registered on the server. Registering an ActiveX DLL file enters information in the operating system's registry to allow the ActiveX component to be used. You can register a DLL file on the Web server using a utility called *regsvr32*. In the Windows Command Prompt on the Web server, type **regsvr32** followed by the name and path of the ActiveX DLL file you want to register.

Example:

```
regsvr32 c:\extra\effects.dll
```

The Web server does not have to have Visual Basic installed to use ActiveX DLL files. However, Visual Basic run-time files must be installed on the server. Visual Basic run-time files are included with Visual Basic 6.0. The run-time files are also available at the support.microsoft.com/support/VBasic/runtime.asp Web site.

When you no longer require an ActiveX DLL file, you can use the *regsvr32* utility to unregister the DLL file. This removes the information about the DLL file from the registry of the Web server's operating system. In the Windows Command Prompt on the Web server, type **regsvr32 /u** followed by the name and path of the DLL file you want to unregister.

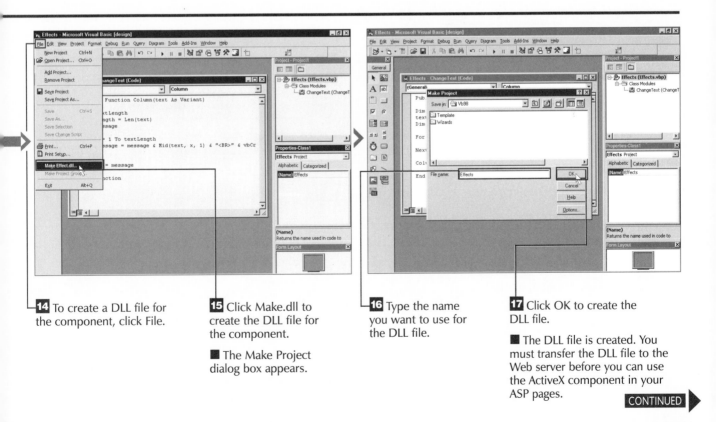

14 To create a DLL file for the component, click File.

15 Click Make.dll to create the DLL file for the component.

■ The Make Project dialog box appears.

16 Type the name you want to use for the DLL file.

17 Click OK to create the DLL file.

■ The DLL file is created. You must transfer the DLL file to the Web server before you can use the ActiveX component in your ASP pages.

CONTINUED ▶

CREATE AN ACTIVEX COMPONENT USING VISUAL BASIC (CONTINUED)

Once the ActiveX component has been created and the ActiveX DLL file has been registered on the Web server, the component can be used in your ASP pages.

The component is used by creating an instance of the ActiveX component and assigning the instance a name. The function created for the ActiveX component can then be accessed and executed. The instance of the ActiveX component is created by using the `Server.CreateObject` statement. The `Server.CreateObject` statement specifies the name of the ActiveX DLL file, followed by the

name of the class you created for the ActiveX component.

To execute the ActiveX component, you specify the name of the instance of the component followed by the function name. For example, if the instance of the ActiveX component is called 'myObject' and the ActiveX component contains a function called 'Print', then you would use the `myObject.Print` statement to use the component. Any values you want to pass to the function must be passed when accessing the function, such as `myObject.Print("This is a test")`.

USE AN ACTIVEX COMPONENT IN AN ASP PAGE

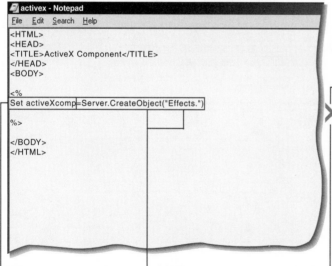

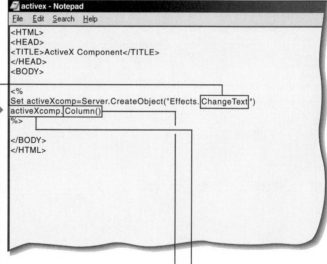

1 Click where you want to use the ActiveX component in an ASP page and type **Set** followed by the name you want to assign to this instance of the ActiveX component.

2 Type **=Server.CreateObject("")** and then press Enter.

3 Position the insertion point between the quotation marks ("") and type the name of the DLL file you created for the component followed by a period (.).

4 Type the name of the class you assigned to the ActiveX component.

5 Click where you want to execute the ActiveX component and type the name for this instance of the ActiveX component followed by a period (.).

6 Type the name of the function you created in the code for the ActiveX component followed by ().

Extra

Visual Basic is not the only programming language that you can use to create ActiveX components. The language you should use depends on the objective of the component and the environment in which it will be used. Visual Basic will meet your needs for creating most ActiveX components; however for busy Web servers where speed and efficiency are major issues, a more powerful programming language, such as C++, may be a better choice. ASP pages access ActiveX DLL files in the same way, regardless of the programming language the DLL files were created with.

If you encounter problems using an ActiveX component that you have created, you should ensure that the class name you are using to access the component in the ASP page is the same class name stored in the registry of the Web server's operating system. Select the Start button and choose Run. In the Run dialog box, type **regedit** and then press Enter. In the Registry Editor window, select the Edit menu and choose Find to display the Find dialog box. Type the class name of the component, ensure the Data option is selected in the Look at area and then click Find Next to begin the search for the name in the registry.

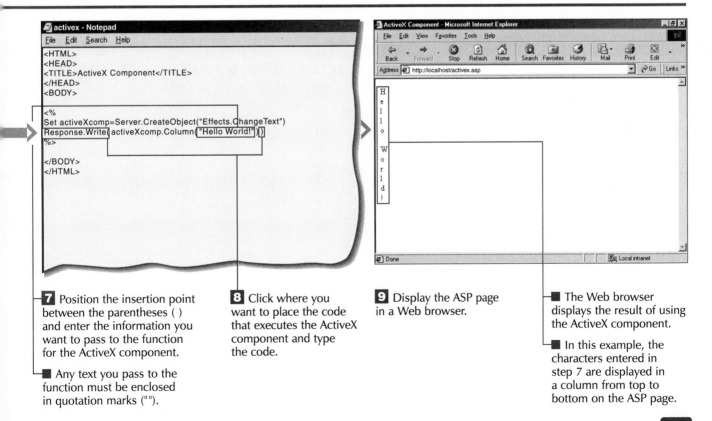

7 Position the insertion point between the parentheses ( ) and enter the information you want to pass to the function for the ActiveX component.

■ Any text you pass to the function must be enclosed in quotation marks ("").

8 Click where you want to place the code that executes the ActiveX component and type the code.

9 Display the ASP page in a Web browser.

■ The Web browser displays the result of using the ActiveX component.

■ In this example, the characters entered in step 7 are displayed in a column from top to bottom on the ASP page.

USING THE ENABLESESSIONSTATE PREPROCESSING DIRECTIVE

A preprocessing directive instructs the Web server to perform an action before the code in an ASP page is executed and the result is sent to the user's Web browser. The ENABLESESSIONSTATE preprocessing directive determines whether session information is enabled or disabled for an ASP page. The Session object stores session information such as a user's name, password and preferences while the user is visiting the Web site. For more information about the Session object, see pages 148 to 155.

The default setting for the ENABLESESSIONSTATE preprocessing directive is True. Changing the value of the preprocessing directive to False disables the use of session information for the ASP page. Disabling the ENABLESESSIONSTATE preprocessing directive also

prevents the ASP page from reading information from or writing information to cookies in the user's Web browser.

It is important to ensure that you have properly set the ENABLESESSIONSTATE preprocessing directive in an ASP page. If the ENABLESESSIONSTATE preprocessing directive is set to False and the ASP page references session information, an error will be generated.

If your ASP pages do not require the use of session information, you should disable the ENABLESESSIONSTATE preprocessing directive to help increase the performance of the Web server.

USING THE ENABLESESSIONSTATE PREPROCESSING DIRECTIVE

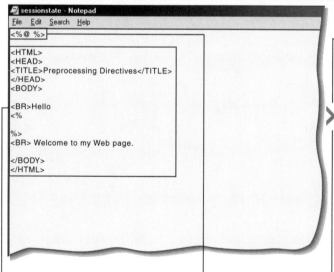

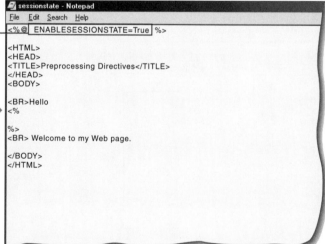

1 Type the HTML and ASP code you want to execute to display information in a user's Web browser.

2 Position the insertion point in front of the first line of code in the ASP page and type **<%@ %>**. Then press Enter.

3 Position the insertion point after the @ symbol and type a space followed by **ENABLESESSIONSTATE=True**.

■ You can type **ENABLESESSIONSTATE=False** to disable the preprocessing directive.

Extra

The value of the ENABLESESSIONSTATE preprocessing directive for Active Server Pages may be set in the registry of the Web server's operating system. Enabling or disabling the ENABLESESSIONSTATE preprocessing directive in an ASP page will override the setting in the registry for that ASP page.

Leaving out the space that follows the @ symbol is a common error when setting preprocessing directives in an ASP page. Another common error is placing a space before and after the equal sign (=) between the directive name and its value. If either of these errors is made, the preprocessing directive may not work properly.

You should not use a preprocessing directive in an ASP page that uses a *Server-Side Include* file. If you do, the code in the Server-Side Include file may not be processed properly. For information on Server-Side Includes, see page 174.

There are other preprocessing directives you can set in an ASP page. See pages 262 to 265 for information about additional preprocessing directives. To set more than one preprocessing directive, you must place all the directives within the same ASP delimiters (<% and %>) on the first line of the ASP page. Each directive must be separated by a space.

Example:

```
<%@ ENABLESESSIONSTATE=False LANGUAGE="JScript" %>
```

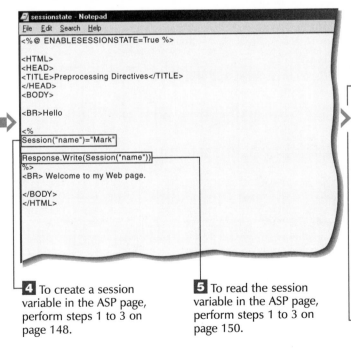

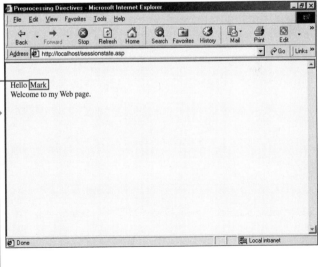

4 To create a session variable in the ASP page, perform steps 1 to 3 on page 148.

5 To read the session variable in the ASP page, perform steps 1 to 3 on page 150.

6 Display the ASP page in a Web browser.

■ The Web browser displays the result of reading the session variable.

■ If the ENABLESESSIONSTATE preprocessing directive is disabled, an error message will appear in the Web browser.

USING THE LCID PREPROCESSING DIRECTIVE

The LCID preprocessing directive is used to specify a locale identifier for the code used in Active Server Pages script. A locale identifier determines settings, such as how dates, times and numbers should be formatted, based on the script author's language and location.

The locale identifier may affect how code generated by the ASP page appears in a user's Web browser. For example, if an ASP page displays a list of product prices using the FormatCurrency function, you can change the locale identifier for the page to change the currency format used.

Common LCID values include 1040 (Italian-Standard), 1036 (French-Standard) and 2057 (English-United Kingdom). You can find a comprehensive list of LCID values at the msdn.microsoft.com/scripting/vbscript/doc/vsmscLCID.htm Web site.

A preprocessing directive must appear in the first line of code in the ASP page you want the directive to affect. You should not use a preprocessing directive in a page that uses a *Server-Side Include* file. For information on Server-Side Includes, see page 174.

USING THE LCID PREPROCESSING DIRECTIVE

lcid - Notepad
File   Edit   Search   Help

```
<%@ %>

<HTML>
<HEAD>
<TITLE>Preprocessing Directives</TITLE>
</HEAD>
<BODY>

<BR>Welcome to my Web page
<BR>The total product price is:

<%
Dim x
x=9.45

Response.Write(FormatCurrency(x))
%>

</BODY>
</HTML>
```

lcid - Notepad
File   Edit   Search   Help

```
<%@   LCID=2057 %>

<HTML>
<HEAD>
<TITLE>Preprocessing Directives</TITLE>
</HEAD>
<BODY>

<BR>Welcome to my Web page
<BR>The total product price is:

<%
Dim x
x=9.45

Response.Write(FormatCurrency(x))
%>

</BODY>
</HTML>
```

1 Type the HTML and ASP code you want to execute to display information in a user's Web browser.

2 Position the insertion point in front of the first line of code in the ASP page and type **<%@ %>**. Then press Enter.

3 Position the insertion point after the @ symbol and type a space followed by **LCID=**.

4 Type the locale ID value you want to use for the ASP page.

USING THE CODEPAGE PREPROCESSING DIRECTIVE

The CODEPAGE preprocessing directive allows you to specify the code page, or character set, used to create the text that makes up the code of an ASP page. Changing the code page may be required when the computer where the ASP code was written and the Web server where the code will be executed do not use the same language. The code page value tells the Web server what language was used to create the code in the ASP page.

The code page specified using the CODEPAGE preprocessing directive applies only to the character set used in the Active Server Pages code. The code page does not affect the display of information in a user's Web browser.

Common code page values include 1252 (Western European), 20127 (US-ASCII) and 936 (Chinese Simplified). You can find a comprehensive list of code page values at the msdn.microsoft.com/workshop/Author/dhtml/reference/charsets/charset4.asp Web site.

A preprocessing directive must appear in the first line of code in the ASP page you want the directive to affect. You should not use a preprocessing directive in a page that uses a *Server-Side Include* file. For information on Server-Side Includes, see page 174.

USING THE CODEPAGE PREPROCESSING DIRECTIVE

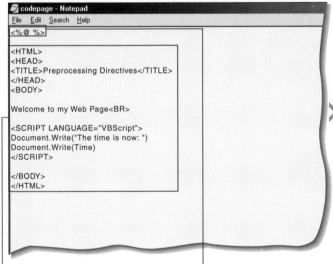

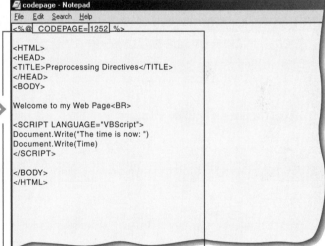

1 Type the HTML and ASP code you want to execute to display information in a user's Web browser.

2 Position the insertion point in front of the first line of code in the ASP page and type **<%@ %>**. Then press Enter.

3 Position the insertion point after the @ symbol and type a space followed by **CODEPAGE=**.

4 Type the code page value you want to use for the ASP page.

USING THE LANGUAGE PREPROCESSING DIRECTIVE

Active Server Pages allows you to write scripts in several different scripting languages. You use the LANGUAGE preprocessing directive to specify the scripting language used to create an ASP page. If the scripting language is not specified using the LANGUAGE preprocessing directive, the Web server assumes that VBScript is used.

ASP pages stored on Personal Web Server or Internet Information Server (IIS) can be written in VBScript or JScript. JScript is Microsoft's version of JavaScript. If you want to use another scripting language, such as PerlScript, in your ASP pages, you must install the scripting language on the Web server.

The Web browser of the user accessing the ASP page does not have to support the scripting language specified by the LANGUAGE preprocessing directive. The script will be processed on the server and then the result will be sent to the user's Web browser.

A preprocessing directive must appear in the first line of code in the ASP page you want the directive to affect. You should not use a preprocessing directive in a page that uses a *Server-Side Include* file. For information on Server-Side Includes, see page 174.

USING THE LANGUAGE PREPROCESSING DIRECTIVE

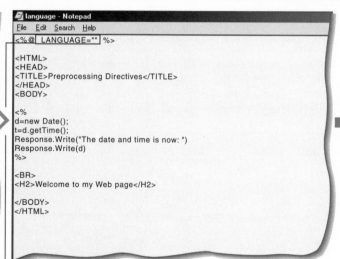

1 Type the HTML and ASP code you want to execute to display information in a user's Web browser.

2 Position the insertion point in front of the first line of code in the ASP page and type **<%@ %>**. Then press Enter.

3 Position the insertion point after the @ symbol and type a space followed by **LANGUAGE=""**.

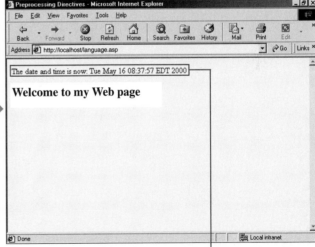

Apply It

Even when the scripting language is specified using the LANGUAGE preprocessing directive, it is possible to use different languages in the ASP page. To use a different scripting language, use the `<SCRIPT>` tag with the LANGUAGE attribute set to the other language you want to use and the RUNAT attribute set to SERVER.

TYPE THIS:

```
<%@ LANGUAGE="JScript" %>
<HTML>
<HEAD>
<TITLE>Tip</TITLE>
</HEAD>
<BODY>

<SCRIPT LANGUAGE="VBScript" RUNAT="SERVER">
Response.Write("<BR>There are ")
Response.Write(DateDiff("ww", Now(), "25-Dec-00"))
Response.Write(" weeks until Christmas.<BR>")
</SCRIPT>

<%
Response.Write("The date and time is: ")
Response.Write(Date())
%>
</BODY>
</HTML>
```

RESULT:

There are 32 weeks until Christmas.

The date and time is: Mon May 15 14:49:57 2000

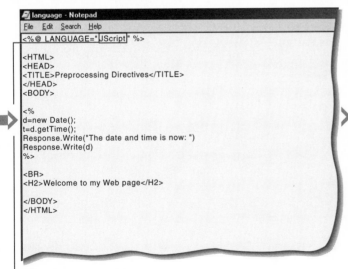

4 Position the insertion point between the quotation marks ("") and type the language you want to use for the code in the ASP page.

5 Display the ASP page in a Web browser.

■ The Web browser displays the results of using JScript to create the ASP code.

CREATE A CUSTOM ERROR MESSAGE

An error occurs when the Web server processes Active Server Pages code that contains a mistake. Common mistakes include typing errors, attempting to access an array element that does not exist or trying to divide a number by 0. When an error occurs in an ASP page, the Web server stops processing the page and sends an error message to the Web browser to notify the user about the error. Creating a custom error message allows you to determine the information a user sees.

When an error occurs, the Web server automatically processes an ASP file named 500-100.asp to send an error message to the Web browser. The type of error that occurs determines the information that is displayed in the error message. You may want to create a custom ASP page to display an error message if you feel the 500-100.asp file reveals too much information about your code or you want to provide users with additional instructions. You can create a custom error message for each directory that stores ASP pages on the Web server.

The code in a custom error message should not send header information to a Web browser.

GENERATE AN ERROR

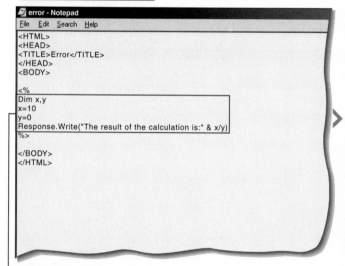

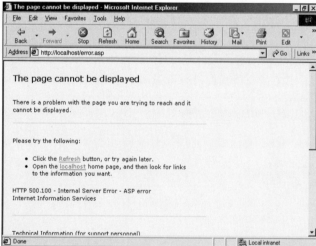

1 Click where you want to place the code that generates an error and type the code.

2 Display the ASP page in a Web browser.

■ The Web browser displays an error message processed by the 500-100.asp file.

Extra

In order for the Web server to use a custom error message you create, you must define the location of the message for each directory you want to use the message. On a Web server running Microsoft Internet Information Server (IIS) 5.0, display the Internet Information Services window and select the directory you want to define the custom error message for. Select the Properties button and then click the Custom Errors tab. Select the 500;100 option from the list and then click the Edit Properties button. In the Message Type area, select the URL option. In the URL area, enter the location of the custom error message.

You can include code in your custom error message that accesses and displays information, such as the session and application variables that were in use at the time an error was generated. This can help pinpoint the cause of an error.

If you do not want to create a custom error message, you can simply modify the 500-100.asp file. The 500-100.asp file is usually located in the Web server's operating system folder in a sub-folder named iisHelp/common. Every user who views an ASP page stored in a directory that uses the modified 500-100.asp file will see your changes when an error occurs.

CREATE A CUSTOM ERROR MESSAGE

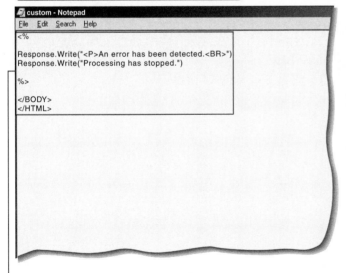

```
<%

Response.Write("<P>An error has been detected.<BR>")
Response.Write("Processing has stopped.")

%>

</BODY>
</HTML>
```

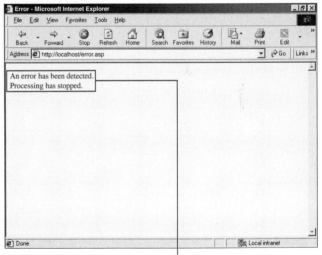

1 Start the text editor you will use to create a custom error message.

2 Type the code for the custom error message.

3 Save the error message on the Web server with the .asp extension.

VIEW THE CUSTOM ERROR MESSAGE

1 Display an ASP page that generates an error in a Web browser.

■ The Web browser displays the custom error message.

CONTINUED ▶

CREATE A CUSTOM ERROR MESSAGE
Display Error Information in a Custom Error Message

After you have created a custom error message, you can have the message display detailed information about errors that occur in your ASP pages. This can help you troubleshoot your pages. The Web server must be running Active Server Pages 3.0 to display error information in a custom error message.

You use the `Server.GetLastError` statement to create an instance of the ASPError object in the custom error message. The ASPError object allows you to access information about an error. The ASPError object must be created before any other ASP data is sent to a Web browser.

Once the ASPError object has been created, there are several properties that can be used to access and display specific information about an error. You can use properties to access information about errors generated by Active Server Pages code, VBScript code or the Web server. You can display information such as the location of an error within a section of code, a description of an error or the name of the file containing an error.

Displaying detailed information about errors reveals information about your code. For security reasons, you may not want to display error information if your Web pages will be available to the general public.

DISPLAY ERROR INFORMATION

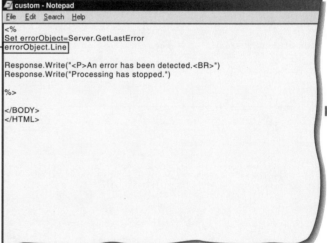

```
custom - Notepad
File   Edit  Search  Help
<%
Set errorObject=Server.GetLastError

Response.Write("<P>An error has been detected.<BR>")
Response.Write("Processing has stopped.")

%>

</BODY>
</HTML>
```

```
custom - Notepad
File   Edit  Search  Help
<%
Set errorObject=Server.GetLastError
errorObject.Line

Response.Write("<P>An error has been detected.<BR>")
Response.Write("Processing has stopped.")

%>

</BODY>
</HTML>
```

1 In a text editor, display the code for the custom error message you created. See page 267 to create a custom error message.

2 Click directly below the opening ASP delimiter (<%) and type **Set** followed by the name you want to use for this instance of the ASPError object.

3 Type **=Server.GetLastError** and then press Enter.

4 Click where you want to access information about an error and type the name for this instance of the ASPError object followed by a period (.). Then type the name of the property you want to use and press Enter.

Extra

ASPError Object Properties

PROPERTY	DESCRIPTION
Line	Returns the number of the line in the ASP page where an error occurred.
Column	Returns the number of the column in the ASP page where an error occurred.
Description	Returns a brief description of an error, such as Division by zero.
Category	Returns the type of error, such as Microsoft VBScript runtime.
File	Returns the name of the .asp file that generated an error.
Source	Returns the line of code that generated an error, if available.
ASPCode	Returns the ASP code the Web server uses to identify an error.
ASPDescription	Returns a detailed description of an ASP-related error, if available.
Number	Returns the number of an error message.

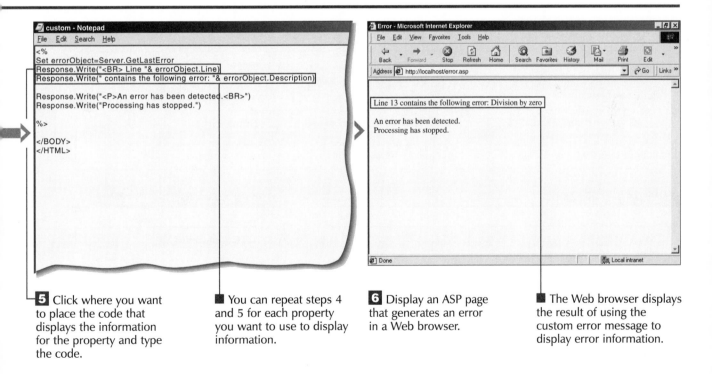

5 Click where you want to place the code that displays the information for the property and type the code.

■ You can repeat steps 4 and 5 for each property you want to use to display information.

6 Display an ASP page that generates an error in a Web browser.

■ The Web browser displays the result of using the custom error message to display error information.

VBSCRIPT ESSENTIALS

OPERATORS

**Operators allow you to manipulate
data in your scripts.**

ARITHMETIC OPERATORS

+ (Addition) Finds the sum of two values.	**/ (Division)** Divides one value by another value.	**Mod (Modulus)** Divides one value by another value and returns only the remainder in the result.
– (Subtraction) Finds the difference between two values.	**\ (Integer Division)** Divides one value by another value and returns only a whole number in the result.	**^ (Exponentiation)** Raises a value to the power of an exponent.
* (Multiplication) Multiplies two values.		

COMPARISON OPERATORS

> (Greater than) Checks if one value is greater than another value.	**< (Less than)** Checks if one value is less than another value.	**<> (Not equal to)** Checks if one value is not equal to another value.
>= (Greater than or equal to) Checks if one value is greater than or equal to another value.	**<= (Less than or equal to)** Checks if one value is less than or equal to another value.	**= (Equal to)** Checks if one value is equal to another value.

LOGICAL OPERATORS

And Checks if two or more statements are true.	**Or** Checks if one of two statements is true.
Eqv Checks if the values of two statements are equal.	**Xor** Checks if the values of two statements are not equal.
Not Checks if a statement is not true.	

CONCATENATION OPERATOR

& (Concatenation) Combines two strings of text.

STATEMENTS

VBScript statements allow you to use
items such as variables, functions and
subroutines in your scripts. Statements
also allow you to control the flow of
a script and check for errors.

DECLARATION STATEMENTS

Const Declares constants. **Dim** Declares variables and assigns storage space. **End** Declares the end of a Function or Sub procedure.	**Exit** Quits a Do...Loop, For...Next, Function or Sub procedure prematurely. **Function** Declares the name, argument list and code for a Function procedure.	**Redim** Declares dynamic array variables and assigns storage space. **Sub** Declares the name, argument list and code for a Sub procedure.

ERROR STATEMENT

On Error
Allows error handling in a script.

OPTION STATEMENT

Option Explicit
Requires a precise declaration of all variables in a script.

PROGRAM FLOW STATEMENTS

Call Executes a Function or Sub procedure. **Do Until** Repeats a section of code until a condition is true. **Do While** Repeats a section of code while a condition is true.	**For...Next** Repeats a section of code a specific number of times. **If...Then** Executes a section of code if a condition is true. **If..Then..Else** Executes one of two sections of code depending on the value of a condition.	**If...Then...ElseIf** Executes one of several sections of code depending on the value of a condition. **Select Case** Executes a section of code depending on the value of a variable. **While...Wend** Executes a section of code as long as a condition is true.

VBSCRIPT ESSENTIALS

FUNCTIONS

VBScript includes a collection of functions
that allow you to work with dates, times,
text strings, number values, objects and
arrays in your scripts.

DATE AND TIME FUNCTIONS

Date Returns the current date.	**MonthName** Returns the name of the month.
DateAdd Returns a date to which a specific time interval has been added.	**Now** Returns the current date and time.
DateDiff Returns the time interval between two dates.	**Second** Returns the second from 0 to 59.
DateSerial Returns a date subtype variant from a specified year, month and day.	**Time** Returns the current time.
DateValue Returns a date subtype variant from a specified date.	**TimeSerial** Returns a date subtype variant containing the time from a specified hour, minute and second.
Day Returns the day of the month from 1 to 31.	**TimeValue** Returns a date subtype variant containing the time from a specified time.
Hour Returns the hour of the day from 0 to 23.	**Weekday** Returns the day of the week from 1 (Sunday) to 7.
Minute Returns the minute from 0 to 59.	
Month Returns the month of the year from 1 to 12.	**Year** Returns the year.

STRING FUNCTIONS

Asc Returns the ANSI code number of a character.	**LCase** Converts text to lowercase.
Chr Returns the character value of a number between 0 and 255.	**Left** Extracts a specific number of characters, starting at the left end of a string.
FormatCurrency Formats a string value as currency.	**Len** Finds the length of a string.
FormatNumber Formats a string value as a number.	**Mid** Extracts a specific number of characters, starting at a specific point.
InStr Finds the position of one string in another, starting the search at the left end of a string.	**Replace** Replaces one string with another string.
InStrRev Finds the position of one string in another, starting the search at the right end of a string.	**Right** Extracts a specific number of characters, starting at the right end of a string.
IsDate Checks if a string contains a valid date.	**Trim** Removes spaces from the beginning and end of a string.
IsNumeric Checks if a string contains a numerical value.	**UCase** Converts text to uppercase.

VBSCRIPT ESSENTIALS

FUNCTIONS (CONTINUED)

OTHER COMMONLY USED FUNCTIONS

Abs Returns the absolute value of a number.	**CreateObject** Creates an object.	**FormatPercent** Formats a specified numerical value as a percent.
Array Creates an array.	**FormatDateTime** Formats a specified date and time.	**Ubound** Returns the largest index number in an array.

INTRINSIC CONSTANTS

VBScript includes several intrinsic, or built-in, constants you can use in your scripts. VBScript sets the value of an intrinsic constant.

COLOR CONSTANTS

Name	Value	Description
vbBlack	&h00	Black
vbRed	&hFF	Red
vbGreen	&hFF00	Green
vbYellow	&hFFFF	Yellow
vbBlue	&hFF0000	Blue
vbMagenta	&hFF00FF	Magenta
vbCyan	&hFFFF00	Cyan
vbWhite	&hFFFFFF	White

COMPARISON CONSTANTS

Name	Value	Description
vbBinaryCompare	0	Performs a binary comparison.
vbTextCompare	1	Performs a text comparison.

TRISTATE CONSTANTS

Name	Value	Description
TristateTrue	-1	True
TristateFalse	0	False
TristateUseDefault	-2	Use default setting.

INTRINSIC CONSTANTS (CONTINUED)

Days of Week

Name	Value	Description
vbSunday	1	Sunday
vbMonday	2	Monday
vbTuesday	3	Tuesday
vbWednesday	4	Wednesday
vbThursday	5	Thursday
vbFriday	6	Friday
vbSaturday	7	Saturday
vbFirstJan1	1	Returns the week of January 1st.
vbFirstFourDays	2	Returns the first week to contain at least 4 days of the year.
vbFirstFullWeek	3	Returns the first full week of the year.
vbUseSystem	0	Uses the date format of the computer.
vbUseSystemDayOfWeek	0	Uses the first day of the week set for the computer.

STRING CONSTANTS

Name	Value	Description
vbCr	Chr(13)	Carriage return.
vbCrLf	Chr(13) & Chr(10)	Carriage return followed by a linefeed.
vbLf	Chr(10)	Line feed.
vbNewLine	Chr(13) & Chr(10) or Chr (10)	New line.
vbNullChar	Chr(0)	Character with a value of 0.
vbNullString	String value of 0	String with a value of 0.
vbTab	Chr(9)	Horizontal tab.

ACTIVE SERVER PAGES QUICK REFERENCE

I. RESPONSE OBJECT

The Response **object sends and controls information from the Web server to a client. For more information, see chapter 5.**

Cookies

Creates a cookie file on a user's computer.

PROPERTIES

Buffer	ContentType	IsClientConnected
Determines if an ASP page should be buffered until complete.	Specifies the type of content an ASP page contains.	Determines if a client has disconnected from the Web server.
CacheControl	**Expires**	**PICS**
Determines if proxy servers can store ASP-generated output in the cache.	Specifies the number of minutes that a Web browser stores an ASP page in its cache.	Sets the content rating for rating services, such as family filtering software.
Charset	**ExpiresAbsolute**	**Status**
Specifies the character set used by an ASP page.	Specifies the date and time that a cached ASP page will expire in a Web browser.	Indicates the status of a client's request for an ASP page.

METHODS

AddHeader	BinaryWrite	End	Redirect
Sends information about an ASP page, such as the location of the page, to a client.	Sends binary information, such as an image file, to a client.	Terminates the processing of code in an ASP page.	Sends a client to a different Web or ASP page.
AppendToLog	**Clear**	**Flush**	**Write**
Adds an entry to the log file on the Web server.	Clears information from the buffer, preventing the information from being sent to a client.	Sends information stored in the buffer to a client immediately.	Sends data to a client.

II. REQUEST OBJECT

The `Request` object retrieves and controls information sent from a client to the Web server. For more information, see chapter 6.

COLLECTIONS

ClientCertificate	**Form**	**ServerVariables**
Retrieves certification information sent by a client when using secure communication between the Web server and the client.	Retrieves information passed by a form that uses the POST method.	Retrieves information stored in a server variable.
Cookies	**QueryString**	
Retrieves information from a cookie stored on a user's computer.	Retrieves information passed to an ASP page by a query string.	

PROPERTY

TotalBytes

Determines the number of bytes sent by a client in a request.

METHOD

BinaryRead

Retrieves binary information, such as an image file, sent to the Web server as part of a POST request.

III. SERVER OBJECT

The `Server` object creates objects and supplies access to methods and properties on the Web server. For more information, see chapter 7.

PROPERTY

ScriptTimeout

Specifies the amount of time the Web server will spend processing an ASP script.

ACTIVE SERVER PAGES QUICK REFERENCE

III. SERVER OBJECT (CONTINUED)

METHODS

CreateObject	GetLastError	MapPath	URLEncode
Creates an instance of an object in an ASP page.	Creates an instance of the ASPError object, which describes an error that occurred.	Identifies where a file is stored on the Web server.	Encodes a URL to allow the URL to be passed from one ASP page to another for processing.
Execute	HTMLEncode	Transfer	
Accesses an ASP page from within another ASP page.	Prevents a client from attempting to process HTML code that is to be processed as plain text.	Transfers control from one ASP page to another.	

IV. SESSION OBJECT

The Session object stores session information for individual clients as they navigate a Web site. For more information, see chapter 8.

COLLECTIONS

Contents
Holds items added to the Session object using script commands.
StaticObjects
Holds objects added to the Session object using the <OBJECT> tag.

PROPERTIES

CodePage	SessionID
Specifies the character set used to create the text that makes up the code of an ASP page.	Uniquely identifies each current user to the Web server.
LCID	Timeout
Sets the locale identifier of the code used in an ASP page.	Specifies, in minutes, the length of time a user's session information is stored on the Web server after the last refresh or request.

METHOD

Abandon

Immediately ends a session for a user and erases the information associated with the session.

EVENTS

OnStart

Specifies an event that occurs when the Web server creates a new session.

OnEnd

Specifies an event that occurs when a session is abandoned or times out.

V. APPLICATION OBJECT

The Application **object stores and shares information for use during an active application. For more information, see chapter 9.**

COLLECTIONS

Contents

Holds items added to the Application object using script commands.

StaticObjects

Holds objects added to the Application object using the <OBJECT> tag.

METHODS

Lock

Locks all variables in an application while the value of a variable is being modified.

Unlock

Unlocks all variables in an application.

EVENTS

OnStart

Specifies an event that occurs when the Web server starts an application.

OnEnd

Specifies an event that occurs when an application ends.

WHAT'S ON THE CD-ROM DISC

The CD-ROM disc included in this book contains many useful files and programs that can be used when working with Active Server Pages. You will find a page providing one-click access to all the Internet links mentioned in the book, as well as several popular programs you can install and use on your computer. Before installing any of the programs on the disc, make sure a newer version of the program is not already installed on your computer. For information on installing different versions of the same program, contact the program's manufacturer.

SYSTEM REQUIREMENTS

To use the contents of the CD-ROM, your computer must be equipped with the following hardware and software:

* A Pentium or faster processor.
* Microsoft Windows 95 or later.
* At least 32MB of RAM.
* At least 200MB of hard drive space.
* A double-speed (2x) or faster CD-ROM drive.
* A monitor capable of displaying at least 256 colors or grayscale.
* A modem with a speed of at least 14,400 bps.

AUTHOR'S SOURCE CODE

The CD provides files that contain all the sample code used throughout the book. You can copy these files to your hard drive and use them as the basis for your own projects. You should open the files using a text editor such as WordPad.

WEB LINKS

This CD provides one-click access to all the Web pages and Internet references in the book. To use these links you must have an Internet connection and a Web browser, such as Internet Explorer, installed.

ACROBAT VERSION

The CD-ROM contains an e-version of this book that you can view and search using Adobe Acrobat Reader. You can also use the hyperlinks provided in the text to access all Web pages and Internet references in the book. You cannot print the pages or copy text from the Acrobat files. An evaluation version of Adobe Acrobat Reader is also included on the disc.

INSTALLING AND USING THE SOFTWARE

This CD-ROM contains several useful programs.

Before installing a program from this CD, you should exit all other programs. In order to use most of the programs, you must accept the license agreement provided with the program. Make sure you read any Readme files provided with each program.

Program Versions

Shareware programs are fully functional, free trial versions of copyrighted programs. If you like a particular program, you can register with its author for a nominal fee and receive licenses, enhanced versions, and technical support. Freeware programs are free, copyrighted games, applications, and utilities. You can copy them to as many PCs as you like, but they have no technical support. GNU software is governed by its own license, which is included inside the folder of the GNU software. There are no restrictions on distribution of this software. See the GNU license for more details. Trial, demo, or evaluation versions are usually limited either by time or functionality. For example, you may not be able to save projects using these versions.

For your convenience, the software titles on the CD are listed alphabetically.

Acrobat Reader

For Microsoft Windows 95/98/NT/2000. Evaluation version.

This disc contains an evaluation version of Acrobat Reader 4.05 from Adobe. You will need this program to access the book files also included on this disc. For more information about using Acrobat Reader, see page 282.

ASP Edit 2000

Build 19 for Microsoft Windows 95/98/NT/2000. Evaluation version.

ASP Edit 2000 is an ASP editor that can also be used for coding in languages such as HTML, Perl and JavaScript. ASP Edit 2000 has features that will appeal to the beginner, such as an easy to access ASP tag list, as well as more sophisticated features, like the SQL Query generator, which will appeal to more experienced programmers.

ASP Edit 2000 is an evaluation program from Tashcom Software. It is fully functional for 30 days or 20 uses, after which you are required to register it with the author. You can download the latest version of ASP Edit 2000 as well as program tools and additions at www.tashcom.com.

ACTIVE SERVER PAGES 3.0:
Your visual blueprint for
developing interactive Web sites

ASP Express

Version 1.81 for Microsoft Windows 95/98/NT/2000. Shareware version.

ASP Express is a text editor specifically tailored for working with ASP and HTML Web pages. ASP Express includes features such as the ability to work directly with ASP files on a remote Web server and special program assistants to simplify creating complex code, such as making a connection to a database or processing information from a form.

ASP Express is a shareware program from David Wier. It is fully functional for 25 days, after which you are required to register it with the author. To ensure you have the latest version of ASP Express, visit the Web site at www.aspexpress.com.

HomeSite

Version 4.5 for Microsoft Windows 95/98/NT/2000. Evaluation version.

HomeSite is a full featured HTML editor that is well-suited for use with other Web-related coding languages, such as Active Server Pages and VBScript. HomeSite also includes powerful Web site management features.

HomeSite is an evaluation program from Allaire. It is fully functional for 30 days, after which time you are required to register it with the author. You can download the latest version of HomeSite as well as participate in message forums with other HomeSite users at www.allaire.com.

Internet Explorer

Version 5.01 for Microsoft Windows 95/98. Commercial version.

Internet Explorer 5 is Microsoft's latest Web browser. It offers new and improved features that make browsing the Web faster and easier. Internet Explorer also includes a VBScript engine which can be used to create and test VBScript scripts.

Internet Explorer is a fully functional program from Microsoft Corporation. There is no charge for its use. You can download support files and additional components from the Internet Explorer Web site at www.microsoft.com/windows/ie.

Netscape Communicator

Version 4.73 for Microsoft Windows 95/98/NT. Commercial version.

Communicator is a suite of applications from Netscape that includes the popular Web browser, Navigator. Communicator also includes other Internet related applications including the Winamp music player, the Messenger e-mail program and the AOL Instant Messenger communication program.

Communicator is a fully functional program from Netscape. There is no charge for its use. The latest version of Communicator, as well as support files and additional components are available on the Web at www.netscape.com.

UltraEdit-32

Version 7.10 for Microsoft Windows 95/98/NT/2000. Shareware version.

UltraEdit-32 is a text editor that can be used to write code in many languages including HTML and Active Server Pages. UltraEdit-32 has many features to make coding easier and more efficient, including syntax highlighting, multi level-undo and customizable templates.

UltraEdit is a shareware program from IDM Computer Solutions, Inc. It is fully functional for 45 days, after which time you are required to register it with the author. Additional spelling dictionaries, macros and support files for UltraEdit-32 are available at www.ultraedit.com.

Visual InterDev Evaluation Copy

Windows 95/98. Trial version.

Visual InterDev is a development tool that includes many powerful tools to help you design and manage Web applications. For more information about the Visual InterDev program from Microsoft Corporation, visit the msdn.microsoft.com/vinterdev Web site.

WEB-ED Webpage and Scripting Editor

Version 2.85 for Microsoft Windows 95/98. Shareware version.

WEB-ED is an editor for use with HTML and VBScript. WEB-ED features keyword highlighting, automatic file saving and VBScript debugging tools. This program requires the use of Microsoft's Visual Basic 6 runtime files, which are available via the WEB-ED Web site at www.jsware.net.

WEB-ED is a shareware program from Joe's Software. It is fully functional for 30 days, after which time you are required to register it with the author.

TROUBLESHOOTING

We have tried our best to compile programs that work on most computers with the minimum system requirements. Your computer, however, may differ and some programs may not work properly for some reason.

The two most likely problems are that you don't have enough memory (RAM) for the programs you want to use or you have other programs running that are affecting the installation or running of a program. If you get error messages while trying to install or use the programs on the CD-ROM disc, try one or more of these methods and then try installing or running the software again:

* Close all running programs.
* Restart your computer.
* Turn off any anti-virus software.
* Close the CD-ROM interface and run demos or installations directly from Windows Explorer.
* Add more RAM to your computer.

If you still have trouble installing the programs from the CD-ROM disc, please call the IDG Books Worldwide Customer Service phone number: 800-762-2974.

USING THE E-VERSION OF THE BOOK

Y ou can view *Active Server Pages 3.0: Your visual blueprint for developing interactive Web sites* on your screen using the CD-ROM disc included at the back of this book. The CD-ROM disc allows you to search the contents of each chapter of the book for a specific word or phrase. The CD-ROM disc also provides a convenient way of keeping the book handy while traveling.

You must install Adobe Acrobat Reader on your computer before you can view the book on the CD-ROM disc. This program is provided on

the disc. Acrobat Reader allows you to view Portable Document Format (PDF) files, which can display books and magazines on your screen exactly as they appear in printed form.

To view the contents of the book using Acrobat Reader, display the contents of the disc. Double-click the BookPDFs folder to display the contents of the folder. In the window that appears, double-click the icon for the chapter of the book you want to review.

USING THE E-VERSION OF THE BOOK

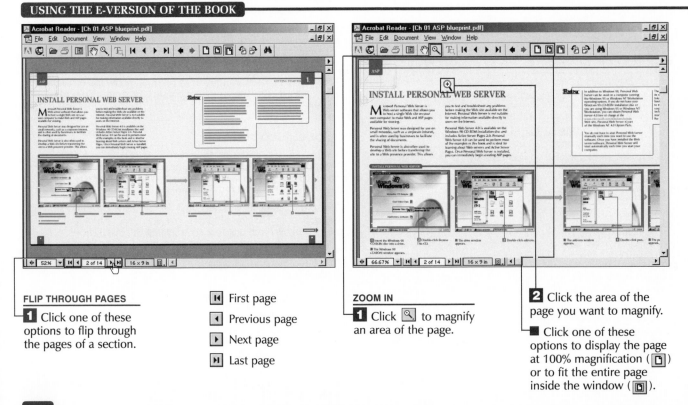

FLIP THROUGH PAGES

1 Click one of these options to flip through the pages of a section.

|◄| First page

|◄| Previous page

|►| Next page

|►| Last page

ZOOM IN

1 Click 🔍 to magnify an area of the page.

2 Click the area of the page you want to magnify.

■ Click one of these options to display the page at 100% magnification (🗋) or to fit the entire page inside the window (🗖).

ACTIVE SERVER PAGES 3.0:
Your visual blueprint for
developing interactive Web sites

Extra

To install Acrobat Reader, insert the CD-ROM disc into a drive. In the screen that appears, click Software. Click Acrobat Reader and then click Install at the bottom of the screen. Then follow the instructions on your screen to install the program.

You can make searching the book more convenient by copying the .pdf files to your own computer. Display the contents of the CD-ROM disc and then copy the BookPDFs folder from the CD to your hard drive. This allows you to easily access the contents of the book at any time.

Acrobat Reader is a popular and useful program. There are many files available on the Web that are designed to be viewed using Acrobat Reader. Look for files with the .pdf extension. For more information about Acrobat Reader, visit the Web site at www.adobe.com/products/acrobat/readermain.html.

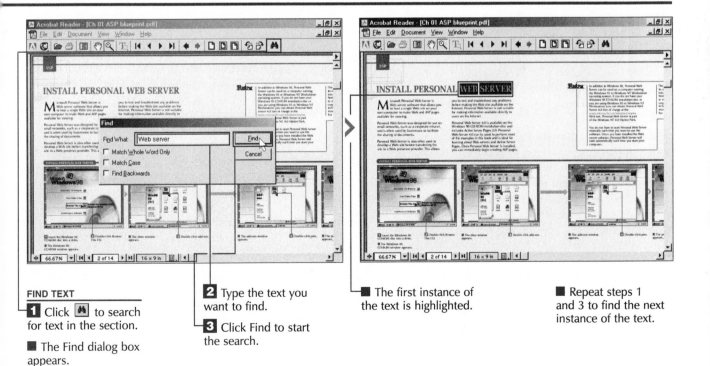

FIND TEXT

1 Click 🔍 to search for text in the section.

■ The Find dialog box appears.

2 Type the text you want to find.

3 Click Find to start the search.

■ The first instance of the text is highlighted.

■ Repeat steps 1 and 3 to find the next instance of the text.

APPENDIX

IDG BOOKS WORLDWIDE, INC.
END-USER LICENSE AGREEMENT

READ THIS. You should carefully read these terms and conditions before opening the software packet(s) included with this book ("Book"). This is a license agreement ("Agreement") between you and IDG Books Worldwide, Inc. ("IDGB"). By opening the accompanying software packet(s), you acknowledge that you have read and accept the following terms and conditions. If you do not agree and do not want to be bound by such terms and conditions, promptly return the Book and the unopened software packet(s) to the place you obtained them for a full refund.

1. License Grant. IDGB grants to you (either an individual or entity) a nonexclusive license to use one copy of the enclosed software program(s) (collectively, the "Software") solely for your own personal or business purposes on a single computer (whether a standard computer or a workstation component of a multi-user network). The Software is in use on a computer when it is loaded into temporary memory (i.e., RAM) or installed into permanent memory (e.g., hard disk, CD-ROM or other storage device). IDGB reserves all rights not expressly granted herein.

2. Ownership. IDGB is the owner of all right, title and interest, including copyright, in and to the compilation of the Software recorded on the CD-ROM. Copyright to the individual programs on the CD-ROM is owned by the author or other authorized copyright owner of each program. Ownership of the Software and all proprietary rights relating thereto remain with IDGB and its licensors.

3. Restrictions on Use and Transfer.

(a) You may only (i) make one copy of the Software for backup or archival purposes, or (ii) transfer the Software to a single hard disk, provided that you keep the original for backup or archival purposes. You may not (i) rent or lease the Software, (ii) copy or reproduce the Software through a LAN or other network system or through any computer subscriber system or bulletin-board system, or (iii) modify, adapt or create derivative works based on the Software.

(b) You may not reverse engineer, decompile, or disassemble the Software. You may transfer the Software and user documentation on a permanent basis, provided that the transferee agrees to accept the terms and conditions of this Agreement and you retain no copies. If the Software is an update or has been updated, any transfer must include the most recent update and all prior versions.

4. Restrictions on Use of Individual Programs. You must follow the individual requirements and restrictions detailed for each individual program in the "What's On The CD-ROM Disc" section of this Book. These limitations are contained in the individual license agreements recorded on the CD-ROM. These restrictions may include a requirement that after using the program for the period of time specified in its text, the user must pay a registration fee or discontinue use. By opening the Software packet(s), you will be agreeing to abide by the licenses and restrictions for these individual programs. None of the material on this disc(s) or listed in this Book may ever be distributed, in original or modified form, for commercial purposes.

5. Limited Warranty.

(a) IDGB warrants that the Software and CD-ROM are free from defects in materials and workmanship under normal use for a period of sixty (60) days from the date of purchase of this Book. If IDGB receives

ACTIVE SERVER PAGES 3.0:
Your visual blueprint for
developing interactive Web sites

notification within the warranty period of defects in materials or workmanship, IDGB will replace the defective CD-ROM.

(b) IDGB AND THE AUTHOR OF THE BOOK DISCLAIM ALL OTHER WARRANTIES, EXPRESS OR IMPLIED, INCLUDING WITHOUT LIMITATION IMPLIED WARRANTIES OF MERCHANTABILITY AND FITNESS FOR A PARTICULAR PURPOSE, WITH RESPECT TO THE SOFTWARE, THE PROGRAMS, THE SOURCE CODE CONTAINED THEREIN, AND/ OR THE TECHNIQUES DESCRIBED IN THIS BOOK. IDGB DOES NOT WARRANT THAT THE FUNCTIONS CONTAINED IN THE SOFTWARE WILL MEET YOUR REQUIREMENTS OR THAT THE OPERATION OF THE SOFTWARE WILL BE ERROR FREE.

(c) This limited warranty gives you specific legal rights, and you may have other rights which vary from jurisdiction to jurisdiction.

6. Remedies.

(a) IDGB's entire liability and your exclusive remedy for defects in materials and workmanship shall be limited to replacement of the Software, which may be returned to IDGB with a copy of your receipt at the following address: Disc Fulfillment Department, Attn: Active Server Pages 3.0: Your visual blueprint for developing interactive Web sites, IDG Books Worldwide, Inc., 10475 Crosspoint Boulevard, Indianapolis, Indiana, 46256, or call 1-800-762-2974. Please allow 3-4 weeks for delivery. This Limited Warranty is void if failure of the Software has resulted from accident, abuse, or misapplication. Any replacement Software will be warranted for the remainder of the original warranty period or thirty (30) days, whichever is longer.

(b) In no event shall IDGB or the author be liable for any damages whatsoever (including without limitation damages for loss of business profits, business interruption, loss of business information, or any other pecuniary loss) arising out of the use of or inability to use the Book or the Software, even if IDGB has been advised of the possibility of such damages.

(c) Because some jurisdictions do not allow the exclusion or limitation of liability for consequential or incidental damages, the above limitation or exclusion may not apply to you.

7. U.S. Government Restricted Rights. Use, duplication, or disclosure of the Software by the U.S. Government is subject to restrictions stated in paragraph (c) (1) (ii) of the Rights in Technical Data and Computer Software clause of DFARS 252.227-7013, and in subparagraphs (a) through (d) of the Commercial Computer—Restricted Rights clause at FAR 52.227-19, and in similar clauses in the NASA FAR supplement, when applicable.

8. General. This Agreement constitutes the entire understanding of the parties, and revokes and supersedes all prior agreements, oral or written, between them and may not be modified or amended except in a writing signed by both parties hereto which specifically refers to this Agreement. This Agreement shall take precedence over any other documents that may be in conflict herewith. If any one or more provisions contained in this Agreement are held by any court or tribunal to be invalid, illegal or otherwise unenforceable, each and every other provision shall remain in full force and effect.

INDEX

Numbers and Symbols

ACTIVE SERVER PAGES 3.0:
Your visual blueprint for
developing interactive Web sites

ACTIVE SERVER PAGES 3.0:
Your visual blueprint for
developing interactive Web sites

ACTIVE SERVER PAGES 3.0:
Your visual blueprint for
developing interactive Web sites

ACTIVE SERVER PAGES 3.0:
Your visual blueprint for
developing interactive Web sites

I

J

INDEX

ACTIVE SERVER PAGES 3.0:
Your visual blueprint for
developing interactive Web sites

ACTIVE SERVER PAGES 3.0:
Your visual blueprint for
developing interactive Web sites

INDEX

ACTIVE SERVER PAGES 3.0:
Your visual blueprint for
developing interactive Web sites

ACTIVE SERVER PAGES 3.0:
Your visual blueprint for
developing interactive Web sites

X

Y